THE FINAL
BATTLE

Hal Lindsey

Western Front, Ltd.
Palos Verdes, California

ISBN 0-9641058-2-9

Western Front, Ltd.

Book design/Typesetting: Skilset Communications
Manufactured in the United States of America.

TABLE OF CONTENTS

JEWISH JERUSALEM
THROUGH THE AGES

Jewish attachment to Jerusalem has spanned thousands of years, and the city has been the capital of independent Jewish states both in antiquity and in the modern day. Though Jerusalem is revered by other faiths, its centrality to Judaism and to the Jewish people is unique. It has, for example, never been the capital of an Islamic state and was often left to decay under Islamic rule. Despite these inescapable truths, the media frequently distort the role of Jerusalem in the political and religious life of the region.

B.C.

1000	King David establishes Jerusalem as the capital of the Jewish Kingdom.
940	First Temple is built under King Solomon.
586	First Temple is destroyed by Babylonians under King Nebuchadnezzer and Jews are expelled.
538	Jews return from exile and rebuild the Temple while under Persian Rule.
444	Walls of Jerusalem are built by Nehemia.
332	Jerusalem is taken by the Greeks under Alexander the Great.
198	Seleucid conquest. Antiochus III rules, allowing Jews to live according to their tradition.
167	Antiochus IV turns Second Temple into a shrine for the Greek god Dionysus. Jews are persecuted.
164	Jews under Judah Maccabee liberate the Temple. Temple is rededicated (Hanukkah). Under Hasmonean dynasty, heirs to the Maccabees, Jewish civic and religious life flourishes.
63	12,000 Jews are massacred as the Romans conquer Jerusalem.
37	King Herod reigns over Jerusalem.

A.D.

33	Jesus is crucified by order of Pontius Pilate.
70	First Jewish revolt against Rome Second Temple is destroyed by Titus.
130	Jerusalem is renamed Aelia Capitolina under the Romans.
132-135	Second Jewish revolt led by Bar Kochba.
135	Romans quell the Bar Kochba revolt and forbid Jews from living in Jerusalem.

324	Constantine establishes Christianity as state religion throughout the Roman Empire, including in Jerusalem.
335	Church of the Holy Sepulchre is built by Helena. Jews are forbidden to enter Jerusalem except to lament the destruction of the Temple on the 9th of the Jewish month of Av.
438	Empress Eudocia allows Jews to return. Christianity flourishes as numerous churches are built.
614	Persians conquer Jerusalem, return it to the Jews. Many churches are destroyed during the conquest, most of which are later rebuilt.
629	Byzantines conquer and expel Jews.
638	Muslim Arabs conquer Jerusalem under Caliph Omar. Omar limits the number of Jewish families allowed to return to seventy.
660	Al Aqsa Mosque is built by Mu'awiya and the Ummayads on the remains of the Second Temple.
691	Abdul el-Malik completes the Dome of the Rock on the Temple Mount.
750	Abbasid conquest. Jerusalem is administered from Baghdad. The city decays.
878	Jerusalem falls to the Egyptian kingdom of Ibn Tulun.
969	Fatimid conquest.
1010	Caliph al-Hakim orders destruction of synagogues and churches, including the Church of the Holy Sepulchre.
1099	Crusaders conquer; Jews and Muslims are massacred. Christian Arabs are brought by the Crusaders from east of the Jordan River and are settled in the Jewish Quarter. Jews are murdered, exiled, or sold into slavery in Europe.
1187	Saladin rules Jerusalem and allows the reentry of Jews.
1212	300 rabbis/scholars from Europe settle in Jerusalem.
1244	Seljuk Turks conquer Jerusalem.

1260   Mamlukes of Egypt conquer Jerusalem, rule for two
        and a half centuries.

1267   Nachmanides arrives from Spain, reviving Jewish
        religious life.

1400   Jews are heavily taxed under the Mamluks.

1516   Ottoman Turks rule Jerusalem.

1535   Suleiman rebuilds the city walls.

1553   Official census counts the number of Jews as 1500,
        exceeding the Ottoman quota for Jews. Jews are forced
        to pay bribes to remain in the city.

1838   Population totals 14,000: 6,000 Jews, 5,000 Muslims,
        3,000 Christians.

1844   First official census in Jerusalem confirms a Jewish
        plurality in Jerusalem: 7,120 Jews, 5,760 Muslims,
        3,390 Christians.

1860   First Jewish Settlement is founded outside the city walls
        in Mishkenot Sha'ananim.

1864   Hurvah Synagogue is reconstructed.

1900   Jews are majority in Jerusalem as population grows
        to 46,500; 28,200 Jews, 8,760 Christians, 8,600
        Muslims

1917   British begin rule over Jerusalem under General
        Allenby.

1922   Haj Amin al-Husseini is appointed Grand Mufti of
        Jerusalem. Population is 33,971 Jews, 13,413 Muslims,
        and 14,699 Christians.

1925   Hebrew University is established on Mount Scopus.

1929   Arabs riot against Jews; 133 Jews and 116
        Arabs are killed.

1932   *Palestine Post* (later *Jerusalem Post*) is established as
         first English daily in Palestine. JNF, Keren Hayesod are
         established.

1938   Hadassah Hospital on Mt. Scopus is erected, later to be
         evacuated after massacre of 78 doctors and nurses in
         1948.

1948   War of Independence. Jerusalem is divided with
         East Jerusalem under Jordanian Rule. Arab Legion
         captures the Old City and destroys the Jewish quarter,
         including 58 Jewish religious sites. Population is 99,320
         Jews, 36,680 Muslims, 31,300 Christians.

1949   Jordan defies armistice treaty that assured free access to
         the Western Wall.

1951   King Abdullah of Jordan is assassinated by Muslim
         Arabs atop the Temple Mount.

1965   Teddy Kollek becomes Mayor, governing for 28 years.

1967   Six Day War. Jerusalem is reunited under Jewish
         sovereignty. Knesset passes law for the protection of
         holy places of all faiths.

*Reprinted from CAMERA Media Report with permission of the Committee for
Accuracy in Middle East Reporting in America.*

THE
FINAL
BATTLE

American Marines and special forces troops are monitoring the decommissioning of three nuclear warheads in the Ukraine. But instead of sending the three missiles to the junk heap, the Russian military officer in charge orders his own troops to open fire on the international observers and hijacks the warheads.

In the U.S., millions of Americans are glued to their television sets keeping up with this hyper-drama that could very easily lead to World War III. But, thankfully, it's not CNN they're watching. It's the network premiere of "Tom Clancy's *Op Center*," a thrilling February 1995 miniseries that showed in graphic and riveting detail just how quickly and easily this international aura of peace could deteriorate into a global nightmare.

The TV show ended happily, with the American military recapturing the warheads. But at least one real-life incident like it has not. You may not have read about it in your daily newspapers, but three nuclear warheads from the old Soviet Union did indeed find their way into the hands of the Islamic extremist nation of Iran. How long will it be before the Islamic bomb is used? When can we expect the first extortion threat to be made? The clock is ticking—and this is no prime-time entertainment production.

The Old Book That Now Looks Familiar

When *The Late Great Planet Earth* was released twenty-five years ago, it reawakened interest in and popularized the subject of Bible prophecy like no other book before or since. I was stunned by its success, as were many other long time students of prophecy. Why was it so successful? How did it reach tens of millions of people the world over, in some fifty-four languages? What was it about that book that touched the hearts and minds of so many? Well, for one thing, it jolted religious and non-religious people alike out of a sense of complacency and into a realization of how little time we have left—any of us, young or old, rich or poor.

That book was particularly effective at reaching younger people, who traditionally didn't think about their own mortality and destiny. *The Late Great Planet Earth* frankly shocked a whole generation into thinking about the possible end of civilization as we know it.

The book you are about to read has the same kind of power—the same punch. It will provoke you by the sheer weight of facts that are fitting into a scenario written by the Hebrew prophets hundreds of years ago. After you read this book, you will not be able to think about international relations in quite the same way again. You will not be able to stop thinking about what lies ahead for the world—perhaps just a few short years away. This book describes in more detail and explicitness than any other just what will happen to humanity and to the Earth, not a thousand years from now, but in our lifetime—indeed in this very generation.

There Is Hope If . . .

Some of it is not a pretty picture. I wish I could offer you some light and entertaining reading. This is not it. If you're looking for what the media call "escapist" entertainment, this doesn't fit the bill. However, despite its focus on the darkest hours of man's inhumanity to man, it does offer an opportunity for the greatest deliverance of all time. And that's my great hope in writing this book—that it will, like *The Late Great Planet Earth* did for many millions, jar this generation awake to the imminent catastrophic events that are about to rock this planet, and also to present a personal hope of a great inner awakening and deliverance from this coming global holocaust.

As always, I have not written this book claiming to be a prophet. Rather I have sought to faithfully interpret the only system of prophecy that has been proven 100 percent accurate in history. It is all contained in the Book of Books.

More than any other work I have done before, this one focuses on how man, using weapons of mass destruction that are now in the arsenals of the world's most dangerous nations, will come very close to committing suicide as a species. You really don't have to be a student of Bible prophecy to see what is coming. Many in the secular world have been seeing the same signs for a long time. Way back in 1860, the French scientist Pierre Berchelt predicted: "Within a hundred years of physical and chemical science, man will know what the atom is. It is my belief that when science reaches this stage, God will come down with His big ring of keys and will say to humanity, 'Gentlemen, it is closing time.'"

This book was largely inspired by an interview with one of the most widely read intelligence experts in the world— the editor of *Intelligence Digest,* Joseph de Courcy, Jr. I have studied Mr. de Courcy's indispensable publication for many years. His *Intelligence Digest* publication is read by some 70 heads of state monthly. There is no more astute analyst of world affairs or geo-strategic developments than Mr. de Courcy. So, for me, it was a great opportunity and pleasure to spend time interviewing him about the subject of this book.

I have been writing about Bible prophecy for more than three decades. I have been teaching about it for even longer. Maybe to some I sound like a broken record. But, lo and behold, along comes de Courcy making many of the same observations about the world and forecasting a strikingly similar scenario—yet relying on completely different sources of information! Mr. de Courcy's sources are rooted in the hard facts of the world of secular intelligence. He has access to most of the world's best political and military "think tanks" and intelligence organizations.

So this book is an unusual kind of effort. De Courcy and I agree about what is happening in the world, and on what is about to happen in the world, but for very different reasons. I rely on the Bible prophecy—on prophecies made over a period of 3,500 years. He relies on some of the best human intelligence sources ever developed by a writer-reporter. Either way—secular intelligence sources or divine intelligence sources—we both have come to the conclusion that the world is headed for a monumental history-altering series of catastrophic events.

This book focuses on a rapidly approaching climactic war—the most brutal, barbaric and destructive conflict ever waged on this planet. I will show how the world is headed inevitably toward a holocaust that can only be halted by an extra-terrestrial intervention. I will show you who will be the key players in this endtimes drama, who will be the worst victims and even the sorts of weapons that will most likely be used.

But keep in mind, the war the Bible prophets and secular intelligence sources warn us is soon coming is just *one* of many signs of the times—just one indication that we have entered the final stage of human history as we know it. All of this material needs to be considered in the context of other profound developments of recent history. Here are a few of the other signs the Hebrew prophets tells us to look for before the climax of history:

- *Famines and plagues*: Does Somalia come to mind? Are the pictures from Ethiopia still vivid? And how about the worldwide spread of AIDs and other sexually transmitted diseases? What about the other new mysterious killer viruses? The prophecies of Matthew 24:7 and Luke 21:11 are being fulfilled right before the eyes of a skeptical world.

- *Earthquakes and volcanoes*: The city of Kobe, Japan, didn't mean much to westerners until the tragic quake that killed over 5,500 people in early 1995. And since then, there has been a dramatic increase in seismic activity around the world. In fact, as I documented in my last book, *Planet Earth—2000 AD,* the incidence of killer quakes worldwide has risen more than 30-fold in the last century. Jesus predicted this exact scenario.

- *Changing weather patterns*: We hear about it everyday—the greenhouse effect, the diminishing ozone layer, the El Nino ocean warming current, deforestation of the planet, drought, floods, hurricanes, tornadoes. The signs are undeniable. Jesus predicted there would be signs in the sun and moon and the earth's atmosphere that would cause horrifying, violent storms to come in from the oceans. It will get worse, folks—so bad that men will drop dead out of sheer fear of the unprecedented magnitude of the storms. (Luke 21:25-26)

- *Sliding morals*: Has there ever been a better description of the times we live in than the one provided by 2 Timothy 3:1-5? **"But realize this, that in the last days**

difficult times will come. For people will be lovers of self, lovers of money, boastful, arrogant, revilers, disobedient to parents, ungrateful, unholy, without natural affection, irreconcilable, malicious gossips, without self-control, brutal, haters of good, treacherous, reckless, conceited, lovers of pleasure rather than lovers of God; holding to a form of godliness, although they have denied its power; avoid such men as these."

- *The rise of false prophets*: Heresy, apostasy, humanism, liberalism, occultism—even Satanism—abound in the latter stages of the 20th century. Jesus clearly warned about an increase in deceiving spirits and false prophets in the endtimes. (Matthew 24:11, 24)

- *Global government*: Just before all hell literally breaks loose on planet Earth, the world will be operating under a global system of government. Do you see the trend toward that goal today? The power and influence of the United Nations is increasing. The European Community has already embraced regional government. The North American Free Trade Agreement is another step   in this direction. And then there is the World Trade Organization—perhaps the first major step toward a one-world order.

- *Increased knowledge*: We've witnessed an explosion of knowledge in the last half-century with the advent of jet planes, space travel, atomic power, miracle drugs and computer technology. The prophet Daniel saw these days coming, **"But as for you, Daniel, conceal these words and seal up the book until the time of the end; many will go back and forth and knowledge will increase."** (Daniel 12:4)

- *The rebirth of the state of Israel and the reclaiming of Jerusalem by the Jews*: Queen Victoria once reportedly asked Prime Minister Benjamin Disraeli to provide just one verse of the Bible that would prove its truth. "Your majesty," he is said to have replied, "I will give you one word—Jew! If there was nothing else to prove the truth of the Bible, the history of the Jews is sufficient." And keep in mind, this is before Israel was reborn as a nation in 1948 after nearly 2,000 years of global exile!

I was once asked by a journalist if there was any event that might change my mind about this period being the endtimes. If Israel ceased to be, I said, that would give me some second thoughts. But I know that cannot happen. I know how God keeps His promises. Israel is in for some very troubled and turbulent times, but the Jewish state will survive for one reason—because Bible prophecy promises it will.

Troubled times are coming? "But Hal," you might say, "peace is breaking out all over the Middle East. Israel has more peace agreements with its neighbors now than it can count! Why are you still preaching doom and gloom?"

Yes, it's true that on Oct. 30, 1991, the Arabs and Israelis began their peace conference in Madrid. It was a natural result of the end of the Cold War a year earlier and the successful 34-nation, U.N.-authorized military operation to oust Saddam Hussein's Iraqi forces from Kuwait in January and February of 1991.

The combination of the fall of the Soviet empire and the swift reversal of Iraq's military aggression led U.S. President George Bush to declare the dawning of a "new world order." It was in this atmosphere that George Bush and his Secretary of State James Baker pushed Israel, its nearest Arab neighbors and the Palestinians to the negotiating table.

Everything seemed possible under the new dispensation, including peace between the Arabs and the Jews.

However, such a peace is not in the cards—not at this time, at least. Based on my interpretation of Bible prophecy and supplemented by Joseph de Courcy's insight into modern-day world affairs, we agree that the Middle East is more unstable and more prone to war than any time in modern history. It's literally on the brink of a catastrophic nuclear war. And the next time, it's not going to be a regional, self-contained conflict. It will touch every part of the globe.

The peace process continues, of course. And we believe it will eventually result in a comprehensive settlement between Israel and much of the Arab world. There will be a psuedo-peace shortly before the final battle begins. But—and this is a big "but"—any such settlement is doomed to ultimate failure for two basic reasons. First, because it doesn't deal with *the principal causes* of war between Arabs and Jews, which are rooted in the Muslim religion. Second, because it at the same time, increases the *opportunities* for war.

The Muslim nations know that Israel must have the territory she has held since 1967 to successfully defend herself with conventional weapons. So when Israel is squeezed down to the presently agreed upon borders, the Muslims will once again figure that an all out attack on Israel would have a high probability of victory.

"A combination of war-weariness and superpower pressure is pushing Israel into dangerous, possibly fatal, territorial compromises in return for formal peace treaties," says de Courcy. "But peace treaties do not guarantee peace. Indeed, as former U.S. Secretary of State Henry Kissinger constantly observes, all wars begin between countries that were, until the outbreak of war, at peace with each other. *It is a stable balance of power, not treaties, that ensures peace.* Yet the settlement that is slowly emerging from the Madrid peace process will upset the delicate balance of Middle East power, shifting it far enough towards the Arabs to make war a rational policy option once again."

De Courcy continues, "Major causes for war will survive any deal that Israel can sign with the Arabs. These include: (1) the continuing presence of a Jewish state bisecting the land root of the African and Asian halves of the Arab world, (2) the continuing rise of radical Islam and (3) the religious issue of who controls Jerusalem. Peace, therefore, will only be maintained if the opportunity for war is lacking. Unfortunately, a combination of geopolitical trends is conspiring to provide exactly the conditions in which the Arabs might calculate that an attack on Israel is a justifiable risk. These trends include American retrenchment, the return of Russia to a traditional pro-Third World foreign policy, the retreat of Israel to its pre-1967 borders and the acquisition by the Arab states and Iran of weapons of mass destruction and the means to deliver them."

About this state of affairs, we heartily agree. In our interview he warned, "If something is not done to reverse these current developments, the result is likely to be a final, catastrophic war between the Arabs and the Jews, *possibly pitting superpower against superpower and possibly including nuclear and other weapons of mass destruction.*" (Emphasis in conversation)

Doesn't this sound like what I have been saying for the last thirty-five years? This book, then, will tie together the views of a prophetic analyst and an intelligence analyst of global affairs—the Biblical and the secular—converging in similar forecasts, yet from very different sources and perspectives.

You won't find another book quite like this one. We will examine why and how the world is hurtling toward disaster. De Courcy's eye for detail—his commitment to accuracy—his vast knowledge of history and current events—all combine to make this book especially appealing to the non-religious person. My background as a student of prophecy allows me to place all this information in perspective in a way that is sure to lead many people to the ultimate truth about the coming global holocaust—and, if they are open, to a wonderful way of escaping it.

Read this book. Learn from it. Pass it on to your friends. It may be the last chance some of them will ever have to avoid the horrible fate this book describes.

Chapter 1

THE NEW ISLAMIC GLOBAL THREAT

"The governments of the world should know that Islam cannot be defeated. Islam will be victorious in all the countries of the world, and Islam and the teachings of the Koran will prevail all over the world."

—Ayatollah Ruhollah Khomeini

While they are saying, "Peace and safety!" then destruction will come upon them suddenly like birth pangs upon a woman with child; and they shall not escape.

—1 Thessalonians 5:3

In Psalm 83, some 3,000 years ago, God gave a warning of what would happen in the last days:

O God, do not remain quiet; do not be silent and, O God do not be still. For, behold, Thine enemies make an uproar; and those who hate Thee have exalted themselves. They make shrewd plans against Thy people, and conspire together against Thy treasured ones. They have said, *"Come, and let us wipe them out as a nation, that the name of Israel be remembered no more."* For they have conspired together with one mind; against Thee do they make a covenant: The tents of *Edom* and the *Ismaelites*; *Moab,* and the *Hagrites; Gebal,* and *Ammom,* and *Amalek; Philistia* and the inhabitants of *Tyre; Assyria* also has joined with them. They have become a help to the children of *Lot.* Deal with them as with Midian, as with Sisera and Jabin, at the torrent of Kishon, Who were destroyed at Endor, who became as dung for the ground.

In these verses, the **Philistia** or Philistines are the modern Palestinians. **Tyre** is modern Lebanon. **Assyria** is modern Syria. I wanted you to read this passage for yourself because it speaks of a time in which there is a concerted effort to wipe out Israel as a nationæwipe them out even from memory. Even then, the Psalmistæunder Divine Inspiration—looked to the last days before the Messiah would come to deliver Israel from the children of Ishmael.

All of the peoples named in those verses make up the various tribes that became known as the Arabs. When you read some of these verses it sounds like modern Radio Tehran, doesn't it? Why? Because this passage of scripture is predicting the modern-day Middle East situation.

"But how could this be, Hal?" you might ask. "The news media are telling us that the Middle East is closer to peace than it has ever been. How do you expect us to believe that the Arabs and Israeli are actually on the brink of total war?"

I don't expect anyone to accept my judgment without evidence. I intend to present the facts with both logic and evidence. People who have been around for awhile understand that the real threats in life are usually the ones you don't know about and are least prepared to deal with. Those of us old enough still have visions of a hostile and belligerent Nikita Khruschev banging his shoe on the table at the United Nations and warning the West that the Communist Soviet Union would destroy America and the free enterprise system.

"We will bury you," Premier Khruschev threatened.

While it's easy to smile nostalgically about such predictions today, the reality of the Cold War for those of us who lived through 40 years of it was no laughing matter. Many Americans gave their lives in Korea, Vietnam and other conflicts that occurred when the Cold War spasmodically turned hot. Hundreds of millions of people around the world knew nothing but fear and repression while living behind the Iron Curtain. The sacrifices were great. And Khruschev's prophecy wasn't as crazy as it may seem today.

A *Pax Sovieticas* Was Possible Then

In fact, the Soviet Union *was* on the verge of dominating the world militarily in the period leading up to 1985. The U.S. economy was in the throes of a major decline. Our defense forces were being unilaterally scaled back. And the Evil Empire was on the march in Afghanistan, Ethiopia, Grenada, Angola, Syria, Iraq, Nicaragua and a dozen other hotspots around the world. Fortunately, a confident and bold leader, Ronald Reagan, was elected president of the United States and set in place policies that resulted in a series of reversals—military and economic—for the Soviet Union.

I believe God's providential hand was working behind the scenes because it was never in the cards for the Kremlin to rule the world. For the Bible clearly spells out the international alliances, tumult and upheavals planet earth will experience in the days leading up to the return of Jesus Christ—an event promised within the general time of the rebirth of the nation of Israel. Prophecy declares the ethnic Russians will indeed play a significant role in those endtime events, but establishing a *Pax Sovieticus* over the world was never in that script.

Meet The New Threat

Today, Communism appears to be on its way to the ash heap of history. But a greater threat—a more evil empire— is quietly, without fanfare, filling the void left by the break-up of the Soviet Union. This movement seeks not only to destroy the state of Israel but also the overthrow of the Judeo-Christian culture—the very foundation of our western civilization.

While Communism was only on the scene for seventy-five years, this evil empire is more than 1,300 years old. It once conquered most of the known world and its zealous adherents have never given up their imperial dreams. They have, like the Communists, at their philosophic core the sworn duty to "bury us."

The name of this movement—the greatest threat to freedom and world peace today—is Islamic fundamentalism. Whether the West wants to face it or not, we are already at war. The media, our diplomatic and political establishment and even our military planners have not been quick to recognize the danger. In fact, tragically, the world's sole remaining superpower for the moment—the United States—has responded to this monumental threat by embarking on a suicidal demilitarization process of unprecedented proportions.

Like the scriptures warned, the West is blithely saying **"Peace and safety"** and talking about "peace dividends." It's not the first time the world was caught napping in the midst of an imminent threat to security and stability coming from the Middle East.

A Pattern Emerges

In the late 1980s, a few insightful intelligence figures in Washington, London and Jerusalem were warning that the Middle East—indeed, the whole world—was facing a terrible danger. A cunning madman by the name of Saddam Hussein had turned the obscure Arab state of Iraq into an armed camp and mobilized the fourth largest standing army in the world. He was rapidly developing nuclear, chemical and biological weapons of mass destruction—including plans for a hydrogen bomb.

He was bellicose, threatened regularly to invade his neighbors and always let it be known his ultimate goal was the destruction of the state of Israel. But, world leaders paid little attention to warnings about Iraq or Hussein. Until, that is, the invasion of Kuwait. Only when Hussein was on the

verge of invading Saudi Arabia and capturing the oil fields
of the Arab gulf states did the world finally wake up.

The Greatest Danger Since WW II

Today, the world is on another precipice. But as
ominous and potentially disastrous as Hussein's antics in
the Persian Gulf were, his blitzkrieg against helpless Kuwait
pales by comparison to this larger, as yet unappreciated,
threat. In fact, the free world today is facing danger greater
than anything since World War II.

"Over the rest of this decade, the divide between radical
Islam and the industrial democracies will become the most
destabilizing factor in world affairs," Joseph de Courcy
reported in *Intelligence Digest* early in 1992. Before the year
was out, it was clear that his prediction was no overstatement.

Still ignored by most so-called experts and the media,
the rise of Islamic fundamentalism threatens most secular
Muslim Middle East countries, sponsors uprisings in many
other nations and is spreading rapidly throughout the world.
While many in the West are still congratulating themselves
on defeat of Communism in the Soviet Union and its
satellites, there is a quiet new menace growing stronger
every day—a force more explosive and dangerous than
simple totalitarianism, Marxism-Leninism or Nazism.

A New World Order

In fact, this new threat is actually billing itself as the
successor to Marxism as the new main agent of change in
the world and the No. 1 challenge to the Judeo-Christian
world order.

Iranian President Akbar Hashemi Rafsanjani says the
movement's goal is to unite all of the Islamic nations under
the leadership of a coalition led by Iran and Syria. They see

themselves as the pure expression of the real meaning of the Koran. Their first declared effort will focus on driving the West out of the Middle East, then to destroy Israel, liberate Palestine and reestablish Muslim authority over holy Jerusalem. The final goal is to replace the Judeo-Christian world order with a Muslim-based world order.

Is this really an agenda we should be concerned with? Is there enough military power in the Islamic world to threaten Israel and the West? Can fundamentalist Islam really take the place of Communism as the greatest danger to world order and peace?

Unfortunately, the answers to all these questions appears to be an emphatic "yes."

In a meeting last year presided over by Rafsanjani, the Iranian leader told Arab political and religious leaders that Islam has replaced Marxism as the No. 1 ideology and power in the world to destroy Western civilization.

Preparing For A Holy War

The strategic objective of the Damascus-Tehran alliance is to unite all of the Islamic countries of the world from Indonesia, Malaysia and Bangladesh to Pakistan, Afghanistan and Turkey to the six former Soviet Islamic republics to Saudi Arabia, Egypt and Libya to all of the nations of Africa. Islamic fundamentalism will lead all of them into "holy war," or *Jihad.* Iran will be the great spiritual leader and Syria, the main military power.

But Islamic unity and control of Middle East oil fields are only the first stop in Iran's plans for conquest. The real prize is Jerusalem. In 1992, Iran's spiritual leader, Ayatollah Ali Khamenei, met leaders of Lebanon's terrorist party *Hezbollah* and endorsed its *jihad* against the Jewish state. Khamenei congratulated Hezbollah on its recent terrorist and electoral victories in Lebanon and "stressed the need to combine *jihad* with political activities," said Tehran radio.

Iran has made little secret of its support for international terrorism. Groups like Lebanon's *Hezbollah* and *Hamas,* the Islamic fundamentalist rival, have been completely underwritten and directed from Tehran. Islamic terrorists— like those that carried out the deadly truck-bombing of the U.S. Marine barracks a few years ago—have demonstrated that their first and foremost concern is not the here and now but the hereafter. Muslim terrorists have been deluded into believing that if they die in the service of Allah that they will immediately go to paradise and have eternal life with their own harem. Therefore, Islamic fundamentalism draws on a vast potential army of fanatics who are more than willing to give their lives for the cause.

The Age Of The Nuclear Terrorist

Imagine what this kind of zealotry means in the nuclear age—in the age when weapons of mass destruction can easily fit into a suitcase. It is this easy acquisition of nuclear, chemical and biological warheads in the post-Soviet world that more than any other factor makes Islam the greatest threat to peace the world has ever known.

Everywhere, it seems, we are witnessing the capitulation of the free world to the dual-edged sword of Islamic fundamentalism—propaganda and terror. Islam has cleverly used two approaches in its war with the Judeo-Christian West. It has convinced most people—including the U.S. State Department and the media establishment— that the problems of the Middle East all revolve around the dispute between the Arabs and the Jews over land. And it has effectively used terror—and the threat of terror—to mute any opposition.

Playing The Blame Game

"Since the end of the Cold War and defeat of Iraq, the American view has been that a lasting Middle East peace can best be achieved by concentrating on the primary cause of Arab discontent—Israel," explains de Courcy. "It is (the American view) that the removal of Israel to its pre-1967 borders would satisfy the Arabs sufficiently to reduce the threat of war to a minimum."

One only need think back to the Persian Gulf War and the images of our troops and news correspondents and Israeli civilians wearing gas masks to understand the reality of the nightmare. But it hasn't gone away with the limited military defeat of Saddam Hussein. Much of Iraq's death-producing infrastructure remains intact as Hussein has toyed with United Nations inspectors searching for his nuclear secrets. Syria is also known to have an active biological warfare program and has gained technical help from North Korea. Libya has a major chemical weapons complex just 50 miles from Tripoli.

But as potentially destructive as those weapons are, they are viewed in Iran and elsewhere in the Middle East as "poor men's nuclear weapons." The emphasis in more than half a dozen Islamic nations is on buying a nuclear capability. Russian President Boris Yeltsin once confided in President Bush that "certain Islamic states" did indeed try to buy tactical nuclear weapons from the former Soviet republic of Kazakhstan. Our intelligence sources say that three of those weapons actually made it to Iran.

You might say, "Come on Hal, you can't really believe that Islam is a threat to us here in the United States? What could the Muslims possibly do to pose a serious challenge to the West?"

Permit me to enlighten you, my friends. Islam is the fastest growing religion in the world. And the increasingly radical fundamentalist brand represents not only the greatest threat to world peace and stability, but also the greatest challenge to Christianity, western civilization and the Judeo-Christian ethic in fifteen hundred years.

Ten years ago, a survey of the largest religions in the world showed Roman Catholicism first with 622 million followers, Islam second with 555 million, Hinduism third with 462 million and Protestantism fourth with 370 million. Today, Islam has catapulted into first place with more than *one billion adherents!* (That's 1,000,000,000 plus)

This means that of the world's 5.2 billion people, 20 percent are Muslims. Though Islam is Arab in origin, only one-fifth of the world's Muslims live in Arab countries. There are 400 million in Pakistan, Bangladesh and India. Iran and Turkey have about 110 million. Africa, too, has large populations of Muslims.

According to demographic estimates, by the year 2025—if we make it—there will be 8.3 billion people in the world and one-quarter of them (2.2 billion) will be Muslims.

But to appreciate the growing power and influence of Islam, you must look beyond the population figures. Muslims now control, to some extent, about fifty of the world's most important countries—from Indonesia in the East, through the oil-rich states of the Middle East, to Senegal on the Atlantic. These countries control vast wealth and unappreciated commercial resources. For instance, Kazakhstan, the former Soviet republic, refers to itself as "the New Klondike."

In Christianity's Back Yard

A total of 70 of the world's 184 countries are considered part of the *Dar al Islam,* or house, or realm, of Islam. It is a religion practiced in the jungles of Africa, the sands of the Sahara, the oil fields of the Middle East, the mountains of Asia and the islands of the Pacific. Islam is also making its impact felt in traditionally Christian parts of the world.

In England today there are now more Muslims than Methodists. There are even more Muslims than there are evangelical Christians.

"Funded by the vast resources of Arab oil money, the Muslims are buying abandoned Anglican churches and turning them into mosques at such a rate that some Muslims claim that England will soon be the first Muslim European country," says author Robert Morey. About ten years ago there were an estimated 150 mosques in England; today there are more than 1,100.

And as their numbers skyrocket, special privileges come with them. Muslims, the English Parliament has been forced to rule, are not subject to English Common Law when it comes to such matters as divorce.

Islam is also growing rapidly in Australia, Canada, Germany and the United States. There are now more than 500 Islamic centers in the U.S. and more Muslims than Episcopalians or Presbyterians, and, by the turn of the century, Islam may well surpass Judaism as America's largest minority religion.

Islam Within Israel's Borders

But maybe the biggest surprise of all—and the biggest threat—is the rapid growth of Islam within the borders of the state of Israel. The faith is uniting Arabs in Judea,

Samaria and Gaza in a way that simple politics—like the kind practiced by Palestine Liberation Organization leader Yasser Arafat—never could. This makes it much less likely that any accommodation involving an autonomous "Palestinian" state could ever be worked out. Even within Israel, most of the Muslims contend that the PLO does not represent them, much less those outside its borders. So with whom are they making peace?

About 1.9 million Arabs live within the borders of territory controlled by Israel. About 92 percent of them are Sunni Muslims, while the other 8 percent are Christian Palestinians. But this minority is shrinking all the time— victims of harassment and persecution by their own Palestinian Muslim majority.

As distasteful as aspects of Islamic life are, the religion is fulfilling a deep spiritual hunger among the people of the Arab world. In some ways it is similar to the spread of Christian fundamentalism in various parts of the world. There is a growing recognition in modern Arab states like Egypt, which have experimented with secularism and socialism, that "man does not live by bread alone." There is a spiritual yearning in every man that even the vast wealth provided by the largest oil reserves in the world cannot satisfy. Though Islam is not a true path to God, it does offer a real alternative to the modern world's reigning deity of moral relativism and materialism.

It's A Real Threat

More than at any time since the Crusades, Islam is posing a serious threat to the Western world. It now possesses the wealth *and the modern lethal weaponry* to supplant the Soviet Union as the greatest challenge to the Judeo-Christian based western world order.

Islam tried to overrun Europe in the eighth century, but was repelled by Charles the Hammer and the Franks at the Battle of Tours. In the 12th, 13th and 14th centuries, Christianity and Islam clashed again in the Crusades. Muslims renewed the attacks in the 15th and 16th centuries as the Muslim Ottoman Turks took Constantinople, invaded Italy and besieged Vienna. Europe's imperialism in Africa and Asia temporarily put a halt to Muslim expansionism in the 19th and 20th centuries.

There is growing evidence of strategic economic alliances between key Muslim nations. One very dangerous bloc involves Iran and the former Soviet republics. Five former Soviet republics and Afghanistan have now joined the Economic Cooperation Organization (ECO) of Iran, Pakistan and Turkey, creating what Pakistani officials say will be a formidable economic bloc. From Iran's point of view, this was the first step toward forming a Muslim military confederacy that will ultimately implement their "Grand Design" mentioned above.

"The ECO had been inching along at a snail's pace for years, but now it will be forced to develop very quickly," Minister of State for Economic Affairs Sardar Asif Ahmad Ali said in an interview.

Five Central Asian republics—Turkmenistan, Kyrgyzstan, Tajikistan, Uzbekistan and Azerbaijan—and Afghanistan all joined in late 1992. Oil-rich Kazakhstan, the largest of the Central Asian states stretching from China as far west as the Urals, has opted for observer status while it tries to gain entry to the European Community, Ali said. (But Turkey is an example of how impossible that will be. So it is inevitable that they will become part of the Muslim ECO). This vastly expanded regional grouping will cover 372 million square miles and include about 300 million people.

The Enormous Danger Of Turkey

One of the most important and dangerous developments is the rapid movement of Turkey into the Iranian sphere of influence. Iran and Turkey are two of the most powerful Islamic nations in the world. They have been historically adversaries. Yet, in a stunning change of Turkish policy, they are putting their differences aside and working together. Turkish and Iranian leaders agreed in late 1992 that it was better to cooperate in central Asia than to compete for influence in the Moslem republics in what was once the Soviet Union.

Turkish Prime Minister Suleyman Demirel, on a visit to Tehran, said Iran and Turkey had a responsibility to cooperate: "As two powerful states in the region, (they) can be effective in promoting peace and calm and in the economic development of the region," he added.

His host, Iranian President Akbar Hashemi Rafsanjani, said, "If joint cooperation is reflected instead of competition, this will greatly benefit Muslims." Demirel and Rafsanjani said it was wrong to think their countries were in fact rivals in central Asia. "Such a fictitious rivalry is to the detriment of Moslems," said Rafsanjani. But he added, "Had Iran and Turkey taken joint actions, the situation of Muslims in Nagorno-Karabakh and the Caucasus would have been different."

Islam And Democracy Are Incompatible

One of the reasons Islam is such a destabilizing force in the world is its lack of commitment to democracy and human rights. In the epilogue to his book *Sandcastles*, Milton Viorst concludes that democracy and human rights in the Arab world "were doomed from the start by the taint of their colonial origins. Arab scholars who sought to legitimize them by citing indigenous precedents, whether historical or religious, failed to persuade the multitudes. The idea of representative government was too unfamiliar. Even now, liberal values carry the burden of foreign rule, as well as of the West's insistent claim to ascendancy in the Middle East. "In fact," Viorst concludes, "a strong claim can be made that Islam, the heart of Arab culture, sets the limits of personal and social development in the Arab world. Despotism, the Arabs' most pervasive political institution, is surely its offshoot, even though Islam has sometimes been at odds with its despots."

It's a fact, often asserted by former United nations Ambassador Jean Kirkpatrick, that democracies tend not to invade one another. Democracy, thus, is a stabilizing factor in international relations. Sadly there is little or no democracy in the Arab world or even on the horizon for the near future.

From Mohammed onward, Islam has been completely rooted in the Seventh century nomadic culture of the Arabian Bedouin. A culture based on the total authority of the tribal sheik or chief. It is a religion of conquest by the sword under the control of powerful dictators.

The Arab nations continue to rely on aggressive use of military power to settle disputes not only with Israel but with each other and with their own people. De Courcy points out that Hosni Mubarak in *Egypt* has invaded Sudan's territory, *Iran's* Rafsanjani has occupied disputed islands in the Persian Gulf and *Syria* has been involved in 26 interstate disputes "that included the threat, display and use of armed force" in the 40 years between 1948 and 1989.

"Saddam Hussein of Iraq of course, launched the war against Iran and the invasion of *Kuwait*," de Courcy adds. "The armed forces of *Libya* under Col. Moammar Gadhafi have fought in *Chad, Sudan* and *Uganda,* and there have been armed clashes in *Tunisia* and *Egypt.* Further afield,

Pryce-Jones points out, Col. Gadhafi has paid for wars, revolutions, coups d'etat and destabilization in the *Philippines, Ireland, Malta, New Caledonia, Surinam, Burkina Faso, Nicaragua, El Salvador, Eritrea, Ghana* and the *Canary Islands."* (Emphasis added)

There have been democratic experiments in the Arab world, but they have not lasted. The most important recent attempt at Western-style democratic process was the Algerian election of December 1991. The Islamic Salvation Front announced that it would participate in the December 26 elections only twelve days before polling day. Its program called for a reform of education, the media and the position of women in society. In other words, the party was calling for the imposition of an Islamic state.

The Islamic fundamentalists won the first round of the two-stage elections with 47.5 percent of the vote, recalls de Courcy, compared with 23.5 percent for the long-time ruling party and 15 percent for the third-place socialists.

"With the Islamic fundamentalists poised to take power, the military intervened to cancel the second round of the elections scheduled for January 1992," explains de Courcy. "An army-backed regime has been in control ever since. It is the only viable alternative to the Islamist despotism that a free election was due to return."

What would happen if the Arab nations opened themselves up generally to free elections? The Algeria model is indicative: *Genuinely free elections in Algeria, Tunisia, Egypt, Jordan and possibly the West Bank and Gaza Strip would put non-democratic Islamists in power.*

The Fateful Turn Of Turkey

De Courcy warns, "Even Turkey, with its 70-year commitment to Ataturkism and secularism, is facing an

Islamist revival because of the perceived failure of its pro-Western foreign policy. It is no coincidence that the countries in the Middle East where Islamists are threatening to take power are those countries that lack, for the moment, a despot. Those that are headed by despots—Libya, Syria and Iraq, for instance—are in little danger from an Islamist takeover, but nor are they in danger of holding democratic elections."

The real choice for these Arab nations is not between despotism and democracy, but between secular or religious despotism.

De Courcy related to me, "The history of Islamic fundamentalism in the Middle East shows that it prospers most in countries that are showing signs of moving toward the West and least in countries that pursue radical anti-Western policies. Apart from pursuing a radical anti-Western policy, the only other way of keeping Islamic fundamentalism at bay is ruthless suppression."

It may sound horrible—it may sound immoral. But I believe that de Courcy is absolutely correct, especially when you consider the long-range objectives of the radical Islamic fundamentalists. All of my middle eastern intelligence sources agree with this.

The rise of radical Islam in the Arab world is important not just because of what it says about Arab attitudes toward Western culture and political standards, but also specifically because of its doctrine of *Dar al Islam* (the realm, or house, of Islam), which recognizes no political or state boundaries. It is the duty of good Muslims to extend the *Dar al Islam* to all those areas where it physically can. It is the central religious doctrine of *Jihad* to conquer all lands possible for the glory of Allah.

The Goal Of Islam—*JIHAD*

"No other religion poses such a challenge to the West at this time," says G. H. Jansen, an expert on Islam. "Islam has confronted the West militarily for 1,300 years. Now, in addition to the military confrontation of the past, an economic confrontation has been added."

The goal of Islam from the days of Mohammed has been to unite all followers in a common brotherhood for the purpose of waging *jihad*, or holy war, on the Judeo-Christian and non-believing (infidel) world.

In Mohammed's original revelations, the Arabic word for *jihad* meant basically a "struggle" for the cause of Islam. It was then expanded to embrace self-defense. And very quickly took on a different, more aggressive denotation—*offensive, military action to conquer or re-conquer land for Allah.*

As recently as 1980, the Saudi Arabian Crown Prince Fahd, in a statement to Riyadh Domestic Service defined *jihad* as "a united, comprehensive, integrated Arab-Islamic confrontation in which we place all our resources and our spiritual, cultural, political, material and military potentials."

Jihad is an on-going concept today in the Islamic world. The struggle is constant, never-ending. The holy war is a crusade that may take 100 years or 1,000. But it will continue on every front—military, economic, propaganda, etc. Every once in a while an important Arab leader will let his guard down and tell the press and public what he really believes. When they do, it's important to be listening and comprehending.

The Writing Is On The Wall

Syrian President Hafez Assad did just that in early 1992. In a very far-reaching address he gave to visitors from

Kuwait, he outlined his long-range policies and what he calls his "100 years war" to liberate Jerusalem and Palestine.

"Wars may be interrupted for hundreds of years, but Syria will never give up as long as one Syrian village remains under occupation," he told the audience in a speech reported by *Intelligence Digest*. However, Assad made it clear that if he does not get everything he wants—namely all of the territory occupied by Israel on the Golan Heights— then war can easily be resumed. *He also made it clear "he does not believe long-term peaceful co-existence with Israel is possible—even if those territorial concessions are made."* (Emphasis added)

What Assad is saying is that there are all kinds of maneuvers that can be made within the political and diplomatic arena. But Syria—along with its allies in Iran— remains committed to the complete destruction of the nation of Israel and the denial of all Western influence in the Middle East.

Israel is a very tiny country in a giant land mass known as the Middle East. "It is the roughest neighborhood in the world," observed the conservative Israeli leader, Benyamin Natanyahu. The Jewish state is less than half the size of San Bernardino County in California. Its Jewish population is about 3.5 million—roughly that of Iowa. Compare this to the 22 Arab states, armed to the teeth, and virtually all of them in a constant state of war with Israel. Together, just these Arab states alone have more than 140 million inhabitants and a land area larger than the United States.

This is the reality that Israel must face every day. This is the reality of the awesome power of Islam that surrounds them. And this is the power that will soon ignite the Final Battle.

Chapter 2

ROOTS OF THE CRISIS

An Ancient Family Feud

"And he [Ishmael] will be a wild ass of a man, his hand will be against everyone, and everyone's hand will be against him."

God Almighty—Genesis 16:12

"Before the Jewish state was established [in 1948], there existed nothing to harm good relations between Arabs and Jews," the late King Faisal of Saudi Arabia told Henry Kissinger in 1973.

Other Arab leaders have made similar claims. It's one of those incomparable and inexplicable myths of the Middle East that frustrate me so. Repeat it often enough and it begins to take on a life of its own. Today, it is accepted widely as conventional wisdomæeven in the most learned circles.

But don't believe it. As difficult as it may be to understand in this day and age of space travel, satellite communications and secular pseudo-sophistication, the current crisis in the Middle East originated in a feud that began in the tents of Abraham—the father of both Ishmael and Isaac.

God promised Abraham an heir who would bless all nations and raise up a mighty people who would spread love, faith and hope around the world. Abraham received this message and believed it. And though Abraham was a great man of faith, as time passed and he and his wife, Sarah, grew elderly, he began to have doubts. Had he misunderstood God's promise?

So Abraham and Sarah decided that God expected them to help Him out. They took matters into their own hands, thinking, "God helps those who help themselves." (This idea is not only not in the Bible, but is diametrically opposite to what it teaches.) Sarah told her husband to impregnate her Egyptian maidservant, Hagar, so they would have a child to raise. This was the standard practice of the region in those days. So a son was soon born, and they named him Ishmael. Sarah realized she had made a mistake almost immediately after Hagar had conceived the child. She relates in the Genesis account that once the pregnancy had occurred, Hagar began to despise the very sight of Sarah. Abraham gave Sarah permission to do whatever she wished with Hagar. So because of her harsh treatment, Hagar fled into the wilderness—the first of two times she was exiled. In this first incident, she was told by God to return and submit herself to Sarah's authority.

So Ishmael was born and raised in the home of Abraham and Sarah. And Abraham grew to love his first son. But fourteen years later, when Abraham was 100 years old and Sarah was 90, she gave birth to the natural heir that God had promised. They named him Isaac.

Ishmael's Prejudice Begins

Conflict between the two sons of Abraham began from the very start. In Genesis, chapter 21:9, it says the conflict began just after Isaac was weaned: **"Now Sarah saw the son of Hagar the Egyptian, whom she had borne to Abraham, mocking."**

Ishmael, now a teenager, was mocking the infant Isaac, the Bible tells us. Ishmael had been "born according to the flesh" and Isaac had been "born according to the promise" (Galatians: 4). Ishmael was replaced by Isaac as the favored son and heir. This made him jealous and bitter. As a result, he mocked and disdained his half-brother. Eventually the

situation became so intolerable that Sarah demanded that
Ishmael and his Egyptian concubine mother, Hagar, be
expelled permanently from Abraham's family.

But the Lord loved Hagar and her son and had mercy
upon them. God promised her son would beget twelve
princes who would become a great nation. Ishmael went to
live in the wilderness region of Hejaz in what became
known as the Arabian Peninsula. He indeed had twelve
patriarchal sons who became associated with the peoples
known as Midianites, Edomites, Egyptians and Assyrians.
Here the Bible and Islamic tradition both agree that Ishmael
became the leader of all the great desert peoples of the
Middle East.

God Tries To Redeem It All

Obviously God provided many opportunities in this
story for redemption of bad situations created mostly out of
disobedience and lack of faith. Abraham agreed to
impregnate Hagar because he doubted God would fulfill his
promise to bear him an heir with Sarah. To be fair to
Ishmael, God provided him a great kingdom of his own to
the east of his brother.

But perhaps because Isaac's descendants and Isaac's
descendants alone—faithful men like Jacob, Joseph, Moses,
Joshua, Gideon and David—were able to claim the full
inheritance of Abraham.

It is this jealously and resentment that have created a
hate that has no parallel in history. This hatred has
continuously set off wars and atrocities for four thousand
years. And it is that title deed to the land of Israel, which
God promised to Abraham's lineage, that has been the
source of the friction between the Jews and the Arabs right
up to this very moment.

The descendants of Ishmael have been at Isaac's descendants' throats for 4,000 years now, and their blood feud has smoldered and frequently flamed into war during all that time. No racial problem in the world can compare with this one in terms of duration and intensity of animosity. They can't even agree on the history of that hatred.

Islam's Distortion

Muslims believe the Jews changed and distorted the Bible in order to establish themselves as the heirs of Abraham's Covenant blessings. However, they fail to explain how the New Testament, written by Christians who had no motive for following Jewish falsifications, clearly teaches that the Covenants were made to Isaac and his descendants.

According to Islamic tradition, Abraham had eight sons rather than two. They say they were reared in Mecca not Hebron. They say it was Ishmael, not Isaac, whom Abraham was about to sacrifice on Mount Moriah when an angel stopped him. According to the Koran, the Abrahamic covenant, with its promises—including the title deed to the land of Israel—was passed down to the Arabs through Ishmael, rather than to the Jews through Isaac.

But, if you believe the Old and New Testaments were written under the inspiration of the Spirit of God as they claim, then there is no question that Israel is the Promised Land of the Jews. And God's words to Abraham in Genesis are some 2,500 years older than the creation of Islam.

"Sarah your wife shall bear you a son," God tells Abraham in Genesis 17:19-21. **"And you shall call his name Isaac; and I will establish my covenant with him for an everlasting covenant for his descendants after**

him. And as for Ishmael, I have heard you; behold, I will bless him, and will make him fruitful, and will multiply him exceedingly. He shall become the father of twelve princes, and I will make him a great nation. But my covenant I will establish with Isaac. . . ."

God fulfilled His promise to Abraham. He fulfilled His promise to Isaac. And He fulfilled His promise to Ishmael. In fact, God gave much more land to Ishmael than He did to Isaac. He also made salvation available to his descendants. But they were never satisfied with God's blessings and few accepted His salvation.

Not Content With Great Nation

Nevertheless, the sons of Ishmael were as rebellious and contrary as Abraham's first son. They were not content to be part of a great nation, as God had provided. They were jealous and envious of the sons of Isaac from the very beginning. They wanted it all. They were not willing to accept the bountiful blessings of God and live in peace and harmony with their brothers.

It's no wonder that such an attitude caused them to lose their way spiritually and their knowledge and understanding of God long before the birth of Mohammed in the seventh century. Before Islam, the descendants of Ishmael believed in a multitude of gods. They were a tribal people to whom it was perfectly appropriate to raid a neighboring community to steal, pillage, find wives and obtain slaves.

"These desert tribes lived by the code of 'an eye for an eye and a tooth for a tooth,'" writes author Robert Morey. "Vengeance was extracted whenever anything was done to hurt any member of the tribe."

It was a rough life lived by the nomadic Arabian tribes, and it was governed by a harsh law. Cutting off hands, feet and heads were standard penalties for crimes. Tongues might be cut out, ears cut off or eyes gouged out, according to the offense.

It was not a law Jews and Christians would be comfortable with or would even understand. Murder was not necessarily wrong. In fact, it was the right thing to do in certain situations. Forcing people into slavery, kidnapping women from other tribes and adding them to your harem were considered manly and admirable pursuits.

These characteristics carried over to the post-Mohammed culture as well. Morey notes, for example, that the term "assassin" is derived from the Arabic *hashshashin,* which literally means "smokers of hashish." Some religious Muslims were known for smoking the drug and working themselves into a frenzy before charging out to kill their enemies. Later a Muslim sect took on the name "The Assassins," because they believed Allah had called them to kill as their sacred duty.

Even today, Islam still commands its followers to kill the infidels—or non-believers. In the Koran, Muslims are instructed to "Fight and slay the pagans wherever ye find them, and seize them, beleaguer them, and lie in wait for them in every stratagem of war."

The First Big Lie

The very basis of Islam—that God's true covenant was with Ishmael rather than Isaac—is based on a lie. And it is a lie meant not only to deceive the world about God's promises to the Arabs, it could well be characterized as Islam's first Big Lie or "blood libel" about the Jews. Islam claims for itself the bloodline inheritance God solemnly promised to the remnant of Israel.

This is the beginning of what has become an all-too-familiar pattern in the relationship between Arabs and Jews. Even in Mohammed's day, the descendants of Ishmael were telling blood libels about their Jewish brothers. George Grant characterizes the hatred and rivalry first expressed in the Sahih Muslim annals back in the seventh century as "the first Palestinian conflict."

"The criminal Jews have brought destruction upon the *Umma* since the earliest times," the annals say. "Their leaders conspired to send the innocent of Canaan away from their homes. They repulsed the pleas of the Philistine widows and Moabite orphans and washed their fields in the blood of the Ammonite poor. Therefore, they shall not stand in the day of judgment, nor shall they prevail against the sure coming of *Jihad*. Allah shall pronounce retribution and the *Umma* shall observe with joy and gladness."

This blood feud lives on today in graphic words that are not dissimilar. But, as Joseph de Courcy says, mutual hatred and distrust—no matter how deep they run—are not necessarily reasons for continuing war.

"History is full of examples of former enemies making peace and even becoming friends," he says. "In the last century Britain and France moved from almost permanent war to permanent peace. In this century, the postwar reconciliations between the French and the Germans and between the Americans and the Japanese have been every bit as unlikely and every bit as successful. It cannot, therefore, be claimed with any force that because the Arabs and Jews have been at war for 100 years, peace is impossible. However, the depth of the Jews' distrust of their Arab neighbors, which is fed by the full knowledge of the deep and abiding nature of the Arab hatred for the Jews, is a highly significant security factor."

De Courcy says that to fully appreciate the significance of this tension, you must remember that Israel is a country only nine miles wide at one point in its pre-1967 borders. It has literally no strategic depth.

"Such a country cannot afford mistaken judgments and must, if it has any doubts about the intentions of its neighbors, rely on pre-emptive military strikes for survival," he explains. "If it distrusts its neighbors, and has good historical reasons for distrusting them, then the balance will always weigh more heavily in favor of pre-emption. This in turn predisposes the enemy toward a first-strike doctrine. It is a vicious circle that is hard to break and incredibly destabilizing."

It is this situation, de Courcy reminds us, that led Israel to launch pre-emptive military strikes in 1956 and 1967. With the increasing speed, accuracy and deadliness of more modern weaponry developed in the last twenty-five years, there is an even greater temptation and necessity to strike first rather than second. In 1973, the Arabs launched a surprise attack on Israel on the holy day of Yom Kippur, that very nearly defeated Israel before reserve troops could be mustered and rushed to the collapsed military fronts. Today, there is grave doubt among military and intelligence experts that Israel could withstand a similar surprise attack.

But the security threat Israel faces is not simply an external one. There are nearly two million Arabs living within the confines of its borders. And even the autonomy granted to these people through negotiations with the Palestine Liberation Organization has not diminished the danger of terrorism and insurrection within the Jewish state and its territories. There is no question that the ancient enmities between the Jews and the Arabs have helped to feed the political and strategic goals of Israel's foes.

"Be assured that the many indignities heaped upon the Palestinian people since ancient times must and shall be avenged," PLO leader Yasser Arafat said before he moved his headquarters to Jericho as part of Israel's peace efforts. "Israel's policy in the occupied territories is little more than an extension of the imperialist tactics of the conqueror Joshua. Surely the judgment of Allah is reserved for them until Palestine is transferred from *Dar al Harb* to *Dar al Islam. Ishmael shall have his revenge!"*

Nevertheless, many revisionists today—such as old King Faisal—like to suggest that the Arab-Jewish hostilities commenced only in 1948 with the rebirth of the state of Israel. However, it is certainly true that Arabs have been persecuting Jews in the Middle East since at least the days of Mohammed—the Arab religious leader who seemed to fine-tune the art of hating Jews. It was Mohammed who beheaded hundreds of Jewish men near the conquered city of Medina and set the precedent for pogroms that have continued even into the 20th century.

Big lies and blood libels have often been at the root of these mindless slaughters. In 1840, Syrians concocted a story about Jews murdering a priest and his servant to collect blood for Passover matzoh. Before the Jews were vindicated of the charges, word had spread far from Damascus and caused terror in the persecuted Jewish communities.

"The trouble with the Arab is that his ruling classes, moved by selfish interests . . . can easily inflame the Muslim masses, who add to a religious fanaticism an inborn if latent hatred of the Jews," wrote historian Ernest Main way back in 1937. "This conflict between Jacob and Esau is as old as history: it is splitting Palestine today."

Demonizing of the Jews was not the exception in Arab countries, it was the rule. It has been repeated in modern times even in *official* government publications in Arab countries. In 1962 the Egyptian Ministry of Education published "Human Sacrifices in the Talmud" as one of a series of "national" books. Bearing the symbol of the Egyptian Institute for Publications on its cover, the book reprints the 1890 work of a writer in Cairo who purports to share conclusive evidence that "this people permits bloodshed and makes it a religious obligation."

Two years later a professor at the University of Damascus apologized for the spread of such stories because they serve a valid purpose: to warn mothers against allowing their children out at night, "lest the Jew . . . come and take their blood for the purpose of making matzoth for Passover." A publication called "The Danger of World Jewry to Islam and Christianity" published in the 1960s alleges that thousands of children disappear each year, "all of them are victims of guess who?"

This blood libel story was celebrated in a 1973 play produced in Egypt by a former foreign minister. At the same time, Saudi Arabian King Faisal stressed the importance of the blood libel of 1840 as a requisite for understanding "Zionist crime." In 1982, after Israel returned the Sinai to Egypt, more blood libel stories began appearing in the official press.

The violence that the PLO's Arafat and others now claim was "only begun against the Jews with the 1948 rebirth of Israel," has a long history in the Middle East.

"'Palestinian terrorism' was actually a critical factor in the early developments that instigated the pivotal population conditions in Palestine," states author Joan Peters. "In their Holy Land, the Jews, as well as Christians, suffered long from harsh discrimination, persecution and pogroms. According to the British Consulate report in 1839, the Jew's life was not 'much above' that of a dog."

Peters also says that the most overlooked collaboration of World War II was "the symbiotic relationship between" Haj Amin al-Husseini, the Grand Mufti of Jerusalem, and the Nazis. She quotes John Gunther writing in "Inside Asia" in 1939 as concluding: "The greatest contemporary hero (in the Arab world) is Hitler." She provides documentation showing that the American Christian Palestine Committee found that "the Arab riots of 1936 in Palestine were carried out by the Mufti with funds supplied by the Nazis."

Husseini, a relative of Yasser Arafat, helped raise two divisions of Yugoslavian Muslims for the Nazi SS during the war. He also recruited Arab agents to be dropped behind Allied lines as saboteurs. Well aware of the final solution, Husseini did his best to ensure that no intended Jewish victims escaped to Palestine.

"The Germans," Husseini said admiringly at a 1943 rally in Berlin, "know how to get rid of the Jews." In 1948, as the state of Israel was reborn, Husseini, the spiritual leader of all of Islam at the time, said: "I declare a holy war my Muslim brothers! Murder them all."

This is the context—the historical backdrop—into which the Jewish state was re-introduced. The blood feud between Ishmael and Isaac may have intensified in 1948, but this was hardly the beginning of the hatred and the violence. The brothers were merely back in the same rough neighborhood—living, literally, within a stone's throw of each other.

Ancient Roots Of Modern Hatred

While today's international leaders attempt to solve the problems of the Middle East by manipulating the political machinery and redrawing maps, the crisis is much deeper. The roots of the problem are not just political, they are profoundly rooted in the ancient racial blood feud, the Muslim religion and culture.

Recent history has only served to further complicate this ancient enmity, as de Courcy points out. Israel and Zionism are now associated, in the Arab mind, with great-power imperialism. Israel is perceived to be a mere artificial creation of the United States and Britain. And making matters far worse is the desire for vengeance for the five straight humiliating military defeats the Jewish state has inflicted upon the Arab world.

"For a nation that covers a region from the Atlantic to the Indian Ocean, with a combined population of some 240 million, to be defeated in five wars by tiny, 4-million-strong Israel is very hurtful indeed," says de Courcy. "It is a humiliation that is crying out for revenge. No deal that can conceivably emerge from the Madrid peace process will undo this legacy."

Jihad By Diplomacy—For Now

The hatred of Israel is ingrained deeply among the Arab populace, according to recent surveys. In 1993, Hilal Khashan, a professor of political science at the American University in Beirut polled 1,000 Muslim Lebanese, Syrians and Palestinians just before the signing of the accord between Israel and the PLO. Of the respondents who favored the peace process, "not one single person gave positive justification for peace with Israel," said Khashan.

"Respondents variously see peace as *the only available alternative at the present,* or as a chance to recover some territory occupied by Israel since the Six Day War, or as an opportunity to put a halt to 'Israeli aggression,'" he wrote in the Wall Street Journal. "But the most popular view sees the peace as *an interim measure* for Arabs to reorganize themselves and strike at Israel later. In all, more than 90 percent of those who support peace say they would cease to support it if Israel were weakened in the future."

Why Jews Are And Should Be Skeptical

But the distrust is by no means one-sided. Jews, too, have historical reasons for skepticism. De Courcy explains: "Particularly important in the nurturing of modern Jewish skepticism about the good intentions of the outside world was the false dawn of Europe's 18th-century Enlightenment. The Enlightenment hastened the spread of religious toleration, but European anti-Jewish sentiment, far from withering as religious toleration spread, mutated into an even more virulent racist strain.

More shocking still than the failure of 19th-century Europe to live up to the promise of the Enlightenment was its failure to live up to the promise of the early 20th century. Universal adult suffrage did not bring an end to Jewish suffering in Europe; it brought Adolf Hitler and the Holocaust. The fact that the Arabs have fought the Jewish return to Palestine at every turn has, if at all possible, deepened still further Jewish distrust of non-Jewish peoples. All Israeli actions, past, present and future, are conditioned by these experiences."

Allegorizing Bible Prophecy Leads To Anti-semitism

Perhaps it's about time for Christians to come to grips with the church's historical role in the persecution of Jews. The early popes instigated religious campaigns against them. St. Augustine, the first Archbishop of Canterbury in the 5th century, described "the image of the Hebrew" as "Judas Iscariot, who sells the Lord for silver," adding, "The Jew can never spiritually understand the scriptures and forever will bear the guilt for the death of Jesus because their fathers killed the Savior."

Later, in 1543, Martin Luther, the great Protestant reformer, would write something as hateful as the most vicious Islamic extremist might come up with: "What then shall we Christians do with this damned rejected race of Jews?. . . Let me give you some honest advice: First, to set fire to their synagogues or schools and to bury and cover with dirt whatever will not burn, so that no man will ever again see a stone or cinder of them. This is to be done in honor of our Lord and Christendom . . . . Second, I advise that their houses also be razed and destroyed . . . . Third, I advise that all their prayer books and Talmudic writings, in which such idolatry, lies, cursing and blasphemy are taught, be taken from them. Fourth, I advise that their rabbis be forbidden to teach henceforth on pain of loss of life and limb . . . . Fifth, I advise that safe conduct on the highways be abolished completely for the Jews. For they have no business in the countryside, since they are not lords, officials, tradesmen, or the like. Let them stay at home . . . . Sixth, I advise that usury be prohibited to them, and that all cash and treasure of silver and gold be taken from them, and put aside for safekeeping . . . . Seventh, I recommend putting a flail, an axe, a hoe, a spade, a distaff or a spindle into the hand of

young strong Jews and Jewesses and letting them earn their
bread in the sweat of their brow."

Pretty scary stuff, huh? It's hard to imagine that this was
a *Christian* leader writing. But it's true. And because it's true,
Jewish mistrust of non-Jews is more than understandable.

As I wrote in my book, *The Road To Holocaust,* the
allegorizing of prophetic passages and the unconditional
covenants made to the believing Jewish remnant, in which
future national blessings are guaranteed to them, open the
door to Christian anti-Jewish attitudes.

Violence From Beginning Of Jews' Return

It's also understandable that the Jews didn't wait for
Hitler to begin a movement in search of their homeland. But
the Jews found little immediate relief in Israel.

"The Mufti of Jerusalem responded to the United
Nations' announcement of the partition plan for Palestine
by declaring *jihad* or holy war against the Jews in
November 1947," recalls de Courcy. "And, on May 16,
1948, one day after the declaration of independence, the
Arab armies of Egypt, Jordan, Iraq, Syria and Lebanon,
accompanied by a Saudi Arabian contingent, attacked the
newly independent state of Israel. This single action has
defined Israel's attitude to its Arab neighbors for nearly fifty
years and will continue to do so until many decades of
peace and mutual toleration have established a confidence
that can only come from long experience, not from
signatures on pieces of paper."

In the fifteen months of that first Arab-Israeli war,
6,000 Jews were killed—about 1 percent of the total
population. When the fighting ended, it stopped with only
an armistice, not a peace treaty. The Arabs and Israelis
remained in an official state of war that has, in some cases,

only recently ended. Since then there have been four more major wars, missile attacks by Saddam Hussein and the relentless terror campaigns.

"Even the experience with Egypt, which signed a peace accord with Israel at Camp David in 1979, has not encouraged Jewish trust of the Arabs," says de Courcy. "It has been a cold peace, as only a cursory glance at the government-controlled Egyptian press is sufficient to demonstrate. Even after the start of the Madrid peace process, since which Egypt has no longer been isolated in the Arab world for being the only Arab country to sign a peace accord with Israel, the government-controlled press has continued to publish strongly anti-Israeli propaganda. Cartoons are constantly published depicting Israelis as Nazis, and the caricatures of Jews are remarkably similar to those used in Nazi Germany. Israel is blamed for every ill in Egypt, from earthquakes [supposedly caused by underground nuclear explosions] to AIDS [supposedly spread by Jewish female tourists]. There has been no normalization of relations between Egypt and Israel despite the promises of Camp David, and there is no warmth in the relationship—let alone trust."

Fifteen years into peace between Egypt and Israel, there are only two major joint economic projects under way. In Jordan, the National Islamic Front issued a religious decree against normalization of relations, declaring that "God has strictly forbidden subservience to those who usurp the land of Muslims or expel them from their homes." In Lebanon, Islamic intellectuals from around the Arab world agreed in 1994 on a program to reject "normalization with the Zionist enemy."

Israelis listen to such rhetoric and are naturally skeptical about meaningful progress with such people. Think of the attitudinal toll of the sustained terror campaign against Israeli and Jewish targets worldwide. De Courcy suspects it has had more impact than even the five wars.

Diary Of Terrorist Outrages

"Outrages like the murder of 11 Israeli athletes at the Munich Olympic Games in 1972, or the bombing of the Israeli Embassy in Argentina in 1992 with 28 deaths and over 200 injured, have made an indelible impression on Jewish minds," he explains. "This technique of warfare is accurately termed 'terror.' In the 20-plus years between the Six Day War of 1967 and the beginning of the current peace process, nearly 600 international acts of terror were either carried out or attempted by PLO groups or organizations with ties to the PLO. Some 500 people were killed as a result of these acts and nearly 2,000 wounded. These terrorist acts were carried out or attempted in some 70 countries."

Has the peace process curtailed the violence as promised? Hardly. De Courcy continues, "In the first seven months after the signing, 44 Israeli civilians and terrorists were killed in terrorist acts despite the specific commitments of PLO Chairman Yasser Arafat. In his September 9, 1993, letter to Israeli Prime Minister Yitzhak Rabin, Arafat declared that 'the PLO renounces the use of terrorism and other acts of violence and will assume responsibility over all PLO elements and personnel in order to assure their compliance, prevent violations and discipline violators . . . .' This broken promise forms just one more, but nevertheless significant, entry in the Jewish mind about the untrustworthiness of non-Jewish commitments to Jewish well-being and security."

To me, after reviewing so much of this history, it's more amazing than ever that the Israelis have seemed to bend over backward to accommodate their enemies. The "peace process," as unlikely as it is to bear fruit, seems even more incredible given the natural and predictable suspicion of most Israelis. It's even harder to believe that some Israeli leaders are prepared to return to the pre-1967 borders.

"Once the Madrid process is through," says de Courcy, "there will be no room for miscalculation. The lessons of history, the realities of geography, and the lethality of modern weaponry will ensure that the trip-wire for an Israeli pre-emptive first strike will be more sensitive than ever. What makes this all so much more worrying is that the latest post-Gulf War military studies suggest that no modern force can suffer a first strike aimed at its command-and-control systems and hope to win the subsequent contest. In other words, all depends on who moves first. So while the Israelis, already historically programmed for extreme suspicion, are bound to rely in the post-Madrid world more and more on a first-strike defense, the Arabs will be forced in the same direction. The effect will be profoundly destabilizing."

So, the peace process you have been reading about in the newspapers is actually leading toward a more dangerous Middle East and a more volatile world for the rest of us. Ishmael and Isaac are still at each other's throats. And, as the Bible shows us, this is one blood feud that only God Himself can end. And He will—but only after the Final Battle.

Chapter 3

THE STRUGGLE FOR THE HEART AND MIND OF ISLAM

"We shall never call for or accept a negotiated peace. We shall only accept war—jihad—the holy war. We have resolved to drench the lands of Palestine and Arabia with the blood of the infidels or to accept martyrdom for the glory of Allah.

—Abdul Aziz Ibn Saud

"Iran, land of ayatollah fundamentalism, is on its way to becoming the most powerful military force in the Mideast, for the moment, perhaps, second only to Israel."

—International affairs analyst **Arnold Beichman**

What is going on inside the world of Islam today has tremendous impact on how the final stages of Bible prophecy concerning Israel are fulfilled. So read this section with care. The implications are enormous.

Conflict between Arabs and Israelis. According to conventional wisdom, that's what the problems of war and peace in the Middle East are all about. If Israel would just give the Palestinians a homeland, the Arabs would be satisfied and peace would reign. If you believe that, I have some lake-front property in the Sahara Desert I'd like to sell you.

The history of the Middle East and Islam is a landscape of tribal warfare, imperial ambitions and oppression for all non-believers. A key component of the Islamic faith is the belief in a continuing struggle, a holy war—or *jihad*—to convert or eliminate every non-Muslim in its path.

And when Islam has not been warring with the "infidels" it has been battling other Muslims. Today a worldwide *jihad* exists within Islam. Never before in the history of the religion has there been such an intense worldwide struggle between nominal or cultural Muslims and the more radical, devout fundamentalists of the Ayatollah variety.

When It All Started

Islam's first civil war was fought outside of Basra, in modern-day Iraq, in December 656 AD. On one side was Ali, Mohammed's son-in-law, on the other was Ayisha, the youngest and favorite of Mohammed's ten wives. When Ayisha, who hated Ali, joined a group of anti-Shiite insurgents, the result was the Battle of the Camel—so-named because Ayisha directed her warriors from atop a camel.

Ali and his forces prevailed. To his credit, in spite of Ayisha's deep hatred, Ali magnanimously spared her, permitting Mohammed's widow to retire in Medina. Ayisha renounced politics and devoted herself to "a long vigil" by the grave of Mohammed, telling stories of the prophet to pilgrims and visitors alike for twenty-two years.

But the internal Islamic fighting was hardly over. While most Arabic tribes accepted their fate once conquered by Muslim invaders, the Persians, a fiercely proud and ancient non-Arab people, did not. With origins dating back to Nimrod and the Tower of Babel, the Persians had gone from master to servant and the transformation did not sit well. After recovering from the initial shock, they set about to destroy the Arab hegemony.

Thus, the early Islamic civil wars were less tribal than the result of a rivalry between the former subjects of the Byzantines and those of the Persian Empire. The forces were represented by the people inhabiting the land now called Iraq, influenced by the Western Greco-Roman culture, and Syria, under the domination of the Persian culture.

Ancient Rivalries Still Live

As evidence that such rivalries have a long shelf life, consider the alignment of nations in the most recent Persian

Gulf War, as Syria chose to oppose Iraq in the multi-national coalition. Likewise, in July 657, Ali and his Iraqi army met Muawiya and his Syrian forces in the city of Siffrin on the Euphrates.

While the battle was not decisive, the two warring parties retreated back to their power bases. Three years later, Muawiya declared himself, like Ali, Caliph of Islam. The following year, Ali was assassinated and Muawiya became the sole Caliph. But, once again, this was not the end of hostilities within Islam—only the beginning of a long blood feud between the Sunnis and the Shiites.

Dreams Of Past Glories

Pre-Islamic cultural enmities were at the root of Saddam Hussein's megalomaniacal imperial ambitions, too. Hussein has long seen himself as the modern-day heir to Nebuchadnezzar, the mightiest of the Babylonian kings who conquered the known world about 600 years before the birth of Christ. Early on in his reign, Hussein announced his intentions to restore Babylon to greatness. He spent billions excavating the ancient city and rebuilding its most significant sites—the temple precinct, the hanging gardens and the grand palace.

While giving lip service to Islam, Hussein rewrote the Iraqi constitution to conform to the law of Hammurabi. He even revived interest in the cult of Ishtar, Babylon's ancient pagan religion. At the reconstructed Ishtar Gate, he said: "Glorious in a glorious time, Babylon is the lady of reviving centuries, rising dignified and holy, showing the great history of Iraq. Added to its magnificence and emphasizing its originality, the phoenix of the new time rises alive from the ashes of the past to face the bright present—thus placing it on a golden throne, bringing back its charm, its charming youth, and unique glory. Babylon is not a city made of rocks and bricks, full of mere human events. It is not a forgotten place of the ancient past. Babylon is something else altogether. Since its birth, Babylon has stretched out its arms to the future—to be the seat of eternal wisdom, to represent the first civilization, and to remain as the glittering lighthouse in the dark night of history. Here is Babylon."

And Saddam Hussein is not the only Middle East leader trying to relive the glories of ancient empires. Syrian President Hafez al Assad has tried to ignite interest among his people in the memory of prouder moments of the Assyrian empire. In 1978, on the 2,750th anniversary of the destruction of Israel by the Assyrians, Assad held a lavish, week-long celebration. At the end of the feast, Assad unveiled a solid gold statue of the Assyrian deity Ashur.

"We are the heirs of Sennacherib and Shalmaneser—the greatest heroes of our nation," said Assad. "We have inherited their glory. We have inherited their wisdom. We have inherited their valor. But most of all, we have inherited their cause. Assyria must once again unite the Arab world against the imperialism of the Infidel, the interloping of the West, and the encroachment of the Jew. Assyria must arise and conquer. Nothing must be able to stand in our path. Indeed nothing can stand in our path. The world is once again divided between *Dar al Islam*—the abode of faith— and *Dar al Harb*—the abode of war. Like Sennacherib, we shall sweep aside every obstacle. Like him, we shall prevail. *Jihad. Insh'allah.*"

Couple the dangerous pipe dreams of heavily armed madmen—like Assad and Hussein—with the explosive ambitions and ancient hatreds of radical fundamentalist Islam and you begin to appreciate why the Middle East is, as Knesset member Benny Begin says, such "a dangerous neighborhood." In Islam, the call to fight the never-ending holy war is a direct commandment of Allah. The reality, more often than not, means that these wars are directed at one another. They have little to do with Israel and nothing whatsoever to do with the theoretically all-important "Palestinian issue."

The *Jihad* Within Islam

There is talk all over the Arab world today about *intifada*—or uprising. But surprisingly, this insurrectionary chant also has nothing to do with the media events in Judea, Samaria and Gaza. This is a different *intifada*—a rebellion not against Jewish authorities in Israel but against secular governments in Algeria, Egypt, Pakistan, Turkey and throughout the Arab and Islamic world. And while the *intifada* by Palestinians has been cheered and underwritten by many Arab regimes, the uprisings in these other nations are causing panic in some of those same capitals.

The rebellion in Algeria is in reaction to the military's intervention to halt the election process which seemed certain to return the Islamic Salvation Front to power. Many intelligence community observers—as well as Algerian government officials—see Iran's hand behind the fundamentalists in Algeria.

But the violent results show just why most astute observers agree that the divide between radical Islam and the industrial democracies of the West has become the most destabilizing factor in world affairs.

No Room For Democracy

Algeria was faced with a critical and troubling decision in its elections process. Should the fledgling democracy allow free elections to place in power a regime that would very likely do away with future elections? Or should it respond in a repressive and undemocratic fashion and call off the vote?

"Islamic fundamentalism of the Sunni or Shia variety in Iran, Iraq, Egypt, Jordan, the West Bank and Gaza, the Maghreb and also Algeria is not merely resistant to democracy but wholly contemptuous of and hostile to the entire democratic political culture," explains political science professor Amos Perlmutter. "Indeed radical fundamentalist elements denounced participation in the electoral process in Algeria even as a necessary and cynical way to gain power, opting instead for violent and revolutionary overthrow. There is no spirit of reconciliation between Islamic fundamentalism and the modern world that is the Christian-secular universe."

But yet the suspension of democracy in Algeria has provided even more fodder for the radicals. The clerics in Iran and throughout the Islamic world are saying that the Algerian experiment shows the West will allow democracy only as long as it provides for a succession of liberal democratic secular rulers.

"The world of blasphemy, in its bid to avert the triumph of Islam in Algeria, has trampled upon all humanitarian and democratic principles which until now it had so brazenly bragged about," said Hojjat ol-Eslam Mehdi Karrubi, Iran's speaker of the Parliament. "Islam today has put to disgrace the empty slogans of global arrogance."

If nothing else, the Algerian experiment should demonstrate once and for all that democracy—while certainly a praiseworthy ideal—is simply not a miracle cure for the complex disorders that plague the politics of the Middle East. It is also, quite simply, probably not in the cards for the region because democracy, as discussed earlier, is not compatible with Islam. Whenever Islamic fundamentalism gains dominance in a nation, it is plunged back into the dark ages of seventh century Arabia, the time and place of the prophet Mohammed. That means one man, one vote, one time.

The Raging Hot Spots

If current trends continue, more seventh-century-style tyrants may soon be in leadership positions in the Arab world:

- Iran has reportedly set up a terrorist training camp in Sudan and is supplying Egypt's neighbor with oil, weapons and military experts who are training a Muslim paramilitary force as Khartoum moves rapidly toward a radical Islamicization program.

- In Turkey, the Refah Party is making headway through the democratic process. There is now an excellent chance that in the 1996 elections, a regime friendly and open to Iran will be in charge.

- Hassan Turabi, the power behind Sudan's Islamic military government, predicts that fundamentalists will take over in most Muslim countries in the next decade, either peacefully or by force. "It is a matter of time, actually," he said in an interview. "In 10 years, you will have quite a number of countries." That was three years ago.

- Islamic fundamentalism is even gaining strength in Europe as its agents have been spotted at work in the teeming, low-cost housing developments around French cities that swarm with North African Arabs. When the time comes, they are expected to join the growing army of the "soldiers of Allah."

A Fight To The Finish

"Islamic fundamentalism is an aggressive revolutionary movement as militant and violent as the Bolshevik, fascist and Nazi movements of the past," explains Perlmutter. "The Jordanian, Pakistani, Algerian and Egyptian movements have managed to deceive the experts into believing that once they are in power, they will become reformist, gradualist and eventually will rule by law."

Indeed, Muslim zealots do seem to be gaining power around the globe. From the Persian Gulf to Morocco, Islamic fundamentalists are gaining strength through elections and violence, to the dismay not only of Israel and the West but even some Arab governments.

There is violent confrontation in Tunisia, Algeria and Egypt between Muslim militants and governments. Extremists launch bloody attacks on the authorities, who predictably react with violence and mass arrests. Hundreds of people are on trial for murder, weapons possession and conspiracy to overthrow governments. Tens of thousands have been arrested, many held for long periods without charge. Once again, such actions reinforce Islam's skepticism in democratic reforms.

"Confrontation will not subside; it's a battle to the end," explained Hussein Amin, a retired diplomat and noted writer on Islamic affairs.

At Israel's Doorstep

The Islamic civil wars are being waged right at Israel's doorstep, giving the Jewish state a second front to worry about in its war on terrorism. The situation in southern Lebanon, on Israel's northern border, is threatening to get out of hand. A limited war is now a growing possibility. Syria is using the Iranian-backed Hezbollah to wage a war of attrition against the Jewish state and its security zone in Lebanon.

And within Israel's borders the situation is not much better. In Judea, Samaria and Gaza, such fundamentalist groups as Islamic Jihad and Hamas are gaining favor among young people angered by unemployment and occupation. Some analysts believe that Yasser Arafat's days as the undisputed leader of the Palestinian movement are numbered thanks to the heightened interest in Islamic fundamentalism.

The Key Is Iran

The key nation to watch, as Islamic fundamentalism becomes an increasing threat, is Iran. Shiite officials make no secret of their desire to become the dominant Persian Gulf power through advanced nuclear research and high-tech weaponry. Egypt and Algeria have openly blamed Iran for their own problems with the radicals who have paralyzed tourism in Cairo and brought Algiers to the crisis point. Egyptian newspapers carry almost daily reports accusing Iran, Sudan and Afghanistan of training and funding fundamentalists to attack tourists and fight an underground war to replace the government with an Islamic Caliphate.

"We have strong evidence that Iran is spending money on the extremist elements through financing training camps set up in Sudan for this purpose," Interior Ministry official Brigadier Bahaeddine Ibrahim told newsmen. He said militants arrested after tourist attacks had confessed and "We were able to follow the source of the money transferred to extremist groups here."

Ibrahim said some of the militants had been trained in Afghanistan. Independent sources agreed that there was a chain of contacts between Egyptian militant leaders and countries where the extremists were in power like Iran and Sudan.

Egypt On The Brink

While a number of foreign tourists have already been killed in ambushes by Muslim terrorists, the Islamic extremists are threatening even more attacks on Egyptian tourism if Cairo continues its crackdown on fundamentalism. The radicals, who want nothing less than to turn secular Egypt into an Islamic state, have attacked foreign tourists in southern Egypt to embarrass the government and strike at one of the nation's most important industries.

For the Islamic fundamentalists, another potential source of expertise and even nuclear technology is the former Soviet republics. One day after Kazakhstan announced its independence, PLO Chairman Yasser Arafat flew there to greet President Nursultan Nazarbayev with a kiss on both cheeks. This set off alarm bells because of Kazakhstan's inheritance of 1,150 strategic nuclear weapons after the collapse of the Soviet Union. The nuclear lamp had let loose a new genie—the Islamic bomb.

Meet The Boys From Hamas

Knowing how Islamic nations treat their own dissidents or even their own loyal *dhimmi*, or non-Muslim, populations, imagine how they would treat the average Israeli if they ever got the chance. In fact, the same brand of Islamic fundamentalist now terrorizing Egypt, Algeria and other Arab nations is now initiating acts of armed insurrection against the Jewish state.

One Sunday afternoon in December 1992, three armed men marched to the middle of Khan Younis refugee camp on the Gaza Strip, fired in the air and announced they had just carried out a deadly ambush on Israeli troops. The Qassam unit—officially the Martyr Sheikh Al Ezz-Edin al Qassam military wing of the Islamic resistance movement Hamas—had quickly established itself as Israel's most deadly adversaries.

Its audacious attacks—two ambushes of Israeli army jeeps and the kidnapping of an Israeli soldier in the heart of Israel—are a dangerous turn of events for troops who had suffered few deaths in battling Arabs in the well-publicized *intifada*. Its attack on an Israeli jeep near the city of Hebron killed a reserve sergeant and critically wounded an officer.

Hamas representatives later told Khan Younis residents it snatched the Israeli weapons from the jeep before driving off, through Israel, back to the Gaza Strip. The attack was almost a carbon copy of an ambush the previous week, when Qassam guerrillas raked a military jeep in the Gaza Strip with fire, killing all three soldiers.

The Israeli censor was just clearing news of the latest jeep attack when word spread of the kidnapping of Sergeant Major Nissim Toledano. The kidnappers—using a facsimile machine to distribute a statement— threatened to kill

Toledano unless Israel quickly freed the jailed founder of Hamas, Sheikh Ahmed Yassin. Yassin, now 57, was jailed for life for ordering the murder of Arabs who have tried to work peacefully with Israeli authorities.

Qassam units are believed to be tightly organized cells, allowing survival when one is caught. Fighters tend to be in their 20s—older and more motivated than most Palestinians fighting the occupation. There appears no shortage of new recruits, driven by religious as well as anti-Israeli zeal. They were known to be trying to organize new cells in Judea and Samaria.

Israel Unifies Muslim Hatred

Arab may fight against Arab throughout the Middle East and Muslim may butcher Muslim over doctrinal differences around the world, but there is one enemy that has the potential of unifying the Islamic world. There is one enemy that can focus the hatred of Sunni and Shiite. There is one enemy that both fundamentalist and secularist can agree on. And that enemy is Israel.

While it is true that "the Palestinian issue" is a mere mirage, an excuse for hating Jews and Israel and turning the world against them, it is also true that the radical Islamic world will never accept the existence of the Jewish state no matter what concessions it makes toward peace. Negotiations and peace talks are merely seen in the Arab world as secondary battlegrounds in the eventual move to exterminate the population of Israel.

It is common knowledge today that the Grand Mufti of Jerusalem during World War II was pro-Nazi. It is not so well understood today that the current Mufti, Sheikh Tamimi, is just as profoundly anti-Jewish. The leader of

Islam in Jerusalem was responsible for organizing the deadly Temple Mount uprising. And he recently called for all Muslims to join arms against Israel.

"The Jews are destined to be persecuted, humiliated and tortured forever, and it is a Muslim duty to see to it that they reap their due," he said. "No petty arguments must be allowed to divide us. *Where Hitler failed, we must succeed.*" (emphasis added)

Yasser Arafat may look like a moderate compared to his rivals in the hyper-fundamentalist group Hamas, but his suggestions for what must be done to the state of Israel are no less blood-curdling.

"Our objective is simply the liberation of the Palestinian soil and the establishment of a Palestinian state over every part of it," he said. "Thus, the Jews must be removed and Israel must be annihilated. We can accept nothing less." This is the man to whom Israel has turned over Jericho, the Gaza Strip and soon more territory.

The Phony Palestinian Issue

With animosity and intractability so blatant, why do the diplomats, professional politicians and media pundits focus so single-mindedly on the Palestinian issue in their Mideast analysis? Isn't it clear that there is a more fundamental obstacle to peace in the region?

Perhaps it is time to listen to what the key players in the Middle East are actually saying and take them at their word. Here's how Hashemi Rafsanjani, sometimes described as the "moderate" leader of Iran, boiled the crisis down to its essence: "Every problem in our region can be traced to this single dilemma: the occupation of *Dar al Islam* by Jewish infidels or Western imperialists. Every political controversy, every boundary dispute and every internal conflict is spawned by the inability of the *Umma* to faithfully and successfully wage *Jihad. The everlasting struggle between Ishmael and Isaac cannot cease until one or the other is utterly vanquished.*" (emphasis added)

Now that is the teaching of a really committed Muslim. If you follow Islam, that is the attitude you will take. It is very interesting to note that Rafsanjani is a Persian, an Iranian, not an Arab. Yet he refers to the ancient origin of this conflict—Ishmael and Isaac. All of Israel's enemies are aware of it. Though Rafsanjani is an Iranian, he adopts the Arab cause as his own because, as a Muslim, he has absorbed the hatred of the Arab world through his religion.

It is clear that the Islamic *jihad* against the West, the Jews and Israel will be the most destabilizing factor in world affairs during the '90s. "It is this divide," warns intelligence expert de Courcy, "that makes the fate of the former USSR's 30,000 nuclear warheads and 1.7 million weapons technologists of such critical importance."

With that in mind, let me tell you what happened in 1991 after the breakup of the Soviet Union. There are five very powerful Muslim republics to the south of Russia. Three of them have a huge store of intercontinental ballistic missiles and nuclear warheads. The Russians, fearing an Iranian alliance with these southern neighbors, made a secret agreement with Tehran. I first heard about this from an Israeli general in the Mossad. It took the rest of the world eight months to find out about it, and most people still don't realize what happened. The agreement between Boris Yeltsin and Rafsanjani offered the best Soviet arms to Iran in exchange for a pledge not to evangelize these Muslim republics. Russia would help itself economically by making available to Iran some of the world's top technicians and scientists—including nuclear engineers—who were unemployed. Iran began with 273 of Russia's top nuke experts, many of whom are still working there. In addition, before Russia shut down the arms fire sale, Iran purchased three nuclear warheads from Kazakhstan.

Iran armed to the teeth with nuclear weapons—that ought to keep you awake at night. But, you might say, given the relative ease with which the United States and its allied forces defeated Saddam Hussein's army in the Persian Gulf War, do the Islamic nations really pose a serious military threat to the West?

Imagine for a moment what might have happened if Saddam Hussein had at his disposal one or more thermo-nuclear devices during the war. Consider the possible results if the U.S. forces had continued the war and marched right into Baghdad. Is there any doubt that Saddam would have considered pushing the nuclear button and, quite possibly, launching World War III?

That is precisely the prospect we may be facing the next time the West is engaged in combat in the Middle East. Iran's plans for neighbors. And the nukes aren't the only weapons of mass destruction in Iran's arsenal.

In November 1991, Iran's Operation Grand Design went into full-scale military maneuvers that included an amphibious invasion in chemical environment. This tactic is clearly designed for the eventual overthrow of the House of Saud. By taking out Saudi Arabia, the Iran-Syria alliance would remove a vital Western military base, control the Islamic holy places and deprive the West of its supply of oil. According to intelligence sources, the plan then calls for an all-out airborne chemical and nuclear assault on the state of Israel. This would also explain why Syria opposed Iraq in the Persian Gulf War. Syria didn't want Iraq to beat it to the Saudi oil fields!

It's Just A Matter Of Time

Meanwhile, the Central Intelligence Agency says that Iran will be able to *produce* its own nuclear weapons by the year 2000. Iran is not relying solely on the republics of the former Soviet Union for technical expertise in its quest for weapons of mass destruction. Another key strategic ally for the Islamic world in this regard is China.

In the spring of 1991, Leonard S. Spector of the Carnegie Endowment for International Peace told a congressional subcommittee that China was helping Algeria in the development of a nuclear weapons program.

"This is a supplier (China) that seems to be operating without restraint and a recipient (Algeria) that seems to be operating as though this was the norm," Spector testified. " (Algeria) is a country that doesn't even have the security problems of, say, Pakistan or Israel. It seems as though a country has entered into a nuclear weapons program rather lightly. It's almost gratuitous."

Intelligence sources say China has already provided at least some sophisticated nuclear technology to both Iraq and Iran. How sophisticated? According to the best intelligence experts, China "is supplying nuclear weapons technology and military advice on how to match nuclear weapons to various aerial and missile delivery systems."

And what does China have to say about these reports? Yes, China admits, it has provided nuclear technology to Iran and other nations in the Middle East. But it was all intended strictly for "peaceful purposes." But of course—we all know China and Iran's commitment to peace, don't we!

Iran Building Missile Industry

Even the mainstream news media are finally beginning to catch on to the Iranian nuclear threat. An in-depth Associated Press report stated that "the Iranians may be trying to develop nuclear weapons, in a clandestine program similar to that unmasked in Iraq after the Gulf War."

"Iran says it seeks nuclear reactors and the associated technology to expand industry and ensure growth once its oil runs out, but denies wanting nuclear weapons," the report said.

Iran is engaged in a major rearmament, the report acknowledged, which includes building chemical weapons and missile industries, aimed at making it the region's strongest power.

"Nuclear weapons would give Tehran's fundamentalist leadership a military strength matched in the Middle East only by Israel, the region's sole nuclear power," the AP dispatch added. "U.S. and European strategists see that as a blueprint for destabilizing an already dangerous region and creating a serious long-term threat to Western interests."

The report quoted Atta'ollah Mohajerani, one of Rafsanjani's vice presidents, who said recently: "Regardless of the United Nations' effort to prevent nuclear proliferation, Muslims must . . . cooperate among themselves and produce their own nuclear bomb because the enemy has nuclear facilities."

Other Iranian leaders have made similar statements. Meanwhile, Western officials believe Iran's recent acquisition of Scud-C ballistic missiles from North Korea could eventually provide a delivery system capable of reaching targets in Israel, Iraq and Saudi Arabia. The Mujahideen Khalq, the main Iranian opposition movement, claims Iran has spent $800 million since 1988 and that $2 billion more has been committed. Much of the money is not declared in budget allocations.

The Nuclear Weapons Black Market

Just as Saddam skirted international controls with a global network of front companies, Iran's nuclear weapons program—known as "the Great Plan"—has its own clandestine procurement system.

Iran purchased a 300-megawatt reactor from China despite U.S. efforts to block the deal, and may be negotiating to buy another. Washington thwarted an earlier attempt to buy a reactor from India was frustrated by Washington. Tehran hopes Russia will honor a 1989 agreement by the former Soviet Union to provide two 450-megawatt nuclear plants despite Moscow's expressed intention to abide by international controls. Years will be needed to build the Chinese reactor, but when completed, it will be the first in Iran capable of producing weapons-grade uranium. Once that is available, experts say, building a bomb is only a step away.

In 1992, Iran demanded enriched uranium from France as part of a settlement in a $1 billion dispute over a loan made by the Shah that was frozen in 1979, after the Islamic revolution. Paris refused. Iran, unlike Iraq, has extensive uranium ore deposits at Saghand in eastern Yazd province and has built a big processing plant there. Some Western officials suspect it is able to sidestep IAEA safeguards by enriching undeclared uranium at secret facilities.

"Any country that can run a nuclear reactor is able to make enriched or purified uranium," said Frank Barnaby, a nuclear-weapons expert based in London. He said fissionable material could be obtained as little as six months after a reactor becomes operational. The Iranians have acquired military nuclear technology from China and Pakistan, as well as a vast range of equipment from the West, despite international controls.

Tehran is building its conventional military forces as rapidly as it is developing and deploying its nuclear assets. On October 25, 1992, one of three Russian Kilo-class submarines purchased by Iran sailed through the Suez Canal on its way to the Persian Gulf.

Further news of Iran's continuing arms buildup comes almost daily, reports *Intelligence Digest*. There are reports that North Korea has shipped to Iran 100-300 km-range Scud missiles (half of which may be due to be passed on to Syria). This shipment is said to be in addition to 250 missiles already received from North Korea, China and Russia.

Tehran's Growing Arsenal

By 1997, Iran plans to have acquired some *2,000 missiles,* intelligence sources say. There are also reports of a massive arms deal imminent between China and Iran that will provide Tehran with "an enormous quantity of arms" including:

- 38 warplanes that will join the 115 combat craft acquired from Iraq during the Persian Gulf War;
- 10 ballistic missile systems, including five Silkworms;
- 50 armored vehicles designed for riot control;
- 400 tanks;
- 400 medium-range 120mm and 122mm artillery pieces;

- A range of light military equipment, including shoulder-held armor-piercing missiles, radars and other surveillance systems.

But China is hardly the only guilty party when it comes to arming the radical nations of the Middle East. Despite former President George Bush's call to limit arms sales to the region, in the first six months after the Persian Gulf War, the U.S. sold $13.2 billion worth of weapons to the nations of the area. Remember, the U.S. played a large role in arming Saddam Hussein prior to Iraq's invasion of Kuwait.

Other Iranian Weapons

Iran is leading this holy war with the West—this *jihad*—on many fronts. For instance, the Iranian and Syrian governments are counterfeiting U.S. dollars by the millions and destabilizing the entire world economy in an aggressive effort to buy their way into a position of military superiority in the Middle East in preparation for a full-scale "holy war" against Israel and eventually America, which Iran's extremists call "the Great Satan."

The ambitious counterfeiting operation used U.S.-trained printing technicians and U.S. note-printing machinery by the Iranian government's central bank to print millions of nearly perfect $100 bills. Syria has used the counterfeit money for the purchase of strategic weapons, the report said. But the larger purpose behind the massive fake money scandal seems to be the undermining of the U.S. dollar and the American banking system.

"It is estimated that the potential is there for billions of dollars in counterfeit currency to soon be in circulation, mainly outside the U.S. banking system," the report said. The report added that if the counterfeiting operation is not thwarted soon "the implications for the dollar's role as the international medium of exchange could be serious."

After they are printed in Tehran, boxes of the bills are flown to Damascus on Iran Air flights and readied for distribution in Lebanon by Syrian intelligence. Syrian operatives have reportedly shipped crateloads and suitcases full of the bills to Czechoslovakia and the Ukraine as payment for high-performance weapons.

Other Monetary Scams

This is not the only way fundamentalist Islam has misused the world's banking system in an effort to gain more influence and power. Rachel Ehrenfeld, an expert on banking and narco-terrorism, reports that the real mission of the scandal-plagued Bank of Credit and Commerce International—or BCCI—was not financial. The real aim of BCCI from the outset, she says, was to put forward a radical-Islamic political agenda and to support subversive Third World causes.

"From the beginning, BCCI's founder, Pakistani businessman Agha Hasan Abedi, a member of the ultra-religious, quasi-secret Sufi sect, made plain the bank's ideological bent," she reported in the New York Times. "He and other bank officials openly discussed their political and religious mission."

The idea was for BCCI to achieve enough political power to compete with—even dominate—Western financial institutions. BCCI bankrolled media outlets such as *South Magazine* and financed opinion columns on the Middle East in the Western press. In the U.S., BCCI aided in the purchase of several cable TV systems.

"BCCI had plenty of cash: millions from drug traffickers and approximately $1 billion of unrecorded banking deposits from Islamic countries, principally Saudi Arabia," Ms. Ehrenfeld charges. "According to British investigators, BCCI was the bank for the Islamic fundamentalists as well as terrorist groups like Abu Nidal and Shining Path, the violent Maoist terrorist organization operating in Peru."

Weapon No. 1: Oil

Clearly, Iran will build its Islamic empire by any means necessary. But, by far, its most effective weapon is still its vast oil riches. After a long decline, Tehran is back in the upper ranks of the world's oil powers.

"A boom-town mentality has taken hold across southern Iran," according to a report in the *Wall Street Journal*. "Some 50 rigs are in action in the region's oil fields, up from eight just three years ago. The state oil company is even drilling under the local airport and the city of Ahwaz itself. It is all part of a $5 billion campaign to expand oil production, known as Val-Fajr, a Farsi expression that loosely translates as 'I swear to the dawn.'"

Faster than the experts predicted, Iran's oil producing crusade is paying big dividends. It is now pumping 4 million barrels a day, a level not seen since the era of the Shah. Thus, Iran is now ranked as the fourth largest oil-producing nation in the world—after Saudi Arabia, the U.S. and Russia. In 1992, Iran collected an estimated $20 billion in oil revenue.

And guess who's helping make it all possible for the Tehran regime? You guessed it: American oil companies. Though Iran remains as viciously anti-American as ever in its rhetoric, U.S. oil companies are putting their pocketbooks ahead of patriotism—and good sense—and rushing in to capitalize on the oil boom in Iran.

These kinds of economic policies—some legitimate, some fraudulent—allow Iran, Syria and other Islamic fundamentalist states to arm themselves to the teeth in pursuit of their policies of "theocratic imperialism and militarism," as international affairs analyst Arnold Beichman describes it. Iran has been on an arms-buying spree since the end of its war with Iraq in 1988.

And what strategic sites are immediately targeted by those weapons? Beichman and other geo-strategic experts believe Iran—like Iraq before her—is preparing to attack Saudi Arabia and the Arab emirate states.

"Its main aim is to dominate the Persian Gulf and, therefore, in addition to wanting to control southern Iraq, it has an interest in seeing Saudi Arabia surrounded with hostile states to the south and west," says de Courcy. "Whether by luck or judgment, anti-Saudi parties are now in control or are gaining control in Somalia, Yemen and Sudan. Islamist radicals are also putting the pro-Western Egyptian regime under increasing pressure."

What does all this mean for Israel and the coming final battle? Although Iranian support for radical forces in these countries is not primarily aimed at Israel, it does have implications for Israeli security. Not only are these forces anti-Saudi, they are even more anti-Israel.

"Tehran sees itself not only as the dominant force in the Persian Gulf but also as the head of the pan-Islamist movement; and playing a leading role in the expulsion of the Jews from Palestine and returning Jerusalem to Islamic control would greatly enhance Tehran's Islamist status, particularly at the expense of the hated House of Saud," says de Courcy.

And who else is selling this military hardware to Iran? A $1 billion contract was signed between Tehran and the Russian Federation last March. It will provide the Iranian armed forces with 400 T-72 tanks. The Russians are also providing the training. Moscow has also contracted to supply Iran with 500 BMP-2 armored fighting vehicles, each equipped with anti-armor laser-guided missiles. Last year, Iran spent $5 billion with China, $4 billion with Russia and $3 billion with North Korea for the best weapons money can buy.

Terror And The War On Jews

The other major weapon in Iran's arsenal is terrorism. And, for now, this is the weapon of choice Tehran employs against the state of Israel. Through such organizations as Islamic Jihad, the Muslim Brotherhood and Hamas, Iran is sponsoring a guerrilla war of attrition against not only the Jewish state, but all Jews.

"The war is open until Israel ceases to exist and until *the last Jew in the world is eliminated*," explains Hamas (emphasis added). This from an organization that is commanding more respect and admiration within Israel's own borders. Roving gangs of Hamas terrorists murder prostitutes, alcoholics or others violating Islamic law within Judea, Samaria and the Gaza Strip. And in recent university and chamber of commerce elections in these territories, Hamas candidates have often outpolled those of the Palestine Liberation Organization.

Terror is also official state policy in Iran. In late 1994, for instance, Western intelligence sources found that

Tehran's secret agents had begun sending large numbers of unaccompanied suitcases through airport security and onto airlines in an effort to gather information on airline security. Obviously, those sources feared that the Iranians could only be trying to find security loopholes that could be exploited by terrorists who would either be transporting illicit materials or placing explosive devices on planes.

Iran's international terrorist web was founded in 1984, according to de Courcy, when the Supreme Coordinating Council was established between the Islamic Revolution in Iran and the Islamic Revolutionary Movements Worldwide. Of all the extremist groups inspired and directed by Iran, the most lethal by far is the Islamic Jihad. Writing in the June 1991 edition of *Matara*, the Israeli magazine for intelligence, weapons, military and security, terrorist expert Boaz Ganor described the group as "one of the most complex and dangerous of the Arab and Palestinian terrorist organizations." Made up of many factions and cells throughout the Middle East and Europe that act independently, all share a common loyalty to Tehran and the Iranian revolution.

"What distinguishes Islamic Jihad from other Islamic-inspired groups aiming to overthrow domestic secular regimes is the priority it gives to the struggle against the Jews," says de Courcy. "The war to remove the Jews from Palestine is seen by Jihad as an essential first step toward fulfilling the wider goals of Islam. The groups stresses that the conflict with the Jews is religious-based and not just a question of territory. Islamic Jihad activists are fanatic in the extreme, and to die in the cause is an honor—a passport to paradise. These fanatics are controlled, and used, by Iran in pursuit of its diplomatic and strategic goals."

There can be no doubt that the terrorism that Iran is able to unleash through its control of a worldwide network of Islamic terrorists is a very potent weapon. But there are more cunning sides to Tehran's foreign policies as well. It is a mistake, de Courcy suggests, to dismiss Iran as just another pariah state like Libya.

"The Iranian regime is much more astute that Colonel Gadhafi, and Iran is an immeasurably more-important country than Libya," he says. "For a start, it has a population of 63 million, which is growing at about 3.5 percent annually. This makes it the most populous state in the Middle East, ahead of both Turkey and Egypt, which have populations of 60 million each. Western observers constantly underestimate Iran, particularly the subtlety of its diplomacy which bears no resemblance at all to the ill-thought-out antics of Colonel Gadhafi or the singular misjudgments of Saddam Hussein. Iran is much more calculated in its foreign policy than the rhetoric at Friday prayers in Tehran would suggest. This pragmatism has enabled Tehran to build a formidable regional alliance in the face of continuing American hostility. It is now quite possible to discern the makings of an Iranian-inspired bloc that includes Pakistan, Turkey, Syria and Lebanon. Iran has also been making overtures to Egypt and has been careful to maintain good relations with India."

Iran has also used its cunning to extort from the West the credit and trade it needs to finance its international *jihad*. In a very real way, the West is selling the Iranians the rope they will use to hang their benefactors. In 1994, the *Jerusalem Report* uncovered details of how France and Germany capitulated to Iran's international extortion.

Blackmail By Terrorists

"Iran is blackmailing the West," the magazine reported. "It is using the threat of terrorism to pressure Western nations to reschedule debts, boost trade and even release jailed Iranian terror suspects. . . . Within under a year, the government of Ali-Akbar Hashemi Rafsanjani has managed to get a massive $6.2 billion of foreign debt repayments postponed—enabling the desperately cash-strapped regime to keep its head above water, and maintain its hundreds of millions of dollars of spending on conventional arms, missile technology, chemical weapons and its nuclear program."

It wasn't that long ago that the free world was literally held hostage by Iran. Americans, in particular, have a short memory. Unless this ornery beast is defanged and declawed pretty soon, the next time Iran tries to blackmail the West, it may have its finger on a nuclear trigger—just in time for the inevitable Final Battle.

Chapter 4

MODERN-DAY ANTI-SEMITISM AND THE ROAD TO HOLOCAUST

"The power struggle between Israel and the Arabs is a long-term historical trial. Victory or defeat are for us questions of existence or annihilation, the outcome of an irreconcilable hatred."

—Al Riyadh Saud

"The Talmud says that if a Jew does not drink every year the blood of a non-Jewish man, he will be damned for eternity."

—Marouf al Dawalibi
Saudi Arabian delegate to 1984 U.N. Human Rights Commission conference on religious tolerance.

What started as a sibling rivalry and evolved into a racial blood feud has escalated into a deadly religious war that threatens the whole planet.

The ancient hatred of Jews has been justified as a religious cause within the Muslim teachings. Islam literally took the old Arab antipathies and jealousies toward the Jews and enshrined them into a basic religious doctrine. This 1,400-year-old hatred is simmering to the boiling point and will soon provoke the worst bloodbath the world has ever seen—what Bible prophecies predict as the greatest war of all times, the Final Battle.

You can't begin to appreciate how violent and terrible this Final Battle will be without fully understanding the roots of the seething hatred that will inspire it. Beginning with Mohammed and continuing today, Islam has contained an inherently anti-Jewish character. Despite propaganda to the contrary, this characteristic has meant centuries of horror for all non-Muslims—especially Jews—unfortunate enough to be forced to live in a Muslim country. These unfortunate refugees are called *dhimmis* by the Muslims.

It was under Caliph Omar that the laws regarding non-believers were firmly established by Islam. As *dhimmis,* Jews were forbidden to touch the Koran, forced to wear distinctive clothes and a yellow badge (Christians wore blue), not permitted to perform religious practices in public, not allowed to own a horse and required to bury their dead without any public grief expressed.

As an expression of gratitude for being allowed to live among Muslims, *dhimmis* were expected to pay special confiscatory taxes prescribed by the Koran.

"Islamic religious law decreed that, although murder of one Muslim by another Muslim was punishable by death, a Muslim who murdered a non-Muslim was given not the death penalty, but only the obligation to pay 'blood money' to the family of the slain infidel," writes Joan Peters in *From Time Immemorial.* "Even this punishment was unlikely, however, because the law held the testimony of a Jew or a Christian invalid against a Muslim, and the penalty could only be exacted under improbably conditions—when two Muslims were willing to testify against a brother Muslim for the sake of an infidel."

This kind of ruthless double-standard in Islam has carried down through the centuries—enforced to varying degrees of cruelty depending on the character of the Muslim ruler and the country. Under the best of circumstances, life was merely intolerable and filled with indignities. In the worst of circumstances, Jews and Christians lived every moment of every day in fear for their very lives.

Slavery And Dehumanization

Life for Jews has always been particularly demeaning. In Yemen, for example, Jews were treated like subhuman slaves, forced to clean the public latrines and clear the streets of animal carcasses without pay on their Sabbath day. A Yemenite law also decreed that fatherless Jewish children under thirteen be taken from their mothers and raised as Muslims.

"Children were torn away from their mothers," according to historian S.D. Goitein. "To my mind this law, which was enforced with new vigor about 50 years ago, more than anything else impelled the Yemenite Jews to quit that country to which they were very much attached. The result was that many families arrived in Israel with one or more of their children lost to them . . . some widows . . . [were] bereaved in this way of all their offspring." Persecution in Yemen was consistent and extreme over the years. Stoning Jews continued as an age-old custom right up until most Yemenite Jews left the country beginning in 1948.

Given Saddam Hussein's propensity to lob SCUD missiles into Israel during the Persian Gulf War, it should not be surprising that Iraq has a long history of persecuting Jews. More than 123,000 Iraqi Jews fled to Israel between 1949 and 1952 alone. In most cases, they were lucky to escape with the clothes on their backs.

There was a large Jewish presence in Babylonia until the Muslim conquest in the year 634. Later, the heavy taxes were imposed, synagogues razed and, ultimately, entire communities were slaughtered.

"The attitude of the Muslims toward the Christians and Jews, to whom . . . they are in a majority of 10 to 1, is that of a master towards slaves whom he treats with a certain lordly tolerance so long as they keep their place," wrote the British vice-consul just after the turn of the century. "Any sign to pretension of equality is promptly repressed. It is often noticed in the streets that almost any Christian submissively makes way even for a Muslim child. Only a few days ago the writer saw two respectable looking, middle-aged Jews walking in a garden. A small Muslim boy, who could not have been more than 8 years old, passed by and, as he did so, picked up a large stone and threw it at them—and then another—with the utmost nonchalance, just as a small boy elsewhere might aim at a dog or a bird. The Jews stopped and avoided the aim, which was a good one, but made no further protest."

Many Jews were put to death for the trumped-up charge of expressing disrespect for the Koran or Mohammed. There were persistent blood libel accusations and persecutions throughout the 19th century.

After The Imperial Powers

When the Europeans finally left their Middle East colonies behind, they helped create a nationalistic group of Arab states that saw the Jews as their biggest political threat. While, in the past, Arabs maintained a disdainful, demeaning yet paternalistic attitude toward "their" Jews, the new situation in the region resulted in "a completely demoniacal and negative stereotype of the Jew," explains Peters.

"Traditional Koranic slurs against the Jews were implemented to incite hostility toward the Jewish national movement," she writes. "The Nazi anti-semitism in the 1930s and 1940s flourished in this already receptive climate."

In 1941, the Jewish community in Baghdad was attacked by Iraqi soldiers, policemen and civilians worked up to a fever pitch by Nazi propaganda. The result was a full-scale massacre—or *Farhud*—in which anywhere from 150 to 600 Jews were killed. After the 1948 victory by Israel, Zionism became a capital crime in Iraq. Jews were publicly hanged in Baghdad on a regular basis to the enthusiastic cheers of Iraqi crowds.

While the Jewish community in Egypt prior to 1948 was considered to live in relative peace and harmony compared to other neighboring Arab nations, the truth is life was no picnic there either. It was not uncommon for Jews to be jostled in the street by Muslims or to be beaten severely merely for passing on the right hand side of a Muslim.

Beginning in the 1940s, spurred by Nazi propaganda and the rise of Zionism, many Jews were killed in anti-Jewish riots. Egypt even passed laws that all but prohibited Jews from being employed. The government confiscated property, and after the 1947 vote to partition Palestine, Jewish homes were looted and synagogues destroyed.

In one 10-day period in 1948, 150 Jews were murdered or seriously wounded in Egyptian bloodletting. As soon as a ban on Jews leaving the country was lifted in 1949, 20,000 fled Egypt mostly for Israel.

Identifying With Hitler

"Our sympathy was with the Germans," explained Egypt's President Gamal Abdel Nasser in 1964. "The president of our Parliament, for instance, Anwar Sadat, was imprisoned for his sympathy with the Germans."

Even in the 1970s, a prominent Egyptian writer was, once more, helping to stir up the old blood libels against the Jews. Anis Mansour assured his readers that the medieval lie that Jews sacrificed children and drank their blood was historically true and that "the Jews confessed." Because of this, he said it was perfectly appropriate to persecute "the wild beasts." Another time he wrote, "People all over the world have come to realize that Hitler was right, since Jews . . . are bloodsuckers . . . interested in destroying the whole world which has . . . expelled them and despised them for centuries . . . and burnt them in Hitler's crematoria . . . one million . . . six millions. Would that he had finished it!"

Mansour is hardly regarded as some kind of renegade nut in Egypt. In 1975 he represented the nation at the 40th International PEN (writers') Conference in Vienna. Whereupon his return he charged that "the Jews are guilty" for Nazism, and that they "have only themselves to blame."

If Egypt was a bad place to be Jewish in the 20th century, Syria was a living hell. Damascus became the headquarters of anti-Jewish activities as Nazism and Zionism arose. During World War II, the Jewish quarter was raided several times as rumors that Churchill and Roosevelt had agreed to make Syria a Jewish state began to circulate. In 1947, anti-Jewish riots resulted in the destruction of most synagogues, more than 150 homes, 5 schools, 50 shops and offices. Even today, the remaining Jewish community lives cloistered in tiny ghettoes, fearing for its collective life.

Teaching Anti-Semitism

In many cases, they reflected official policies of the Arab governments. Such was also the case with a pattern of anti-Jewish propaganda distributed and taught in the public schools of Arab countries. For example:

- "The Jews in Europe were persecuted and despised because of their corruption, meanness and treachery," history students in Jordan were taught in 1966 and after.

- "Israel was born to die. Prove it," high school students in the same country were instructed.

- "The Jews . . . lived exiled and despised since by their nature they are vile, greedy and enemies of mankind," a Syrian junior high school reader stated.

- "We shall expel all the Jews," a fifth year elementary school syntax exercise suggested.

- "The Arabs do not cease to act for the extermination of Israel," an Egyptian junior high grammar exercise stated.

- "Israel hopes to be the homeland of the Jew, and they have the stubbornness of 4,000 years of history behind them. But Israel shall not live if the Arabs stand fast in their hatred. She shall wither and decline. Even if all the human race, and the devil in Hell, conspire to aid her, she shall not exist," said an Egyptian ninth-grade text.

Official Anti-Jewishness

"The anti-Semitic literature published by the Arabs since World War II has been voluminous, and is continually increasing, despite the almost total evacuation of the Arab world's Jews," writes Peters. "The virulence of this literature is disturbing, but even more significant is the official or governmental origin of the publications—not from an extremist fringe, which might be lightly dismissed, but from Arab governments, including those called 'moderate.'"

The Arab press, in most cases government-sponsored and always government approved, is the most vicious propagator of anti-Jewish slurs today. Here are samples of what the official and semi-official media in the so-called "moderate" land of Egypt are saying:

- *El-Ahram*, the leading daily with over 700,000 readers, carried a book review of *The First Terrorists*, in which the critic, Abd El-Muneim Qandil, asserted March 3, 1987: "I lower my pen in respect to the author who presents proof from Israeli books to the malice of the Jews who wish to kill all male newborns and pregnant women in order to uproot the Palestinians . . . The author speaks about turning facts upside down . . . such as their claim that the gas chambers used by Hitler to get rid of people infected by plague were especially built to burn Jews alive."

- *El Masa*, a daily of 100,000, reported April 21, 1987: "Jews distributed a 'ridiculous lie' after the Second World War concerning the Holocaust. They started with the claim that 100,000 Jews were exterminated but later reached the figure of 8 million. Jews are inflating these numbers in order to achieve bigger help from the U.S.A. . . . We can expect, therefore, that very soon the number of Jews killed by the Nazis will reach 10 million."

- *Sawt El-Arab*, a daily with 100,000 circulation on March 15, 1987: "Israel sells to Egypt seeds, plants and cattle infected with diseases in order to destroy the local agriculture."

- *El Mukhtar El-Islami*, a monthly religious publication in April 1986: "The Jews were responsible for World War II. They initiated this war in order to crush Nazi Germany which was the last obstacle before Jewish domination of the world. Europe was indeed destroyed and Zionist strategy had its victory. The Jews were also behind the murder of President Abraham Lincoln."

- *El-Nur*, weekly publication of the Muslim Brotherhood, circulated 100,000, said October 22, 1986: "We wait for the moment that all Jews will gather in Palestine and that will be the great day for enormous massacre."

- *Sawt Filastin*, a semi-official weekly published for Palestinians in August 1987, the fifth anniversary of the Sabra and Shatilla massacre: "Deception and treason are basic components of Jewish character. Jews always

used tricks and plots to spread terror and death all over
the world."

- *El-Tawhid*, a fundamentalist Islamic monthly stated in
  February 1987: The children of Israel are "garbage,
  allied with Satan, purulence causing pain and infection,
  a deposit of germs."

Fundamentalism Inspired By Israel?

While the Islamic world has shown a tremendous
amount of hatred toward Jews and Israel, many analysts
strongly suspect that Islamic fundamentalism is actually
growing in large part out of an odd sort of respect for the
faith of the Jews. The secular revolution of Nasser in Egypt
failed in the Six-Day War and the Arabs reflected soberly
about that. Why, they wondered, would Allah desert them?

"We lost," said the Islamists, "because we had wandered
away from religion; our enemy prevailed because it could
combine faith and modern warfare."

A *U.S. News & World Report* analysis continued: "The
Islamists did not understand the modern and worldly basis of
Israel's triumph. They saw the exterior of things. Thus, when
Gen. Shlomo Goren, the chief Army chaplain, turned up at
the Temple Mount on June 7, a *sefer torah* under his arm and
a shofar (ram's horn) in his left hand, the Islamicists saw in
him a vindication of a belief in the power of faith. The
defeated Arab states would cater to the new Islamic
sensibility. It was one way of offering solace and consolation,
of absorbing the wrath of the young who had believed that
the men at the helm had built a more competent world. Two
months after the defeat, the Egyptian press reported that
booklets explaining the meaning of the *jihad* (holy war) and
recounting the military campaigns of the Prophet had been

distributed to the armed forces. But the new religious zeal would prove difficult to harness and contain."

Christians Also Targeted

Indeed it has been difficult to contain. And just like the Jews that were driven out of Islamic lands, Christians are the newest targets. Here are just a few examples of the kinds of persecution occurring through the Islamic world:

- In Egypt, Muslim extremists burned 15 houses and shops owned by Christians in the southern part of the country in the summer of 1992. Casualties from that round of religious fighting rose to 9 dead and 22 wounded.

- Coptic Christians in Egypt have been forced to stay inside their mud hovels for months at a time due to the intensity of persecution by Muslims. "Life for Christians here is over," said one Copt. "Now we must figure out how to get out." Coptic Christians, who number 7 million to 8 million of Egypt's 56 million people belong to one of the oldest denominations in Christendom.

- A Pakistani court sentenced a Christian to death for blasphemy against the Prophet Mohammed, a charge brought by a private party.

The Koranic Verses

Where does this kind of hatred originate? Much of it comes from the Koran itself. The Muslim holy book pulls no punches in its denunciations of Jews, Christians and their faiths:

- "Take neither Jews, nor Christians for your friends with one another. Whosoever of you seeks their friendship shall become one of their number. Allah does not guide the wrongdoers."

- "Ignominy shall be their portion (the Jews) wheresoever they are found . . . . They have incurred anger from their Lord, and wretchedness is laid upon them . . . because they . . . disbelieve the revelations of Allah and slew the Prophets wrongfully . . . because they were rebellious and used to transgress."

- "And though wilt find them (the Jews) the greediest of mankind. . . ."

- "Evil is that for which they sell their souls . . . . For disbelievers is a terrible doom."

- "Taste ye (Jews) the punishment of burning."

- "Those who disbelieve Our revelations, We shall expose them to the fire. As often as their skins are consumed We shall exchange them for fresh skins that they may taste the torment."

- "Because of the wrongdoing of the Jews. . . . And of their taking usury . . . and of their devouring people's wealth by false pretenses. We have prepared for those of them who disbelieve a painful doom."

- "Allah hath cursed them (the Jews) for their disbelief."

- "They (the Jews) will spare no pains to corrupt you. They desire nothing but your ruin. Their hatred is clear from what they say, but more violent is the hatred which their breasts conceal."

- "The most vehement of mankind in hostility (are) the Jews and the idolators."

- "You shall surely find the most violent of all men in enmity against the *Umma* to be the Jews."
- "The Jews are smitten with vileness and misery and drew on themselves indignation from Allah."
- "Wherever they are found, the Jews reek of destruction—which is their just reward."

With that kind of Hitlerian institutionalized anti-semitism justified by religion, is it any wonder that nearly all the Jews living under that system have gladly left their possessions behind to escape the intolerance?

The demonization of the Jewish people by the Arabs should seem ludicrous on the face of it. More than 100 years ago—in a *Turkish* court, of all places—the blood libel story was proven to be without any merit. The problem is, even today, these atrocious lies are still being spread and, apparently, believed by many.

No other action than the spreading of the blood libel by well-educated and respected members of the Arab political and cultural elite so perfectly illustrates why all the peace talks in the world can't solve the Arab-Israeli conflict. It also put to the lie any suggestion that today's radical Arab leadership will accept any compromise short of the annihilation of the entire Jewish state.

Long before Israel's statehood was reconstituted in 1948, leaders of Arab thought began recycling the most vicious anti-Semitic stories that had circulated through the Christian world in less enlightened times and combined and embellished those blood libels with the voluminous anti-Jewish Koranic and Islamic teachings writings. That combination of hate-filled rhetoric formed an explosive series of myths against which reason alone seems helpless.

The Jews, they said, were the lowest form of life. They are, the new mythology contended, characteristically arrogant, domineering, cunning, treacherous, cowardly, liars and cheats. If that wasn't enough, the Arabs have frequently revived the blood libel—the satanically false charge that the Jews use the blood of non-Jewish children for religious purposes, especially on Passover. This is a lie from the pit of hell, yet it is believed by a large portion of the Muslim world.

While this rumor was spread through the Arab world, resulting in occasional riots and mass lynchings, for more than 100 years before the rebirth of Israel, it got the official stamp of approval after 1948.

"Everything that was ever written by European haters of the Jews in order to provoke pogroms, and by the Christian anti-Semites who, to the same end, introduced the blood libel into the Ottoman Empire in the 19th century, is now reproduced by the Arabs," writes Samuel Katz. "A book designed to indoctrinate the blood libel was published under the authority of the Egyptian government in 1962."

The Bible Of Anti-Semitism

The bible of modern anti-semitism is a book called the "Protocols of the Elders of Zion." More than any other written work from the early part of the 20th century, it "provides the ideological justification for the physical destruction of the Jewish people."

The Czar in Russia used it. Hitler used it. And it is still being circulated by hate groups like the Ku Klux Klan and neo-Nazis. The book has been called "one of the textbooks of German Nazism" and the "father of the Holocaust." Incredibly, this hate-filled diatribe was approved by respected

Arab leaders and educators as a propaganda weapon in their war against Israel and the Jews.

It is transparently false and filled with vicious lies. Yet between 1949 and 1967, the Arabs published seven different translations of the book. At least five other books contain parts of the Protocols and thirty-three others quote the book with approval. The former prime minister of Iraq formally expressed his appreciation to one of the translators in 1967. And Gamal Abdel-Nasser, at the time the leader of the Arab world, called the book to the attention of a visiting Indian writer and assured him that it "proved beyond any shadow of doubt that 300 Zionists control the destinies of Europe."

In 1992 this book began circulating in Europe again. And where was it being published? In the recently "liberated" nation of Kuwait!

Schoolchildren Indoctrinated In Hate

Even Arab children are indoctrinated with the blood libel story and other heinous anti-Semitic myths. In 1962, the Egyptian government published for schoolchildren a reprint of "Talmudic Human Sacrifices," containing a forward which reads: "The Talmud believes that the Jews are made of different material from the rest of mankind, those who do not share the beliefs of the Jews being animals devoid of sense or they are servants and chattels of the Jews. . . . Their wise men laid it down that there is no law but their own desire, and no doctrine but their own lust. They commanded their people to bring harm to the other peoples, to kill their children, to suck their blood, and take away their wealth."

It is with this kind of instruction that Arab children are officially taught to hate and despise the Jews. They are also

taught to believe that the Jewish state must be destroyed and
its inhabitants exterminated.

"The annihilation of Israel and of its people is thus not
merely a convenient political objective," writes Katz. "It
has become a self-understood purpose demanded by the
Arab future no less than by Arab history, by Arab honor
and pride no less than by Arab pragmatic interest. It has
become basic to all Arab thinking, and it is not kept secret.
No Arab politician and—with the exception of one or two
notable exiles—no Arab intellectual has expressed
contradictory opinions."

The Psychology Of The Big Lie

The continued exploitation of the blood libel and
discredited anti-Semitic tracts like the "Protocols of the Elders
of Zion" should illustrate how far the Arab world is willing to
go in its use of mythology to score political points among its
own people. But why would the Arabs resort to such big lies?
What in the Arab character would make them think they could
get away with such "whoppers"?

One important ingredient in this recipe, without getting
overly psychoanalytical, is what has been recognized down
through the centuries as the "Oriental imagination." The
modern world, with television, radio and international news
agencies, has presented the Arabs with influence even
beyond their own fertile imaginations.

Students of Islam are instructed that lies, in and of
themselves, are not wrong. Al-Ghazzali, the 11th-century
Muslim theologian, wrote, "We must lie when truth leads to
unpleasant results." Even an Arab sociologist, Sania Hamady,
has recognized that "Lying is a widespread habit among the
Arabs and they have a low idea of truth. . . . The Arab has no

scruples about lying if by it he obtains his objective. . . . He is more interested in feeling than facts, in conveying an impression than in giving a report. The Arab language, moreover, provides its users with the tool, for assertion (*tarokid*) and exaggeration (*mubalong*)."

The Arab language is so colorful and prone to overstatement that if an Arab says only what he means, without the expected exaggeration, those hearing him are apt to doubt his basic premise or even suspect he means just the opposite, some Arab linguistic scholars explain.

Exaggeration Boomeranged In The 1967 War

For those old enough to remember, just think back to the days of the 1967 Arab-Israeli war. If you believed the Arab reports of how the battles were progressing, you would certainly be under the impression that Arab forces had all but obliterated Israeli forces. The joyfully awaited massacre of the Jews was about to take place.

The Egyptian air force, which never got off the ground, was said to be bombing Tel Aviv and other Israeli cities and shooting down hundreds of enemy planes. Massive armored battles were taking place in the Sinai and the Israelis were facing huge losses and casualties. Of course, nothing could have been further from the truth.

King Hussein of Jordan joined the battle against his better judgment because of the propaganda. He feared reprisals from his own people if he failed to join in the glorious Muslim victory that was in progress.

The international media were almost completely deceived by the frequency and intensity of the fabrications. Surely some of it must be true, they reasoned. Perhaps it is exaggerated, but there must be some basis in reality, they thought. That's where they made their mistake.

After the war, even many Arabs began to question whether their own imaginations were beginning to deceive even themselves and pose a danger to their cause. They had greatly sabotaged the effectiveness of their own military control and command because they fed such exaggerated information to them that they were not able to assess their true over-all situation until it was too late.

This concern arose again in the 1970s when Yasser Arafat's Palestine Liberation Organization began to regale the world media with tales of its heroic exploits in battle with the Israeli military. The terrorists would stage full-scale, night-time battles in Jordan just for the benefit of the press. And correspondents with little combat experience would be so impressed they would file misleading dispatches about the imminence of war between the Israelis and the PLO.

The rhetoric and ruthlessness of the Iran-backed Islamic Jihad terrorist organization has trumped even Arafat in its fanaticism. The group views the war against the Jews and Israel as an essential pre-requisite for achieving the wider goals of Islam, according to Joseph de Courcy.

De Courcy continues, "One of the leaders of Islamic Jihad, Sheikh Tamimi, spelled this out in his 1990 booklet, *The Obliteration of Israel: A Koranic Imperative,* when he wrote: 'The Jews have to return to the countries from which they came. We shall not accede to a Jewish state on our land, even if it is only one village.' It is the fanaticism of the Jihad recruits that is so alarming. They are indoctrinated with Islamic fervor as to be prepared to die for what they see as a divine command: the war against the infidels. Suicide attacks are common, and it is the use of this strategy, designed to maximize casualties, that makes the Jihad and its associated groups so dangerous."

Anti-Semitism is alive and well, all right. It is thriving—not just in the Middle East and in Muslim countries, but literally throughout the world. What's even scarier is that as it grows more strident and more vicious, it actually gains some respectability—at least in some circles. Consider the following:

- National socialist Vladimir Zhirinovsky captured 25 percent of the vote for Russia's lower house of parliament while unleashing a rash of incredibly vicious anti-Semitic rhetoric, even saying, "I'll act as Hitler did in 1932."

- Neo-Nazi video games circulating throughout Europe teach young people to hate Jews and other minorities by rewarding players with points for torturing prisoners, making their skin into lampshades and selling their remains as dog food.

- In the United States, a top aide to popular Nation of Islam leader Louis Farrakhan praised Hitler to an audience of students and called Jews the "bloodsuckers of the black nation." Earlier, Farrakhan himself had referred to Judaism as a "gutter religion."

- In Japan, anti-Semitic books and tracts are enjoying robust sales. The country's most respected financial newspaper ran an ad claiming that there was a plot by Jews to destroy and enslave Japan.

Who would have thought all of this was possible just 50 years after the Holocaust? But there seems to be no doubt that we are witnessing a worldwide surge of anti-semitism—

at the very moment prophetic fulfillments indicate we are very near the time when the attention of all nations will be riveted on Israel and attacks from three regions of the Earth on the Middle East are imminent. Coincidence? I don't think so.

"The human race seems to be suffering more frequent attacks of selective memory-loss, in which the horrors of the death camps recede and ancient hatreds are revived," explains Rabbi Marvin Hier, dean and founder of the Simon Wiesenthal Center. "It would be difficult to imagine a development with more disturbing implications for humanity."

Yes, it would be hard to imagine a more disturbing development. Ancient hatreds and blood feuds are being revived. And they are inevitably setting the stage for a clash of unimaginable dimensions and unthinkable violence. They are leading to mankind's Final Battle.

Chapter 5

JERUSALEM, O JERUSALEM

"No empire can ever be wrought without the peace of Jerusalem at its center because that is the hinge of history. But then, no empire can ever be wrought with the peace of Jerusalem at its center because such peace is humanly unattainable. It is an impossible mysterious mistress."

—Napoleon Bonaparte

"I tell you that a pledge is a pledge . . . to carry on the march until our children hoist the Palestinian flag over Jerusalem, the walls of Jerusalem, the minarets of Jerusalem and churches of Jerusalem."

—Yasser Arafat, March 5, 1995 speech in Gaza

The *The Berlitz Pocket Guide to Jerusalem* warns its readers that, "This is sacred ground and has had more blood spilled on it for its own sake than any other place in the world. Rivalries lie dormant and do not disappear." Berlitz is right. Jerusalem has been fought over for centuries; it will be fought over again.

No other city on this planet has ever stirred such fervor and passions as sacred Jerusalem. Hundreds of songs and poems have been written about her. The world's three greatest religions all lay claim to Jerusalem and have fought many battles for her. In fact, great wars and crusades have been waged over her for over 3,000 years.

Yet Jerusalem has none of the things that normally make a great city. It is not on a river. It is not a seaport. It is not on any major trade route or important road. It is not on the way to any great destination. Its nearest port is over 60 miles away. It is on a mountain, but the ones that surround it are higher. Fresh water is scarce.

No! None of the natural or normal phenomena that made great cities are present in Jerusalem's history.

Jerusalem is great for one reason only—Jerusalem is a spiritual city. It was founded to be the spiritual capital of the world. About this city alone the Almighty God said: it is **"My city"** [Isaiah 45:13] **". . . Jerusalem, the city where I chose to put my Name."** [1 Kings11:36] **" . . . the LORD**

had said, 'My Name will remain in Jerusalem forever.'"
(2 Chron. 33:4)

Jerusalem, The Heart Of The Jew

To the Jew, Old Jerusalem, with its Temple Mount, is
the Holiest Place on earth:

* It was here that God directed Abraham to sacrifice his
  only son Isaac and then provided a substitute sacrifice—
  2,000 years before Christ, and 1,000 years before King
  David.

* It was here that God directed David to place the
  Tabernacle, with the Ark of the Covenant, over which
  was the visible manifestation of God's presence. David
  made preparations to build the Temple, but was directed
  to let Solomon build it.

* It was about this city that hundreds of inspired songs,
  Psalms and Scripture verses were written.

* It was toward this city that millions of Jews prayed
  while dispersed in every country on earth for over a
  period of nearly 2,000 years.

* It was to this city that the hopes and longings of
  downtrodden, dispersed Jews were expressed every
  passover with the prayer, "Next year in Jerusalem."

The End Of An Agonizing Odyssey

Finally—against all odds—in June of 1967, when the
Jews took back sovereign control over the old city of
Jerusalem for the first time in over 2,000 years, General
Moshe Dayan went to the Western Wall of the Temple

Mount and proclaimed, "We have returned to our holiest of holy places, *never to leave her again.*"

No other people has ever had such a love affair with a land and a city. God Himself has placed within the Jews' heart a virtual symbiotic relationship with Jerusalem. The prophet Ezekiel predicted that their casting out from the land and Jerusalem and scattering among the gentile nations would be like dry bones lying in open graves—their return like life from the dead. (Ezekiel 37)

"Whatever Israel's secular Labour government might be planning by way of compromise with the Palestinians over Jerusalem, the Jewish attachment to the Holy City cannot be exaggerated," explains Joseph de Courcy. "Even if the Labour government, under pressure from the Americans, were to contemplate a return of East Jerusalem to international, let alone Palestinian, control it must be doubted whether the Jewish public would bear it."

Some 18 percent of Jews in Israel are deeply religious, with another 30 percent to 40 percent moderately so. And even the non-religious Israeli has an almost mystical attachment to Jerusalem. So of all the issues that could bring down a "peace-making" Israeli government, including an evacuation of the Jewish settlements in Judea and Samaria, none would be more certain in its effect than an attempt to relinquish Jewish control of East Jerusalem.

Al Quds, The Muslims' Third Holiest Site

The Muslims' love for Jerusalem is also religiously based and held with a fervent passion and fanatical zeal. Their history with Jerusalem began with the teaching that Mohammed and his horse were transported by Allah to the Temple Mount in Jerusalem. They believe fervently that

Mohammed and his horse ascended into heaven from the great rock over which there is now built a beautiful Mosque.

The Muslim's sacred name for Jerusalem is *Al Quds*, which roughly translated from Arabic means "the farthest point." They believe this was the farthest point Mohammed traveled from Mecca before ascending to heaven.

Various movements of Islam held undisputed control over Jerusalem until the Christian Crusades in the 10th through 12th centuries. Then, after three centuries of victories and defeats, the Muslims—under the brilliant leadership of Caliph Saladin—finally drove off the Crusaders. Muslims of one sect or another then retained control over Jerusalem until June of 1967.

Unresolvable Religious Passions

Given these kinds of fanatical religious racial passions that have smoldered and flamed for over so many centuries, you can count on the dispute between Muslims and Jews concerning the sovereign control of Jerusalem to only get worse. The Temple Mount site in Jerusalem is by far the most strategic and potentially explosive piece of land on Earth. Judaism and Islam are on a collision course toward an ultimate showdown with global and heavenly repercussions over that 35-acre plot. This dispute is quite simply the fuse that will ignite the final battle—Armageddon.

As the Bible tells us, the dispute over Jerusalem and Israel's borders will never be settled by any peace agreements nor any whiz-bang diplomatic breakthrough. Jerusalem, the Bible says, will be a stumbling block for the entire world.

The prophet Zechariah describes the horrific battle over Jerusalem that will take place just before the end of history as we know it, **"Behold, I will make Jerusalem a cup of drunkenness to all the surrounding peoples, when they lay siege against Judah and Jerusalem. And it shall happen in that day that I will make Jerusalem a very heavy stone for all peoples; all who would heave it away will surely be cut in pieces, though all nations of the earth are going to be gathered against it."** (Zechariah 12:2, 3, about 550 BC) This prophecy indicates that all the surrounding nations i.e., Syria, Egypt, Jordan, Iraq, Saudi Arabia, Iran, etc., would be intoxicated with Jerusalem. This will result in a war of such magnitude that all the nations of the world will be dragged into it.

Zechariah chapters twelve through fourteen focus on this war to end all wars.

Jerusalem's Centrality To Prophecy

Jesus also predicted that Jerusalem would be the key to all future events related to His coming. He said, **"When you see Jerusalem being surrounded by armies, you will know that its desolation is near. Then let those who are in Judea flee to the mountains, let those in the city get out, and let those in the country not enter the city. For this is the time of punishment in fulfillment of all that has been written. How dreadful it will be in those days for pregnant women and nursing mothers! There will be great distress in the land and wrath against this people. They will fall by the sword and will be taken as prisoners to all the nations. Jerusalem will be trampled on by the Gentiles until the times of the Gentiles are fulfilled."** (Luke 21:20-24 NIV).

Note the scope of this prophecy. In Verses 20 through 23, Jesus predicted the Roman destruction of Jerusalem of 70 A.D. He then predicted this would begin a world wide dispersion of the Jewish people *until* **the times of the Gentiles are fulfilled.** This refers to, among other things, this present age in which the Gentiles have control over Jerusalem and world government. Those days began drawing to a close in June of 1967.

We are literally witnessing the last hours of **the times of the Gentiles.** God's focus is shifting back to His people, Israel. This is why the whole world has its attention riveted on Israel and the struggle for Jerusalem.

Today's media attention has placed Israel center stage in the court of world opinion and helped to make the Jewish state something of a pariah nation. Some might think that this is just a coincidence. But to those who understand the precisely predicted scenario of the Bible concerning Israel in the last days, it is exactly what was anticipated.

REVIEW OF JERUSALEM'S CRITICAL HISTORY
Importance Of The Ark

One cannot overstate the importance of the Ark of the Covenant to the history of Jerusalem as the center of Judaism. It is only necessary to read the books of Samuel, where there are 61 references to the Ark (variously referred to as the "Ark of God," the "Ark of Yahweh," the "Ark of the God of Israel") to understand the importance of the Ark of the Covenant to the Jews. The Ark was the vessel that held the Ten Commandments carved into two tablets of stone that were broken when Moses threw them down in anger at Israel's sin.

So when David brought the Ark to Jerusalem, he thus began creating Israel's most important city. The transformation of Jerusalem was completed by David's son Solomon who constructed the First Temple on the spot where Abraham prepared to sacrifice Isaac. From that time on, Jerusalem has been central to Judaism; and it has remained central through numerous wars, cruel overlords and exile. It was so after Nebuchadnezzar destroyed the Temple in 587 B.C. and carried the Jews off to Babylon; it became even more so after the Persians returned the Jews to Jerusalem and allowed them to construct the Second Temple in the fifth century B.C.; and the city remained central to Judaism even after the Romans destroyed the Temple for the final time in A.D. 70 and drove the Jews into 2,000 years of exile.

Jerusalem was rebuilt by Hadrian in the second century A.D., and it regained some political significance when Constantine was converted and he made Christianity the official religion of the Roman Empire, especially after Empress Helena traveled to the Holy Land to identify and mark the Holy places in the fourth century.

After that came the Muslims, the Crusaders and then the Muslims again—first Mamelukes from Egypt and afterwards the Ottomans from Turkey.

Throughout all the terrible conditions and dangerous times there has always been a Jewish religious colony living in the city. Their spiritual and physical attachment to the city has always been maintained.

The "Wailing Wall"—A Symbol

After the Temple Mount, the most revered site for the Jews is the Western Wall, the only surviving part of the

Temple not destroyed by the Romans. It is actually part of the original retaining wall which enabled the builders to make a level platform. Jews have come to the Western Wall to pray ever since the loss of the Temple. It became known as the "Wailing Wall" because of the impassioned lamentations of Jews mourning the destruction of the Temple through the centuries. For Orthodox Jews, who consider it a desecration to walk over the Ark's former resting place, the Wall is the closest they can get to the site of Solomon's Temple without walking on sacred ground.

The Unrecognized Majority

The Jews have constituted the majority of the population of Jerusalem since at least the 1800s, well before the dawn of the Zionist movement. By 1946, the Jewish population of British-designated Jerusalem had reached 100,000, against a non-Jewish population of some 65,000. Since the 1967 war, the Jerusalem city limits have been extended to include a population of 355,000 Jews and 140,000 Arabs in an area covering 105 square kilometers. Major new Jewish settlements beyond the 1949 armistice line now include Gillo and Givat HaMatos to the southwest; East Talpiyot to the southeast; Ramot Allon to the northwest and a series of ten or more developments in a direct line northwards toward Jerusalem airport and Ramallah.

"These are the demographic and geographic facts that Israel's partial victory of 1948 and complete victory of 1967 have imposed on Jerusalem," explains de Courcy. "Muslims and Christians are still guaranteed access to their holy places, with the Muslims maintaining actual control over the Temple Mount as they have done for 12 out of the last 13 centuries. But in 1967 the Israelis moved

government offices, including the National Police
Headquarters, the Ministry of Justice and the Supreme
Court to the newly expanded East Jerusalem. In July 1980,
the Israelis annexed East Jerusalem and declared the city to
be the united capital of Israel, a status it had not had since
Roman times."

The Muslim's Mastery Of Myths

You know, some Arab propaganda is subtle. Some of it
is based on half-truths. Some of it, however, is so
outrageous, so preposterous and so imaginative that you
have to admire it for sheer inventiveness.

One of the Mideast myths made up from whole cloth is
the notion that Jerusalem is really an Arab city. Some of the
more creative minds in the Arab propaganda machine have
actually managed to convince the world media and
diplomatic establishments that Jerusalem is as important to
Muslims as it is to Jews.

While one important Islamic shrine is indeed located in
Jerusalem, built, as it were, on top of the Jews' old Temple,
it was never an important *city* to Muslims—as population
trends alone should illustrate. As the population figures
above demonstrate, Arabs have never been particularly
attracted to the holy city of the Jews.

Remember, the founder of Islam wanted to convert Jews
and Christians in the holy land to his new faith. In wooing
the Jews, Mohammed first suggested that daily prayers be
directed to Jerusalem rather than Mecca. When he realized
this approach was having little success with either
Christians or Jews, he rescinded it after eighteen months.
Ever since then, Muslims have bowed in prayer toward
Mecca—the undisputed holiest city in Islam.

Long after Mohammed was dead, an Islamic legend arose that contended he ascended into the seventh heaven at the Temple Mount area in Jerusalem. The Koran says only that the event took place at the "uttermost mosque." But there was no mosque in Jerusalem at the time. The Al Aksa Mosque and the Dome of the Rock were built later after Jerusalem was captured by warring Muslim Caliphate Omar. There is no evidence, in fact, that Mohammed ever set foot in Jerusalem.

Jews' History In Jerusalem

"It was not Mohammed's dream that conferred sanctity on the Temple Mount," explains author Samuel Katz. "On the contrary, it was the existing sanctity of the place—it had been holy to the Jews for nearly 2,000 years before Mohammed—that inspired the weavers of the legend to choose it as lending a fittingly awesome station for Mohammed's ascent."

Again, remember, Mohammed and the Koran contended that Islam, though created in the 7th century A.D., was actually the *original*, unadulterated religion of the Middle East. So, naturally, any holy place in the Middle East could and should, in the eyes of Muslims, be co-opted. And that is what Islam tried to do with Jerusalem.

The Al Aksa Mosque and the Dome of the Rock may, indeed, be the third holiest shrines in the world to Muslims, but there is nothing about the city of Jerusalem that would compare it with the cities of Mecca and Medina.

"To the Muslims, it is not Jerusalem, but a certain site in Jerusalem which is venerated," explains Christopher Sykes, author of *Holy Sites*. "To a Muslim there is a profound difference between Jerusalem and Mecca or Medina. The latter are holy places containing holy sites.

Apart from the hallowed rock, Jerusalem has no major Islamic significance."

Arabs Rediscover Jerusalem

Nevertheless, in justifying their claim on "Palestine" and everything else Jewish in the holy land, the Arabs now contend they have a stake in Jerusalem that pre-dates Israel. It was not, however, until the rebirth of Israel in 1948 that the Arabs realized just how important Jerusalem was to them.

"Then, suddenly for the first time in history, the Arabs discovered and revealed to the world the vehement, passionate, almost desperate, accents of a deep-rooted, long-standing and undying attachment to Jerusalem," observes Katz.

Since there is little historical evidence to back up the Arab claim for Jerusalem, one might be tempted to think that the passion for the city—the life-or-death-struggle for it—might wane. Not likely, according to some Arabic scholars.

Middle East Myth Power

"What a people believes, even if untrue, has the same influence over their lives as if it were true," writes Philip K. Hitti, author of *The Temperament of the Arabs*.

So, despite the fact that Islam doesn't really have much of a legitimate claim on Jerusalem, many Muslims believe they do. That's the riddle of the Middle East today. Sometimes what people believe is even more powerful than the truth.

The Jews have much invested in Jerusalem, however. The investment is more than spiritual, too. The reunification of the city was achieved only with the spilling of much blood. The November 1947 United Nations partition plan for Palestine foresaw the internationalization of Jerusalem within extended boundaries which were to include the Christian holy places of Bethlehem. This was an intentional form of gerrymandering designed to balance the Arab and Jewish populations of the internationalized city at approximately 100,000 each.

Under a Swedish amendment to the plan, accepted by the U.N., the extended city was to receive a special status under the control of the U.N. Trusteeship Council for a 10-year period, after which time the council would reexamine the city's status by means of a plebiscite of the inhabitants. A two-thirds majority was to be required for any change in status. On December 2, 1947, de Courcy recalls, the U.N. Trusteeship Council set up a six-man subcommittee to draw up detailed plans for the international status of Jerusalem.

Arabs' All Or Nothing Policy

"It never happened," says de Courcy. "The Palestinian Arab Higher Committee had met in Jerusalem on November 30 and rejected the partition plan, ordering a general strike by all Arabs throughout Palestine to begin December 2. This was a fatal blow to the U.N.'s plans for Jerusalem, as the British refused to implement any U.N. decision that was not accepted by both parties in Palestine."

On the first day of that strike there was widespread violence through the country, but particularly in Jerusalem, where mobs of young Arabs set fire to Jewish businesses, attacked Jews and threw stones at buses and trucks. The fighting continued and escalated for months. By March 26, the Jewish Agency warned that there was a "grave danger that Jerusalem will become a battlefield and that the Holy Places will be damaged by bombardment and street fighting." The agency castigated the U.N. for not taking its responsibilities sufficiently seriously and warned that the Arabs were planning to attack Jerusalem and to isolate the city's 100,000 Jews.

"Throughout this period," reminds de Courcy, "there was fierce fighting on the road from Tel Aviv to Jerusalem, which the Arabs sought to close in an effort to isolate the 100,000 Jewish population in Jerusalem and which the Jews fought to keep open as a vital supply line. On April 13, the Arabs made a ferocious attack on a Jewish convoy on the road up to the Jewish enclave on Mount Scopus. The convoy was transporting doctors, nurses and university staff to Hadassah Hospital and the Hebrew University. Many of the dead were burned alive in their trucks. Thirty-nine Jews were killed and their bodies mutilated."

Fighting between Jews and Arabs went on for six months, culminating in the Arab invasion on May 15, 1948 when the armies of Transjordan, Egypt and Syria-Lebanon attacked from three sides. Once again, it is interesting to note the way the Arabs objected strenuously and violently back in 1948 to the idea of "sharing" Jerusalem in anyway—or to even an internationalization of the city. *Today, of course, the Arabs are demanding just that.*

Why Is What Was Rejected In Past Acceptable Today?

It reminds me of the way the Arabs today call for the establishment of a Palestinian state in Judea and Samaria as the lynchpin of a peace settlement with Israel. But while the Arabs controlled those lands prior to 1967, there was no talk among them of creating a Palestinian state. All of that became academic, however, on June 6, 1967, when, in dramatic style, Israel gained control over the Old City of Jerusalem on the first day of fighting.

As related earlier, "The Israel Defense Forces have today liberated Jerusalem," said General Moshe Dayan to his troops, many of whom were weeping with emotion. "We have returned to our holiest of holy places, never to part from them again. . . ."

To keep that promise, Israelis will have to resist in perpetuity the strong desires of the Islamic world. Because, even though Islam's claim on Jerusalem is tenuous, there is something, very real, very tangible, that Muslims covet inside Jerusalem. It is the 35-acre area known as the Temple Mount. But it is also the most sacred real estate in the world to the Jews. It is not only the spot on which God asked Abraham to sacrifice his son. This is the place the Lord established His name forever. At the Temple Mount now sits the Dome of the Rock. And where Solomon's porch once stood, there is the Al Aksa Mosque.

It is this Temple Mount that will serve as the center stage for the Final Battle. Right now, as you read this, preparations are being made to rebuild the Third Temple— an act that almost certainly will set off massive protests, gnashing of teeth and lamentations in the Muslim world. And it will most certainly set off their last *Jihad.*

Although the Jews now control the entire city of Jerusalem, Israeli authorities have permitted the Muslims to maintain the Temple Mount. Anyone who has visited Jerusalem knows how the Dome of the Rock and the Al Aksa Mosque tower over the Western Wall and the rest of the city, imposing a constant visual and psychological incentive to devout Jews to rebuild the Temple.

The Temple Will Be Rebuilt

Jews can never forget about rebuilding the Temple. Number 20 of the 613 commandments in the Torah calls for the building of a Temple in Jerusalem if one does not exist and orders the maintenance of the Temple if it does exist.

For nineteen centuries, Jews have prayed three times a day: "May it be Thy will that the Temple be speedily rebuilt in our days. . . ." To the Jew, the Temple is central to the essence of Judaism. Of the Torah's 613 commandments catalogued in the Talmud, approximately one-third refer directly to rituals that can only be performed in the Temple rebuilt on its official site.

What's so important about rebuilding the Temple and the Temple rituals? Daniel predicted that three and a half years before the Messiah's coming, sacrifice and offering would be stopped by the treachery of the Roman Antichrist (Daniel 9:27). That means that the Temple must be rebuilt before the beginning of the seven-year Tribulation period leading to the return of Jesus Christ.

The Abomination That Causes Desolation

So the rebuilding of the Temple is significant not only because of the potential firestorm it will create between Jews and Muslims in the Middle East. It is also a critical development in the entire prophetic scenario. The Bible makes it clear that in the last days the Antichrist will establish his reign in the Temple of Jerusalem. Therefore, the Temple must and will be rebuilt.

The Lord Jesus confirmed Daniel's earlier prophecy (Daniel 9:27 and 12:11) and foretold of **"an abomination of [that causes] desolation"** set up in the Holy Place of the Temple (Matthew 24:15). That abomination will occur when the infamous Man of Lawlessness—or Antichrist—takes his seat in the Temple of God.

The Apostle Paul explained what is the abomination that causes desolation and said that it would be one of the unmistakable prophetic signs that the Day of the Lord's judgment had arrived, **"Who opposes and exalts himself above every so-called god or object of worship, so that he takes his seat in the Temple of God, displaying himself as being God,"** we read in 2 Thessalonians 2:3,4. Jesus predicted this is that moment in history when, **"For then there will be great distress, unequaled from the beginning of the world until now—and never to be equaled again. If those days had not been cut short, no one would survive, but for the sake of the elect** [believers in Jesus] **those days will be shortened."** (Matthew 24:21-22)

Islam's Dream Of Jerusalem

Though there is nothing monolithic about Islam, there is one thing that unifies all Muslims in the world today—from the most fundamentalist to the most secular. That one thing is a vision of "liberated" Jerusalem.

Hanan Ashrawi was the official spokeswoman for the original Palestinian team that negotiated with Israel. She is not a radical Islamist zealot or a hopeless Palestinian nationalist. She is, in fact, something of a voice of reason as far as the Palestinian cause goes. Urbane, well-educated and sophisticated, Ashrawi once dated ABC anchorman Peter Jennings. Lately she has been critical of Arafat's heavyhanded censorship of the Arab press and his undemocratic rhetoric. Here's what she says dispassionately about the city: "Jerusalem is an indivisible part of the occupied territories and it is a fundamental issue. It is the heart of occupied Palestine. It is the heart of the Arab world. It is the heart of the Islamic world, and no person, group, or Palestinian leadership can relinquish it. Because without Jerusalem we would have given up the source of strength and self-momentum of the Palestinian cause. . . . We also see Jerusalem as the capital of the Palestinian state and reject any attempts at defining its future in advance. . . . Arab Jerusalem remains the Jerusalem of the Arabs, the Jerusalem of Palestine, and the essence and beating heart of Palestine."

Does it look like any compromise in the world is going to change her opinion about that? Has she left any room for negotiation? I don't think so. And, keep in mind, this is by far "the most reasonable" voice of the Palestinian cause.

Arafat's True Feelings

Let's hear from another renowned Palestinian "moderate," Arafat himself. Here's what he told followers in a mosque in Johannesburg nine months after signing his peace treaty with Israel: "The jihad will continue. And Jerusalem is not for the Palestinian people; it is for the Muslim nation. . . . [The] battle is not to get how much we can achieve from them [Israelis] here or there. Our main battle is Jerusalem; Jerusalem, the first shrine of the Muslims. . . ."

Arafat is not the only Palestinian leader who sees himself conducting a holy war against Israel. The new Islamic mufti of Jerusalem, Ikrema Sabri told an Associated Press reporter in March 1995: "I am one of the holy warriors for Jerusalem. Jerusalem is part of our religion, it is part of the religion of every Muslim. We consider ourselves holy warriors for this city, and we will not abandon it." The cleric adds that Muslims should employ "all means" necessary to protect their interests in the city.

Israeli journalist David Bedein interviewed Heitem Eid, a spokesman for Orient House, the Palestinian organization most concerned with Jerusalem. Here's what this "moderate" Palestinian voice had to say about the city: "Without giving the Palestinians East Jerusalem, *the Israelis will never have peace with the Arabs*. Signing peace agreements does not mean we have real peace."

How true! This is precisely what I have been saying for years. It's what the Bible says. It's what the greatest intelligence minds of the Western world say. Yet, it is not the conventional wisdom of our day. Read the newspapers, listen to the network news, and you would think that peace in the Middle East is about clever diplomacy and compromise and give-and-take. Recent U.S. Presidents and Secretaries of State seem to all think that they can gain a place in history by forcing a peace in this most volatile area. They don't seem to have a clue as to the critical issues involved.

It's just not going to happen. The Jews will never give up Jerusalem and the Arabs will never stop coveting it. Thus, just as the Bible predicted, Jerusalem will remain that burdensome stone for the entire world. The Antichrist will make a temporary solution. Then, it will be the powder keg that sets off the greatest explosion of war the world has ever known.

Prediction Of Secular Intelligence

"And this, from the point of view of world stability, is the critical point," concludes de Courcy. "If the Arab world achieves some form of nuclear parity with Israel (via the ex-USSR or China), an Islamic coalition will in all probability unite behind one more attempt to regain Jerusalem by force. That is the cliff-edge the world seems destined to face sometime in the middle years of this decade." It is certain that the Muslims will have deliverable nuclear weapons in the very new future, according to the most reliable intelligence sources.

Truly, the footsteps of our Lord and Savior, Jesus Christ, can already be heard as He approaches the doors of heaven to return. But before He comes to rule the world from Jerusalem for 1,000 years, the Final Battle—the battle for Jerusalem, the war to end all wars—will have to be fought.

Chapter 6

THE FALSE PEACE AND ISRAEL'S VULNERABILITY

"And you will be hearing of wars and rumors of wars; see that you are not frightened, for those things must take place, but that is not yet the end."

—Matthew 24:6

"For when they say, 'Peace and safety!' then sudden destruction comes upon them, as labor pains upon a pregnant woman. And they shall not escape."

—I Thessalonians 5:3

Ahhhh, peace. Isn't it wonderful? It's so nice to have the world protected from war by all these peace treaties that are being worked out in Madrid, Cairo, Damascus, Ammon, Washington and elsewhere. Isn't it pleasant just basking in the warm glow of world tranquility? Don't you feel so much safer?

Oh, you don't? Then you're like me. You're beginning to see through the veil of wishful thinking that is clouding the minds of the world's political leaders, the press and, to a great extent, the people as well. Don't be fooled by the relative peace in today's world. It's predicted in the Bible. It's called the calm before the storm.

As I wrote in *Planet Earth—2000 AD,* the 20th century has been the bloodiest in the history of mankind. Two great world wars killed millions of combatants and non-combatants alike. The Nazi Holocaust claimed the lives of at least 7 million. Communism, over the last 75 years, killed perhaps 100 million in the gulags of the Soviet Union, the cultural revolution in China, the killing fields of Cambodia, the intentional genocidal famines of Ethiopia, etc.

The revolutions and wars of the 20th century surely fulfilled Jesus' prophecy as recorded in Matthew 24: **"For nation** [ethnic groups] **will rise against nation** [ethnic groups]**, and kingdom against kingdom. . . ."** But, as I have said before, the most striking world development of the 1990s has been the *absence* of any full-blown conflagrations in the world and the great hope that has emerged for a period of lasting peace.

Western leaders are apparently so impressed with their own diplomatic skills that they are on a hell-bent crusade to unilaterally disarm, cash in their "peace dividend" and scrap plans for a space-based missile-defense system that could protect their people and their military infrastructure.

The world is also dividing into regional coalitions and broad alliances—just the places the Bible predicted it would in the last days. Unfortunately—not just for Americans but for the entire free world—the United States is also on the decline in power and influence. Poor leadership, moral decay and a betrayal of many of the Biblical principles upon which the nation was founded have contributed to America's fall from grace.

In addition, in a very real way, I believe America's fate is tied directly to the way it relates to the nation of Israel. Think of the way America prospered from 1948 through 1967 when its support of the Jewish state was virtually unconditional. Today the United States has joined the worldwide chorus urging Israel to make concession after concession to the Arabs for nothing more than promises— promises the Arabs themselves vow to break when addressing their own people away from the glare of Western TV cameras.

Munich Shadow Over Middle East

Appeasement never pays. The free world supposedly learned that lesson in World War II when England's Neville Chamberlain tried at the infamous Munich Conference to give Adolf Hitler whatever he wanted to avoid war. It didn't work then and it won't work now. In fact, you could make

the case based on historical precedent that appeasement is
nearly always more likely to bring about war than to avert it.
An appearance of weakness always encourages would-be
conquerors to go for more. This is especially true in the
Muslim arena.

Let me state this as plainly as I can: The territorial
concessions Israel is being coaxed and coerced into
making have *no chance* of appeasing their Arab neighbors.
Their quarrel with Israel is much deeper than that. As we
have pointed out earlier in this book, this dispute is the
result of a blood feud that dates back to the tents of
Abraham. And there are reasons based on religious
conviction that make it impossible for Islam to accept the
existence of Israel—now or ever.

Israel Is A Blasphemy Against Islam

"The rebirth of the Jewish state right in the midst of the
Arab countries is a direct insult and contradiction to Islamic
teaching," explains author Elishua Davidson. "Has not
Allah *finished* with the Jewish people? And if Allah has
predetermined all things, how is it possible that a Jewish
state should have come into existence once again?" The
existence of Israel has been viewed as blasphemy in their
minds. It is a threat to the very faith of Islam.

This is a feeling—rational or not—that has permeated
the entire Arabic culture. Hilal Khashan's scientific survey
of Arab opinion mentioned earlier in this book showed that
*the overwhelming number believe peace agreements with
Israel should be broken as soon as it is militarily expedient.*
In addition, the political scientist's poll found that three-
quarters of Arabs would support immediate military
confrontation with Israel. The remaining one-fourth call for

maintaining the current situation of no peace, no war, pending the time the Arabs can attain their objectives.

"When three-quarters of the respondents look forward to war, it hardly augurs well for the cause of true peace," writes Khashan in the *Wall Street Journal*. "And when Arabs call for military action against Israel, they demonstrate themselves to be out of touch with reality."

Permanent Peace Toward Israel Unthinkable

Khashan concludes from his data that the Arabs are simply not psychologically prepared for peaceful coexistence with the Israelis.

"This study has produced sobering results," he says. "The respondents show little understanding of the meaning of peace, much less an appreciation of its possible benefits. Quite the contrary, they see peace as surrender and display attitudes that suggest that the conflict with Israel has yet a long life ahead. The survey findings point to strong anti-Israel sentiments remaining in Arab political culture."

The anti-Israel feeling pervades all facets of Arabic society—from the lowest rung to the most well-educated elite. For example, at the end of 1994, as peace treaties between Arab and Israeli were being signed and the prospects for more were great, the Cairo International Film Festival was held featuring top filmmakers from all over the Middle East—except, of course, Israel.

"Only donkeys, monkeys and foxes are interested in normalizing relations with Israel," scoffed Saad Eddin Eahba, director of the film festival.

The film festival snub was not the exception, but the rule, insofar as interpersonal Arab-Israeli relations. No Israeli film has even been shown in Egypt. Artists, directors, actors, musicians, lawyers, engineers, doctors and journalists syndicates all forbid members to travel to the Jewish state. After fifteen years of cold peace between Egypt and Israel, there are only two major joint economic projects under way.

"The momentous peace agreement signed at the White House (in 1993) by Israeli Prime Minister Yitzhak Rabin and Palestinian leader Yasser Arafat raised hopes that have yet to be met, or even approached," the *Los Angeles Times* reported at the end of 1994. "The hands that clasped in Washington, that led to the Nobel Peace Prize for Israeli Foreign Minister Shimon Peres, Arafat and Rabin, remain firmly pocketed most of the time back home in the Middle East."

But it's not just a matter of rhetoric and cold shoulders. *In Tehran, the new leader of the Islamic confederation is determined to do Allah's will and destroy Israel and thereby prove to the world that its creation was merely a historical anomaly.* Here's the plan: Iran's Operation Grand Design includes a a strategic amphibious invasion in a chemical weapons environment. The first step is clearly the overthrow of the House of Saud. By taking out Saudi Arabia, the Iran-Syria alliance would remove a vital Western military base, control the Islamic holy places and deprive the West of its supply of oil. According to intelligence sources, the plan then calls for an all-out airborne chemical and nuclear assault on the state of Israel. Such draconian plans become all the more achievable as Israel's borders shrink.

That's the policy America is promoting today for Israel. And some leaders in Israel appear to be buying into this hopeless plan. *Instead of peace, appeasement will lead to war in the Middle East.* But not just war. This time it will lead to catastrophe, to nightmare, to unprecedented bloodshed and human suffering. In other words, it will lead to the Final Battle.

A Time To Remember

How? Let's travel back in time for a minute to October 6, 1973. The Egyptian army attacked Israel from across the Sinai Desert. On the same day, Syria invaded from the Golan Heights. It was Yom Kippur, the Day of Atonement, and the holiest day on the Jewish calendar. To say the Israelis were surprised would be an understatement.

In the early days of the war, there were unprecedented and stunning victories for the Arabs. Israeli casualties were very high. Hardened and confident combat units were so outnumbered and outflanked they were fleeing in disarray. The clash resulted in the loss of 500 tanks and 49 aircraft with all their seasoned crews in the first three days.

The modernized Egyptian forces used missiles and electronic defenses to blast their way to the eastern bank of the canal. Israeli counterattacks by three tanks divisions were repelled. The Syrians used 1,400 tanks to roll through the Israeli defenses on the Golan and moved to the edge of Galilee and Israel's heavily populated valleys. Only a handful of Israeli tanks stood in their way.

Israeli Defense Minister Moshe Dayan, for one, thought it was all over. "This is the end of the Third Temple," he said. "The situation is desperate. Everything is lost. We must withdraw." On Monday, October 8, 1973, Israel called its first nuclear alert, armed their nuclear missiles and bombs and ordered "Operation Samson" to be launched.

Only some heroic bluffing by an Israeli tank commander and some surprise hesitation by the Syrian forces prevented what would have surely been a nuclear holocaust in the Middle East. But here is the real reason—it just wasn't the right prophetic time. But that is a historical scenario that is worthy of much more consideration than it is generally given by policymakers in Washington—and now, even Jerusalem.

Setting Up For Disaster

Israel is facing world pressure like never before. Because the Muslim nations have been successful at framing the debate over the Middle East as a struggle between downtrodden Palestinians and powerful, heavily armed Jews, Israel is precipitously close to compromising its own security needs. Imagine, "four million Jews beating up on a potential manpower pool of one billion Muslims."

"Land for peace!" is the cry heard 'round the world. Even in Israel, more and more people seem willing to be blackmailed into turning over the lands of Judea, Samaria, Gaza and the strategic Golan Heights. So what's likely to happen? Listen to intelligence expert Joseph de Courcy: "The Madrid peace conference ushered in a series of bilateral negotiations between Israel on the one hand and Jordan, the Palestinians, Syria and Lebanon on the other. It also instigated a series of multilateral negotiations, with a wider participation, to cover arms control, water, economic development, refugee issues and the environment. The first major breakthrough in the Madrid peace process came almost two years later, on September 13, 1993, with the signing of a declaration of principles on Palestinian self-rule by the Palestine Liberation Organization and Israel. The schedule incorporated into the declaration of principles envisions a five-year period of limited autonomy for the Palestinians of the Gaza Strip and the West Bank leading to a permanent settlement coming into effect on December 13, 1998."

Israel Gambles With Survival, Not Just Land

De Courcy does believe that the peace process currently under way will lead to a comprehensive peace settlement between Israel and the Arabs. However, it will not last long. And any objective military and intelligence expert in the world could explain why Israel would be foolhardy to proceed.

"The absolute minimum territory Israel requires to deter war is the territory it is controlling today," concludes de Courcy. "The fundamental problem is that Israel is a small state located in one of the most tempestuous geographical locations imaginable. It occupies a thin sliver of land at the juncture of Asia and Africa, that has been buffeted throughout history by the ambitions of powerful neighbors. From the north, the Hyskos, Assyrians, Babylonians, Persians, Macedonians, Romans and Ottoman Turks had to sweep through on their way to the conquest of Egypt and the extension of their empires into Africa. From the east, it was the Arabs who first had to cross on their way to conquests in North Africa and Spain. And from the south, it was the Egyptians [many times], and in this century the British, to whom Palestine represented the first obstacle on the way from Africa to Asia."

De Courcy points to the period in Jewish history between the fall of the northern kingdom in 722 B.C. and the carrying away of Judah to Babylon in 586 B.C. as particularly instructive.

"The Jewish state constantly had to make the right political choices between support for a declining Assyria, an Egypt that was regaining some but not all of its old strength, and the thrusting neo-Babylonian empire," he says. "In such circumstances, a wrong political choice could have the direst consequences, and it was just such a wrong choice that led directly to the Babylonian exile. By 605 B.C., with its defeat at the battle of Charchemish, it was clear that any realistic hope Egypt might have had of inheriting the Assyrian empire was ended, yet the pro-Egyptian party in Judah remained strong enough to provoke Nebuchadnezzar into carrying off the leading Jews to Babylon. Eleven years later this first Babylonian captivity was followed by the fall of Jerusalem, the end of the kingdom of Judah and the second Jewish exile in Babylon."

Historically, the Jewish state also benefited from close relationships to friendly superpowers. For instance, in what de Courcy describes as "an early foretaste of this century's British-American patronage of Zionism," one of the most fruitful periods for Judah was the period of Persian hegemony following the defeat of the Babylonians in 539 B.C. Not only did the Persians allow the Jews to return to Jerusalem from Babylon in 536 B.C., but they allowed them to restore the Temple and to establish a national renaissance centered around Judaism that would carry the Jews through to the Roman expulsion and beyond.

"The historical experience of Palestine provides important pointers to the future," explains de Courcy. "Indeed, the whole modern history of the Middle East, following the defeat of the Ottoman empire in World War I and the subsequent return of the Jews under British patronage, echoes the earlier defeat of Babylon by the Persians and the Persian-facilitated return of the Jews to Judah. It is evident that the wheel continues to revolve on its old axle. Israel is once again facing an adverse combination of reducing imperial (American-Western) protection; internal weakness (as a result of the Arab uprisings); and a shifting balance of military power in favor of its neighbors. This period of relative Israeli weakness, which will only increase following the conclusion of the Madrid peace process, is unlikely to be different from other similar periods in history. It will provide temptations for Israel's neighbors that they will find almost impossible to resist."

De Courcy believes there are four main ways the peace process can now evolve. The first—however, unlikely—is that everything works out according to the Madrid blueprint with peace treaties between Jews and Arabs that everyone observes. But, he correctly points out, the PLO leadership has made it clear to its own people that they see the peace process as "a stepping stone not the final destination."

The Mecca Model: Make Peace; Get Strong; Annihilate

"The evidence for this is overwhelming," de Courcy continues. "For example, in his now infamous May 1994 speech in a mosque in Johannesburg, Yasser Arafat not only called for a continuing holy war to liberate Jerusalem, he added the following about the PLO-Israel accord: 'This agreement, *I am not considering it more than the agreement which had been signed between our Prophet Mohammed and the Quraysh [Mecca]. . .'* This was a reference to the non-belligerency agreement Mohammed signed with the Quraysh tribe which controlled Mecca. Two years later, Mohammed violated the agreement, conquered Mecca and killed the leaders of the tribe."

A few months before Arafat's speech, Mahgoub Omar, one of his former close associates, had made a similar point in an article in a Palestinian newspaper. He characterized the peace accord as part of a "phased progress," leading eventually to a complete victory. Omar said the program was conceived by PLO leaders in 1973. Omar's article pointed out that despite all the rhetoric concerning the liberation of Palestine from the river to the sea, no major Palestinian organization had argued for years that the job would be completed in one round. Omar argued that the establishment of Palestinian autonomy in as little 2.5 percent of Israeli territory represented "a major gain" which had breached "the walls that the Zionist enemy had succeeded in building around his occupation." But, he cautioned, the accord itself should not be celebrated as a "historic victory" because "the real victory is the recovery of all of Palestine. Anything short of that is a partial victory, to be assessed in points pending the round of the *coup de grace*. The conflict will continue even after the final settlement. The Zionist Israeii presence will remain a source of tension, friction and conflict until the Israeli population melts into the Arab Islamic milieu."

From Their Own Mouths

"This," de Courcy comments, "is explicit stuff and almost certainly reflects the true Palestinian intentions, particularly because radical Islamic Palestinian groups such as Hamas and the Islamic Jihad and the various nationalist rejectionist groups such as the Democratic and Popular Fronts for the Liberation of Palestine are constantly pressing Arafat from behind. Palestinian opponents of the peace process command perhaps 60 percent support in the West Bank and Gaza Strip. So, the scenario that sees Israel completing a *safe* retreat to its pre-

1967 borders, with the Palestinians sufficiently satisfied with what they have got to cause no further trouble for the Jewish state, is an unlikely one."

"At the opposite end of the spectrum," de Courcy says, "is a pessimistic scenario gaining credence in right-wing Jewish circles: that concession after concession by Israel could bring an end to the Jewish state almost without a fight. Jews, they say, are becoming demoralized and are losing their desire to struggle."

"It is certainly true that the Jewish state has become defeatist," says de Courcy. "However, history would suggest that even if Israel has made, and is making, grave errors of judgment, it is unlikely to become *suicidally* defeatist."

A third scenario, according to de Courcy, is that the peace process is halted dead in its tracks by a new government of hard-liners in Israel. He adds: "This would not be an easy option for Israel to take, but it might be the least bad option and is therefore a strong possibility."

Three Determinative Issues

He says there are three issues that could likely bring down the Labor government in Israel: retreat from the strategic Golan Heights, abandoning and evacuating settlements and concessions on the future of Jerusalem.

"It is almost certain that Prime Minister Yitzhak Rabin has already made the decision to abandon the Golan Heights in return for a peace treaty with Syria," says de Courcy. "But he does not have the Israeli public with him on this, partly because the Israeli public does not believe that President Hafez Assad's signature on a peace treaty is worth very much and partly because of a special attachment to the Heights themselves.

"Although the Israeli public's attachment to the Golan Heights cannot in any way be compared with the historical and religious ties that bind the Jews to Judea and Samaria and to Jerusalem, the Jewish public has an instinctive (and well-informed) understanding of the area's strategic importance. Because the Golan Heights have a population of only 33,000, made up of 18,000 Druze and 15,000 Jewish settlers, there are none of the human problems that have so undermined the Jewish hold on the West Bank and Gaza Strip. The problem of the Golan Heights is entirely a strategic one, and the Israeli public is not persuaded that Rabin has correctly calculated the cost-benefit equation."

What the average Israeli understands—in part because their sons and fathers and brothers fought so gallantly to gain this high ground—is that the east-to-west slope of the Golan Heights makes the eastern border the strongest defense point in the country. Giving away the Golan might be enough to cause a political uprising among the Israeli people.

But, if it isn't, surely concessions that involve Judea and Samaria would be. There are 100,000 Jewish settlers living in these lands now. They are biblically Jewish lands. To evacuate Jews from them would be an enormous psychological blow to the whole concept of Jewish nationhood. Frankly, such an attempt might be enough to trigger a civil war. The government is well aware of the risk and has begun assembling a special army unit made up of soldiers who have no relatives in Judea and Samaria and who are not political supporters of the conservative Likud Party, which has opposed any negotiations on these territories. The special unit is being trained in urban warfare techniques. I will leave it to your imaginations to decide what the government is planning. But as difficult a task as abandoning Judea and Samaria would be, it would be even more problematic to implement a retreat from East Jerusalem, as we saw in the previous chapter.

"It might be thought that in view of Jerusalem's historic significance for the Jews, and after so much blood has been spilled to bring it once more under Jewish control, no Israeli government could ever contemplate a surrender, however partial, of the Jewish state's sovereignty over the Holy City," says de Courcy. "But the peace camp in Israel is increasingly arguing for a compromise. As General Dayan's daughter Yael said in an interview published in the1994 New Year's Eve special edition of *Maariv*: 'Holiness of a place is not something over which we have a monopoly. A symbol can't be a way of life. When it clashes with reality, it will be superseded.'"

The point is, it is no longer unthinkable in Israel to talk about compromising away part of Jerusalem.

"In politics the world over," says de Courcy, "the salami-slicing tactic can be highly effective, and Yitzhak Rabin calculates that, given time, the Israeli public can be induced to accept even previously inconceivable concessions. But there is also the possibility that he has miscalculated and that on one of the big issues (the Golan, the settlements and Jerusalem) or a combination of them all, the Jewish public will rebel. The danger signals for Rabin are already visible, and, if he does not heed them, his government could easily fall."

The fourth and most likely scenario for the peace process, according to de Courcy, is that Israel will make the strategic concessions and risk living in a far more dangerous environment.

"If this scenario is correct, it is likely to unfold more or less according to the schedule outlined in the 1993 Oslo accord," he says. "This schedule calls for the permanent settlement between the Palestinians and Israel to come into effect on December 13 1998."

This, he says, is by far the most likely scenario. Either of the last two outcomes is more likely than the first two, he says. Either would result in a much less stable Middle East. Either could also lead to a renewed Arab-Israeli conflict. *But scenario four, de Courcy says, would make war in the Middle East almost unavoidable because of the premium it would put on a pre-emptive military first strike.*

Way back in 1967, when the level of military technology and sophistication available to the Arab states was much lower, a Pentagon study found that Israel needed control of the land just east of Jerusalem, the central West Bank of the Jordan River and part of the Sinai including Sharm esh Sheikh. Israel can overcome its frightening security problems and territorial inferiority only by maintaining a strong deterrence factor.

Pushing Israel Into Nuclear Box

In the late 1970s, Israel agreed to give up the Sinai peninsula to Egypt in exchange only for a peace treaty. Before returning the Sinai, Israel was in control of a territory covering 34,493 square miles; it now occupies just 10,860 square miles. If Israel gives up Judea and Samaria, the Gaza Strip and the Golan Heights, it will be confined to a territory of just 7,993 square miles. In contrast, the frontline Arab states of Egypt, Jordan, Lebanon and Syria cover an area of 497,026 square miles. The land area of the entire Arab world is 5.1 million square miles.

Some suggest that modern technology has rendered territory an irrelevance in warfare. But experience suggests otherwise, and there is strong evidence to suggest that the reverse is true—that the increasing speed and lethality of modern weaponry have *increased* the importance of territory. Thus, many military and intelligence experts agree that further land concessions would leave Israel with hopelessly indefensible borders and no effective *conventional* deterrent against attack.

Notice the emphasis on the word *conventional*. Because Israel still has its *non*-conventional form of deterrent— nuclear weapons. Does the world really want to force Israel to rely exclusively on nuclear weapons for its defense? Tragically, this is exactly where things are headed in the Middle East today.

In the 1990s, it is more critical than ever that Israel hold on to the strategic lands it captured in 1967. Why?

- As weapons of mass destruction become more widely available in the region, the area needed to wage war expands.

- Topography and control of the high ground have become more important in an age when all sophisticated weapons require the transmission of electromagnetic radiation and guiding sensors and antennae deployed from line-of-sight locations.

- The speed of modern aircraft calls for greater warning space.

- The precision and destruction capabilities of modern weapons systems require the dispersal of military airfields, emergency depots and other military facilities.

Intelligence experts point out that if Israel withdraws to its pre-1967 borders, every military airfield will be covered by enemy radar and be within reach of modern artillery. In addition, Israel's major population and industrial centers would be within range of conventional artillery, not to mention missiles.

If the Arab states, with their superior numbers, deployed a massive attack including tanks, conventional artillery and ground-to-ground missiles, Israel would literally have only one choice—go nuclear immediately.

As de Courcy puts it: "The choice which will face Israel's decision-makers if Israel retreats to indefensible borders is between two options: (a) They can respond to the mobilization of Arab forces by a risky conventional pre-emptive strike and be condemned by the rest of the world as aggressors. (b) They can wait until the Arabs attack and depend on the use of nuclear weapons for survival."

The pre-emptive first strike has always played a prominent role in Israeli military thinking, but the greater the territorial retreat (especially given the development of modern weaponry) the greater the reliance that must be placed on pre-emption, says de Courcy.

"In 1956 [the Suez War], 1967 [the Six-Day War], 1981 [the destruction of Iraq's Osirak nuclear reactor] and 1982 [Operation Peace for Galilee] Israel attacked its neighbors because of provocations or fear of imminent attack," he recalls. "Only October 1973 [the Yom Kippur War] was different, when Israel was the subject of a surprise Arab attack on two fronts, and it stands out in Israeli military history as an exception that must never be repeated."

While the Israelis, already historically programmed for extreme suspicion, are bound to rely in the post-Madrid world more and more on a first-strike defense, the Arabs will be forced in the same direction. The effect will be to make war all but inevitable.

Driven Toward "Samson Option"

"Whether such a war escalates beyond the conventional to produce the first use of nuclear weapons since World War II will depend largely on the attitudes of the Jewish state," says de Courcy. "The Arabs will calculate that their own non-conventional armory neutralizes Israel's and that Israel will not, therefore, use its nuclear weapons to counter an Arab conventional attack, however overwhelming. But Israel is not a normal nation. The Jews, having experienced 2,000 years of miserable exile, would probably prefer, like Samson, to "die with the Philistines" rather than risk another term as outcasts in the Gentile world. In other words, the ultimate disaster—nuclear war in the Middle East—*could* happen. In all events, the likelihood of such a disaster is greatly *increased* by a peace process which increases the opportunities for war without removing the causes for war."

This is amazing to me. Here is a world renowned, gifted, sophisticated, secular, highly regarded intelligence expert saying just what I have been saying about the imminent future of the Middle East. He comes to the same conclusions based on different evidence—mine Biblical prophecy, his the dispassionate pragmatism of a political and military scientist with awe-some sources of intelligence information.

I agree absolutely with Joe de Courcy's findings. If Israel gives back Judea, Samaria, the Gaza Strip and the Golan Heights, it will simply no longer be able to defend itself against the Muslim nations with conventional weapons, which as you will see in subsequent chapters, are better armed and equipped than they have ever been before. Israel will simply not have conventional weapons or an army that can be mustered in time. The Israelis would have only one option—and it would be no solution. Instead of just Jewish corpses, there would be millions of Arab corpses.

The option is to launch an all-out nuclear attack on all the Arab capitals. I have seen and read the "Samson Option," a special paper that outlines a military doctrine now in force. If Israel is being overrun, they will use the nuclear option. Like Samson, they may go down, but so will all of their enemies. And that's just a preview of how terrible things will be in the Final Battle.

Chapter 7

THE
LAST
DASH
TO THE
SOUTH

"And you will come from your place out of the remote parts of the north [the extreme north], you and many peoples with you . . . a great assembly [confederacy] and a mighty army. And you will come against My people Israel like a cloud to cover the land. It will come about in the last days that I shall bring you against My land . . . ."

—Ezekiel 38:15-16

It's a cold November night in Moscow. A train is pulling out of the station. The last wagon—a cattle car—is jammed with famous Russian political and cultural leaders, from former President Mikhail Gorbachev to reformer and economist Yegor Gaidar to dissident Andrei Sakharov's widow, Yelena Bonner. It's bound for Siberia.

What's going on here? It's not a movie of the week, folks. This is the fantasy laid out in a new book by Russian "national socialist" Vladimir Zhirinovsky. It's a chilling insight into what life might be like in the new Russia should this megalomaniac, in the near future, be catapulted to power.

Just as too many in the West tend to disregard the actual words expressed by radical Muslim leaders in the Middle East, they also tend to give too little credence to what potential Russian dictators like Zhirinovsky are saying.

General "Zero"

Who is Zhirinovsky and what does he stand for? Well, for starters, he is strongly anti-Semitic and fascistic, yet received the largest number of votes in Russia's December 1993 parliamentary elections. This man, sometimes called the "Russian Hitler," is poised for a presidential run in 1996. He enjoys good support among the Russian military. And his autobiography, apocalyptically titled *The Last Dash to the South,* promotes the idea of Russian expansion into the Middle East and Persian Gulf.

Keep in mind, now, that 2,600 years ago, the Hebrew prophet Ezekiel predicted that in the last days Russia would launch an ill-fated invasion of the Middle East. I'm not saying that Zhirinovksy is the biblical leader named "Gog," but this is clearly evidence that prophetic fulfillment of this critical endtimes development is very near.

"Let Russia successfully accomplish its last dash to the South," he writes in his book. "I see Russian soldiers gathering for this last campaign. I see Russian commanding officers in the headquarters of Russian divisions and armies, sketching the lines of troop movements. . . . I see planes at air bases in the southern districts of Russia. I see submarines surfacing off the shores of the Indian Ocean and landing crafts approaching shores where soldiers of the Russian Army are already marching. . . . Infantry combat vehicles are advancing and vast numbers of tanks are on the move. Russia is at last accomplishing its final military campaign."

If I didn't know better, I would say that Zhirinovksy has been inspired by Ezekiel 38 and 39. But I do know better. This is a man of sin, not a man of God. He promises to be a brutal dictator if he is elected, or if he comes to power by coup, certainly another possibility.

"I'll start by squeezing the Baltics and other small nations," he says. "I don't care if they are recognized by the U.N. I'm not going to invade them or anything. I'll bury radioactive waste along the Lithuanian border and put up powerful fans and blow the stuff across the border at night. I'll turn the fans off during the day. They'll all get radiation sickness. They'll die of it. When they either die of it or get down on their knees, I'll stop it. I'm a dictator. What I'm going to do is bad, but it'll be good for Russia. The Slavs are going to get anything they want if I'm elected."

Sound like the rantings of a madman? You bet. But this is a madman who has a good chance of becoming leader of Russia—and soon.

"I will send troops to Afghanistan again, and this time they'll win," he says. "I will restore the foreign policy of the czars. I won't make Russians fight. I'll make Uzbeks and Tajiks do the fighting. Russian officers will just give the orders. Like Napolean. 'Uzbeks, forward to Kabul!' And when the Uzbeks are all dead, it'll be, 'Tajiks, forward to Kabul!' The Baskirs can go to Mongolia where there's TB and syphilis. The other republics will be Russia's kitchen garden. Russia will be the brains."

This Is Not A Joke

This may sound like a comedy routine, but believe me, it's no joke. This man is deadly serious. And the common Russians are buying his spiel. In fact, they love it.

"I say it plainly: When I come to power, there will be a dictatorship," he says. "I will beat the Americans in space. I will surround the planet with our space stations, so that they'll be scared of our space weapons. I don't care if they call me a fascist or a Nazi. Workers in Leningrad told me, 'Even if you wear five swastikas, we'll vote for you all the same. You promise a clear plan.' There's nothing like fear to make people work better. The stick, not the carrot. I'll do it all without tanks in the streets. Those who have to be arrested will be arrested quietly at night. I may have to shoot 100,000 people, but the other 300 million will live peacefully. I have the right to shoot 100,000. I have this right as president."

Listen to more of Zhirinovsky:

- "I am the almighty! I am a tyrant! I will follow in Hitler's footsteps."
- "From time to time, Russia is overwhelmed with anti-Semitism. This phenomenon is provoked only by the Jews themselves."
- "We will create new Hiroshimas and Nagasakis. I will not hesitate to deploy atomic weapons."
- "History has shown that in Europe, our faithful ally should have been Germany. We could have avoided the two world wars with them. We needed a war against France."
- "What price Paris? How about London? Washington? Los Angeles? How much are you willing to pay so I don't wipe them from the face of the Earth with my SS-18s? You doubt me? Want to take a chance? Let's get started."

Russia, as we learned in recent years, is a country where anything can happen—even Zhirinovksy, as scary as that prospect may seem. But Zhirinovksy is not alone in understanding that anything can happen. Gorbachev certainly recognizes it, too. That's why he has put aside for the moment his position as an international celebrity commanding huge speaking fees and book advances to launch a political comeback in his native country.

Convinced that the nation is disillusioned with President Boris Yeltsin, Gorbachev is mapping out a campaign strategy and a travel itinerary designed to give him the kind of recognition in Russia that he enjoys throughout the West. Gorbachev, by the way, is emphasizing the need to create a new union of former

Soviet republics. And he won't be alone pushing that program on the campaign trail. Zhirinovsky, too, believes the old Soviet Union needs to be re-formed. And Communist Party leader Gennady Zyuganov espouses similar ideas.

One way or another, there are going to be some serious changes in Russia in the next several years. What a difference a few years make. In the dark hours immediately following the attempted coup of 1991, as the Russian people milled about uncertainly, images of Boris Yeltsin, denouncing the plotters from atop a tank, flashed around the world. He was the man of the hour—the hero of free Russia. Yeltsin was the man the West pinned their hopes on for the new era of post-Cold War peace.

Russia, after all, had been beaten to its knees— economically and spiritually, collapsing from within under the weight of its military budget. The arms race broke the back of Russia. So they turned eagerly toward the West in search of their salvation. But the "peace dividend" never really materialized—not for the West or for Russia.

Oh, it's true that the United States has often unwisely thrown money at Russia—but not anywhere close to the amounts dreamed of by Russians, not in the amounts necessary to rescue the nation from calamity. The United States is paying Russian scientists not to sell their nuclear secrets to Libya, Iran and North Korea, for instance. But, I assure you, those nations are willing to outbid the United States—and are doing so. All the West has accomplished is to raise the price a little.

So the Russians are now officially selling their services to Iran in building its nuclear infrastructure in a way that will ensure Tehran can produce its own atomic weapons. About 3,000 Russian workers are assisting in the

construction of a nuclear plant that will provide Tehran with
the plutonium and the technical know-how to build its own
bombs by the end of the decade. When House Speaker
Newt Gingrich threatened in early 1995 to cut off U.S. aid if
Russia pressed ahead with its plan to develop Iran's nuclear
power program, the Russians didn't flinch.

"I'm not worried," said Viktor N. Mikhailov, minister
for nuclear power. "What's $215 million for Russia?" He
knew a lot more money is available from Iran. This boast
proved not to be an idle one. Over the protests of the United
States, Russia concluded a deal to build nuclear reactors in
Iran in March of 1995.

Russia is also eager to sell arms to Iran's ally, Syria.
This is interesting, the *Jerusalem Post* has pointed out
because one of the main arguments for reaching a quick
peace agreement with Syria's Hafez Assad is that his regime
can no longer rely on the Soviet umbrella for support—that
Russia is out of the Middle East politics game.

First of all, this theory falls short because it
presupposes that decisions in the Middle East are always
well-reasoned. But Saddam Hussein did not have the
support of a Soviet umbrella either, yet he marched into
Kuwait and stood fast against hopeless odds. But Russia
also, contrary to conventional wisdom, continues to build
up its own strategic nuclear force and has reportedly
developed a new generation of ballistic missiles,
more accurate and powerful than anything currently on
the market.

Since the Gulf War, the Arab regimes have spent $60
billion on arms purchases. Unlike the Gulf states, Syria
could not pay cash and has accumulated over $10 billion
in debt to Russia. Until recently, Russia insisted that the

debt be repaid before more arms purchases could be negotiated. But Russia is now so eager to sell Syria weapons that it has canceled the debt.

Democracy Is Hypocracy To "Ivan"

The Russian people have given up waiting for the West to somehow magically transform their economy. Let's look at Ivan Q. Public, an average Russian. To him, "democracy" just isn't living up to its hype. Under Communist rule, every Russian had a job, a home and, albeit predictable and colorless, a future. Democracy has introduced the people to unemployment, inflation and homelessness. The disintegration of internal security systems, coupled with the opportunities the free market brings to criminal enterprises, has introduced a new term to the global vocabulary—the Russian Mafia.

Corrupt officials and organized crime groups have extended their control over a vast number of businesses. An *Izvestia* report in 1994 stated that more than half of all capital and 80 percent of voting shares in private enterprises "pass into the possession of criminal structures." It also said that "Mafia clans" control more than 40,000 businesses in Russia and that $20 billion made from criminal activity has been laundered in the West.

The people now believe—and they may well be right— that the mob runs the country. Contract killings of businessmen, investigative reporters and bankers are routine. Most of Russia's biggest banks are now linked directly to the mob, according to the CIA.

Crime, Chaos And Poverty = Coup

"In Russia, there is a real threat that the surge in crime will sour the Russian people on Yeltsin's reform program and drive them into the arms of Russia's hard-line political forces," said CIA Director R. James Woolsey.

But this is just the start of the problems facing the staggering Russian republic. In 1994, the gross national product was at just 46 percent of the 1990 level. In market economies like the United States, such a drop would translate into a situation comparable to the Great Depression, when one of four workers couldn't find a job. In Russia, however, the government continues to subsidize many enterprises, continuing a form of the old state socialism. The federal government in Moscow estimates that some 9 million people are searching for jobs. Another 8 million are underemployed. Millions of others are employed only in black-market activities.

Then there's the problem of a cash-strapped and demoralized military, with leadership talking openly about a coup. The sad state of affairs in the military establishment made international headlines in 1994 when a Moscow utility company shut off electricity to the command center of Russia's Strategic Rocket Forces in an effort to induce payment of back bills.

In 1994, Russia's military needed 60 trillion rubles to maintain minimal standards of readiness and meet payroll. But the government budgeted only 40.6 trillion and then only turned over 14 trillion to the Defense Ministry. Soldiers are reportedly living on starvation rations.

"The mood in Russia's armed forces is one of complete dejection," said *Krasnaya Zvezda,* a publication that speaks for army leadership. ". . . The pockets of some 30 percent of Russian army officers are empty. Many officers are compelled to work as janitors and street cleaners after completing their daily service."

It was in this condition that Yeltsin sent his troops and officers into Chechnya. Is it any wonder it took them so long to subdue the tiny republic and secure its capital? Is it any wonder they experienced so many casualties against a rag-tag civilian militia force?

Humiliated Red Army Dangerous

General Alexander Lebed is one officer who has hinted openly of a coup. He said unless the state "takes necessary steps to provide the army with normal conditions," there is a 50 percent chance of a military revolt.

"Military officers lay the blame . . . squarely on the president's door, and it is said that only 20 percent of the Russian officer corps supports President Yeltsin," says Joseph de Courcy. "Support for hard-liners like General Lebed, commander of the 14th Army stationed in the breakaway Trans-Dnestr region of Moldova, is strong and growing. Lebed, an Afghan war hero, advocates the use of force in dealings with former Soviet republics and to stamp out internal strife in Russia itself."

It is against this backdrop that we examine the role of Russia in the latter part of the 1990s. Yeltsin is not the haloed democratic reformer the world had hoped for. Though he initially recognized little Chechnya's claim on independence, he ruthlessly ordered the invasion of the ethnic enclave later. Why? Chechnya has vast oil reserves, and Russia cannot afford to allow those reserves outside of her control.

The Muslim world condemned Russia's action against the predominantly Muslim Chechnya—but not too loudly. After all, most of the Arab guns trained on Israel are stamped "made in Moscow"—and all require continued Russian parts and technical support to remain operational. But, most of all, the Islamic world has big plans for

Russia. And they wouldn't want a little playground scrap to come between such good friends.

Russia And Islam

Russia is being linked more closely than ever before to the Islamic world. Iran is looking forward to a time when the Islamic world can draw Russia into a war against Israel. An agreement that ultimately will draw Russia into just such a war was signed with Iran in February of 1991. Russia seems to be led into this conflagration reluctantly, almost against its will. I believe it will be the strong Islamic influence on Moscow that places those "hooks into the jaws" of Magog, or Russia, as Ezekiel predicted twenty-six hundred years ago.

"Son of man, set your face toward Gog of the land of Magog, the prince of Rosh, Meshech, and Tubal, and prophesy against him, and say, 'Thus says the Lord God, "Behold, I am against you, O Gog, prince of Rosh, Meshech, and Tubal," the Bible foretells in Ezekiel 38:2-6. **"And I will turn you about, and put hooks into your jaws, and I will bring you out, and all your army, horses and horsemen, all of them splendidly attired, a great company with buckler and shield, all of them wielding swords; Persia, Ethiopia [Cush], and Put with them, all of them with shield and helmet; Gomer with all its troops; Beth-togarmah from the remote parts of the north with all its troops—many peoples with you."**

The Muslims know that Russia's long-term interests cannot be met just by Chechnya's oil. She needs a warm water port, like the Persian Gulf. She needs financial aid— aid that is not coming from the West. That only leaves the Arab oil emirates.

Ezekiel 38 also talks about a confederacy of powers—
including Russia and Germany—coming against Israel. It's
worth noting that Zhirinovsky, as well as other potential
Russian rulers, are talking about forming a closer strategic
alliance with Germany. Coincidence? I don't think so.
Russia has a long-term national interest in moving
the center of gravity in Europe to the East. That's why the
U.S. and Russia—these wonderful new friends—have been
sniping over plans for the future of the North Atlantic
Treaty Organization. You see, NATO ties Europe to the
United States. The Soviets have been working overtime
trying to subordinate NATO to the Conference on Security
and Cooperation in Europe (CSCE).

"The CSCE is a net we have thrown over the whole of
Europe, for the purpose of entangling the European states in
it," said Russian Foreign Minister Andrei Kozyrev in an
unguarded moment. Russia will not be successful in its
effort to achieve strategic hegemony over Europe. But this
struggle will no doubt lead to the kinds of tensions and
frictions that will ultimately cause a showdown in the
Middle East between a European power, the Russians and
their allies and the Asian powers. This Final Battle will be
touched off by Russia, seduced into invasion by its Muslim
allies in the South.

Russia More Unstable Than Ever
The Soviet Union may be gone, but Russia—despite
dramatic moves toward democracy and freedom—is, in this
increasingly volatile world, more dangerous than ever. This
is the kind of environment—combined with the remnants of
a colossal military infrastructure—that breeds coups.

"The American Defense Department held a seminar
called "Scenarios of Russian Futures" in the summer of
1993 which sought to assess the likely path of Russia over
the years up to the turn of the century," recalls Joseph de
Courcy. "The Defense Department's assembled experts saw
three main possibilities for Russia in the year 2000. Only
one variant of the least-likely scenario foresaw the
establishment of a stable, pro-Western Russia. The other
scenarios and sub-scenarios all foresaw the re-
establishment of authoritarian, militaristic, anti-Western
rule in Moscow—or complete disintegration. The most
likely scenario for Russia in the years leading up to 2000
[to which the experts attached a 55 percent probability]
was a nationalist backlash to a Zhirinovsky-style
dictatorship. But regardless of whether President Yeltsin is
eventually replaced by a Zhirinovsky/ Rutskoi/Lebed
figure, signs are already appearing of a hardening Russian
attitude on foreign-policy issues."

It's not too hard to imagine another Kremlin conspiracy
seizing power from Yeltsin and imposing a totalitarian,
military-style dictatorship. Even if there is no coup, once
again the world finds itself relying on one man—Yeltsin—
to hold together the disintegrating and unstable Russian
Republic. How long will his health hold out? Yes, the Evil
Empire may be gone, but Russia's role in the endtimes
scenario remains the same.

The mainstream media may not be tracking
developments in Russia with much scrutiny and clarity, but,
behind the scenes, there are momentous and profound events
taking place in Moscow today. The great bear may not look
as dangerous as it once did, but looks can be deceiving.

Ezekiel Chapter 38, verse 8 describes modern-day Israel, after the Jews have returned from many nations and "are living securely." Today, the Jewish population of the former Soviet Union and East Bloc nations has moved to Israel in record numbers. There they believe they are living more securely than ever before.

In fact, Ezekiel 38 forecasts a period of pseudo-peace for the world. Then God is going to cause the Russian leader—whomever it may be—to make a great tactical error. He is going to side with the Muslims against Israel and attack. As a result, the whole world will be engulfed in the greatest holocaust in history.

Notice that even Zhirinovsky seems to recognize that Russia's "dash to the South" will be the last great military move the nation ever makes. They know it but they can't resist the temptation. The Russians are drawn to fulfill their own biblical destiny.

"Russia is going through one of its periodic attempts to become a Western country," explains Joseph de Courcy. "It tried it in the early 18th century under Peter the Great, it had another go after losing the Crimean War in 1856, and now it is trying again. Every attempt has brought some improvements, but Russia has never managed to make a full conversion. It is unlikely to happen this time, and in due course the most likely outcome of the reform-phase started by Mikhail Gorbachev is that Russia will, as in the past, fall back into a uniquely Russian way of life having come to the realization, once more, that it is *not* a Western country. Russia's future is as a commodity-based economy relying for its continued importance in the world on its geographical extent and location, its large population, its store of raw materials, Third World alliances and, above all, the strength of its armed forces. The signs of such a reversion can already be seen."

De Courcy makes the point that "Iran and Russia need each other." Throughout history, these two nations have courted one another no matter which personality was in power. Under the pro-Western Shah in the late 1960s, Iran was the second-largest recipient of Soviet economic aid," de Courcy recalls. And under the Ayatollah Khomeini, Moscow continued to be supportive.

Just as Russia and Iran need each other, Turkey is also beginning to realize it, too, needs Iran. A change in relations between the two nations began in 1993. At the beginning of the year, Ankara was accusing Iran of encouraging assassins to attempt the murder of Turkish industrialist Jak Kamhi, and, as late as November 1993, Turkish Prime Minister Tansu Ciller was naming Iran, along with Syria, Iraq and Armenia, as providing sanctuary for Kurdish Workers' Party guerrillas.

"But following a visit to Ankara in December 1993 by Iranian Vice President Hassan Habibi, and an earlier one by Foreign Minister Valayati, a far-reaching memorandum of understanding and cooperation was signed between the two countries," says de Courcy. That agreement included:

- A Turkish commitment to purchase between 3 million and 4 million tons of crude oil from Iran in 1994;

- The Turkish Pipeline and Petroleum Transport Corporation to enter into talks about the transport of Iranian natural gas to Europe by way of a pipeline through Turkey;

- The volume of border trade between Iran and Turkey to increase to $50 million in 1994;

- All restrictions on road transit through the two countries to be lifted;
- The Turkish and Iranian rail network to be connected with the railroad system of Central Asian republics. The rail connection between Mashhad in Iran and Serakhs in Turkmenistan, as well as the connection from south of Lake Van to Iran, to be completed by the end of 1996. Railway freight fees to be standardized;
- A road to be constructed linking Central Asia and Europe by way of Turkey and Iran.

The Iranians also mediated a secret agreement between Turkey and Syria in 1993, according to de Courcy. It included the following commitment:

- Turkey to supply Syria with water requirements unconditionally;
- Turkey and Syria to act in unison on the Kurdish problem;
- Turkey and Syria to cooperate against destructive activities threatening national unity and the regimes in both countries;
- Turkey to help Syria oppose international initiatives aimed against Syria;
- Turkey to support Syria's position on Lebanon.

"This trend in Turkish foreign policy, away from its unquestioning pro-Westernism, was given clear expression by the appointment in July 1994 of Mumtaz Soysal as Turkey's foreign minister," observes de Courcy. "Soysal is a long-standing nationalist critic of the West and is referred to in some sections of the German press as 'Turkey's Zhirinovsky.'"

The most important reason for Turkey's new direction is the new influence of Islam on government policy and in cultural areas as well.

"These are dramatic changes," says de Courcy. "They appear to be genuine changes in response to changing circumstances, not just temporary fashion. As Turkey was one of the first countries to recognize the State of Israel in 1949, as it has always provided an important counterweight to Syria, these developments are of immense concern for Israel. It cannot yet be said that Turkey is an enemy of Israel, but the direction of its foreign policy is clear and in any future Arab-Israeli war it would at best be a hostile neutral. If the Islamists take control after the 1996 elections, even that would be optimistic."

During the Cold War, Turkey was considered by the West a bullwark in its frontline defense against the Soviet Union. Today, Iran has coyly drawn this key state into an alliance. How long will it be before Turkey and Russia discover their own mutual interests? How long will it be before Turkey joins the Muslim alliance that will lure Russia into its inevitable invasion of the Middle East—their final dash to the South?

Despite all their talk about "peace and safety" and "the new Russia," Moscow has demonstrated its willingness to move militarily and ruthlessly in Chechnya. To the man on the street, democracy is already a failed experiment, and the old ways are looking pretty good. The West is sufficiently preoccupied with its own problems. Russia will milk that for all it's worth.

As America looks inward to address its social ills, Russia looks to the Middle East to address its own. This is the scenario facing us in the latter half of the 1990s—and it is precisely the one predicted for the last generation before the return of Christ twenty-five hundred years ago by the Hebrew prophets.

Russia will invade Israel at a time when war is least expected. It's easy to see the pieces fitting together now. But this is the same scenario that students of Bible prophecy have been expecting for hundreds of years. In the early part of this century, for instance, H. A. Ironside wrote in his book Ezekiel. In the last days, the final head of the Russia people will look with covetous eyes upon the great developments in the land of Palestine. They will determine that Russia must have her part of the wealth there produced. Consequently, we have the picture of a vast army, augmented by warriors from Persia, Cush, Put, marching down toward Palestine."

Get ready, my friends, for this last dash to the South. The Final Battle is near.

Chapter 8

EUROPE'S COMING PRINCE

"And it was given to him to make war with the saints and to overcome them; and authority over every tribe and people and tongue and nation was given to him."

—Revelation 13:7

News flash: "*Foreign ministers meeting in Brussels approved a law that could lead to a Frenchman being elected mayor in Italy or a German voting for a local official in Spain. Legislation set in train by the Maastricht treaty will allow European Union citizens to vote or run in local elections wherever they live.*"

—*The European,* Dec. 22, 1994

News flash: "BRUSSELS—The European Union, facing mounting instability near its borders, should centralize its defense planning and create a European Intervention Force, a group of independent experts said. The group, which was appointed by the European Commission, said it was vital to crystallize the links between the Commission, the Council of Ministers and the Western European Union as well as between the WEU and NATO."

—*Reuters,* Jan. 27, 1995

News flash: "BRUSSELS—For the European Union, the era of relatively painless expansion has ended and the treacherous march eastward has begun. Not only will the process be difficult and costly, but the danger of failure could create a security vacuum in Central and Eastern Europe."

—*Toronto Globe and Mail,* February 1995.

Things are happening in Europe. Things are happening *fast*. January 1, 1995, saw the ringing in of a whole new set of European Union rules and regulations that still have the people of the entire continent shaking their heads. And there's plenty of new laws on the way.

The "Eurocrats" in Brussels are relishing their new powers and exercising them with glee. No one is out of their reach—not even Santa Claus. Ib Groth Rasmussen, the president of the Father Christmas World Congress, says time is running out on the differing holiday traditions of nations ranging from the Netherlands to Great Britain, as the European Commission develops rules for a new Euro-Santa.

"Children's behavior will probably have to be standardized, too," he frets, saying that the EU seeks to make every aspect of life on the continent conform to a one-size-fits-all model.

Just A Matter Of time

Twenty-five years ago, when I would tell audiences that Europe would soon be uniting to form one of the most powerful political, economic and military blocs on the planet, people would look at at me in disbelief. "Is this guy crazy? A United States of Europe? With all the ancient hostilities pulling these people apart?" Well, today, it is so close to reality that no one doubts it anymore. It's just a matter of time before total integration is in place.

As we've learned in recent years as witnesses to the breakup of the Soviet Union, the tearing down of the Berlin Wall and other profound developments, things can happen very fast. Changes can take place overnight.

Yet, I am still questioned all the time about how Europe can possibly rise to the status of superstate—leader of the world—in the near future. Some recent news events have given me insight into this question.

Many years ago, most of the western European nations began experimenting with socialism. What they found, universally, is that it doesn't work. And every single one of the key European Community nations is currently involved, in some way, at some stage, in dismantling the welfare state.

Even the United States has come to the realization that centralization of power in a federal government and constantly increased social spending are recipes for disaster. Europe, too, is throwing in the towel on socialism. The increase in rules and regulations from Brussels may seem like a contradiction to what I am saying. But not really. That is merely evidence of the coming unification. Each state within the European Union is turning away from government solutions to every social problem under the sun.

The Coming Boom

So what will this trend mean to the future of Europe? Take a guess. It will mean economic resurgence. It will mean growth. It will mean prosperity. And it could also mean *imminent greatness* for Europe.

Am I exaggerating the extent of this trend? No way. Perhaps you haven't read much about this in the liberal press, but the fact remains that European socialism is retreating. Here are some examples:

- Germany has already cut a wide array of welfare state programs including unemployment compensation, paid sick days, student grants, child-care subsidies and holiday pay. The state is also raising the pension age from 63 to 65.

- France has frozen maximum social security pensions at $1,100 a month and increased the length of time required to receive a pension from 37.5 to 40 years. It has also cut government reimbursements of doctor visits from 75 percent to 70 percent and expanded the array of drugs for which no reimbursements are made at all.

- Britain has ordered a complete review of all welfare spending, including its National Health Service. It is considering raising the minimum social security age for women from 60 to 65 and putting teen mothers in hostels rather than apartments.

- Even Sweden—the one-time model for democratic socialism—has reduced sick-leave benefits from 90 percent to 75 percent of regular salaries and eliminated it for the first day's absence. Not surprisingly, absenteeism fell from three in ten workers to one in ten. Swedes also eliminated unemployment compensation for a worker's first five days of joblessness and lowered benefits from 90 percent to 80 percent of the previous salary.

What has the result been so far? There are already signs of economic revival throughout the continent: "Asia is ascendant," a February 14, 1995, *Wall Street Journal* story reported. "American industry is lean and potent. And Europe is commonly viewed as a lost continent of high costs, high unemployment and meddlesome governments. For another perspective, drive down the A14 Autobahn in Austria's Rhine Valley, near the German and Swiss borders. This 50-kilometer stretch is lined with evidence of a reawakening, of growing strength in European industry."

Relaxed regulations are just one reason for the recovery. The highly skilled work force in Europe is even more important. European industry is moving into high-end market niches where cost is less important than quality.

Growing Confidence In Europe

"There is growing confidence in Europe right now," says Betty Thayer, a consultant for Arthur Andersen & Company who has studied manufacturing competitiveness worldwide. "The Europeans are coming back."

Meanwhile, there is another trend at work that will stimulate growth and lessen the economic burdens on the European Community. While the EC once considered adding 20, 30 or more members to its club, the thinking has changed. In fact, the EC is increasingly wary of accepting any new member states.

Why will this help stabilize Europe and move it toward greater prosperity? Because most potential new members are more interested in what benefits they can derive from belonging to the EC than in what they bring to the table. Again, this gets right back to the welfare debate. Europe is looking toward greater productivity for the future—not greater drains on growth.

New Alliances

This new selectivity has also helped to create new alliances. Turkey, for instance, was one of the very first nations to apply for membership in the EC. Yet it has consistently been snubbed. Europeans believe there are too many cultural differences between the existing EC nations and Muslim Turkey. Thus, Turkey, as we have already discussed, is moving into closer alliance with Iran, Syria and, possibly, later with Russia.

I don't believe we have seen the final shaking out of the United States of Europe by any stretch of the imagination. I believe, for instance, that a split is very likely that will cause either Britain and/or Germany to leave the EC. Germany could forge a closer relationship with Russia, while Britain may turn toward the United States of America. The Bible is very clear, as we will see, that this union will be a confederation of ten nations.

But whatever the final breakdown of nations is, Rome will be the center stage and, for a time, the entire world economy will be controlled from Europe. As far back as two years ago, the Club of Rome—the organization which first envisioned a unified Europe—issued a report predicting a "brave new world" and forecasting much of what is going on in the world right now. *The First Global Revolution,* by Bertrand Schneider and Alexander King, illustrated how Europe was on the ascendancy and the United States of America was in decline due to "stagnation," a crushing burden of debt and financial instability that threatens the whole capitalist world.

The Revived Roman Empire

That is precisely the direction in which Europe—or, one might call it, "the revived Roman Empire"—is moving.

Bigger, stronger, more tightly controlled. What is happening there has almost guaranteed the economic dominance of Western Europe in the New World Order.

How could such a thing happen? Well, it will take chemistry—personal chemistry and dynamic leadership. A leader will emerge on the scene who will rally everyone around him. He will be seen as a savior—as humanity's great white hope.

Over the years, I have probably been asked more questions about the rise of the anti-Christ than any other subject. How, people want to know, could a political leader arise and assume so much power in skeptical times like these? With all the division and turmoil in the world, why won't people be suspect of turning over so much authority to one individual? Aren't people simply too distrustful of government these days to fall prey to the vainglorious ambitions of a power-mad tyrant?

Searching For A Leader

Good questions, indeed. Sometimes it is difficult to imagine such a scenario. But, just for example, not too long ago a political leader emerged in Europe who literally swept the populace off their feet and garnered almost universal praise and admiration. How did he do it? What kind of magical spells did he cast? Was he the most gifted orator in the world? Did he resort to the kinds of miraculous and supernatural wonders that the Bible prophesies the anti-Christ will invoke?

No, in fact, the politician who captured the imaginations of the French people is a rather mediocre figure in most ways. Most Americans, who don't pay much attention to events in Europe, have probably not even heard his name before. Prime Minister Edouard Balladur, 64, has been, until fairly recently, only an obscure, behind-the-scenes player in French politics. He does not possess the kind of magnetism or charisma that might be expected of someone commanding positive reviews from the right and left. But, nevertheless, he dazzled nearly everyone.

For instance, France's leading political cartoonist recently portrayed Balladur walking on water. A commentator on the French political scene characterized his meteoric ascension as nothing short of "leviathan." A popular TV puppet show mimicked his regular calls for trust and patience by satirizing him as a hypnotist who puts the nation to sleep. An American newspaper said the prime minister could give Teflon lessons to Ronald Reagan.

That's how fast someone—even someone with nothing but the most mortal appeal—can emerge and take power in this topsy-turvy world of ours. What has propelled Balladur to the top of the political heap in France? Little more than his manner, which seems to put people at ease. He presents something of a father-figure role in a world desperate for comfort and reassurance. He combines an old-fashioned sobriety and severity with "tranquil conviction," explained one American foreign correspondent.

Balladur has addressed the social upheaval in his country by calmly and quietly proposing sweeping change and by promising to rebuild French society by "restoring the nation's economic and military might" as well as reforming runaway welfare and health-care programs. Balladur has decried more than a decade of socialist permissiveness, which, he says, has tolerated lawlessness.

"Nothing is more important," Balladur says, "than restoring a feeling of safety for the vitality and equilibrium of our society."

He is being hailed far and wide for his unique brand of "courteous authority." People are said to appreciate the fact that he represents "a certain kind of order."

And what is behind this demeanor? "He fears social outbursts that could degenerate into violence or spread," explains one legislator.

"We have a very fragile society in which anything can happen at any moment," Balladur says. "My role is to protect people so they are not crushed by this world in which we live."

Imagine The Real Thing

Ahhhhh, the father-figure again. People throughout this world—the United States included—are looking for comfort, for security, as never before. It's easy to see why someone like Balladur would be so appealing and rise so fast.

Is it any more difficult to imagine how someone combining these characteristics with others even more appealing could rise even faster and assume even greater authority? Heed my words very carefully. I am not suggesting Balladur is anything more than an interesting French politician on the rise. It's his universal appeal that is important and illustrative for those of us interested in Bible prophecy.

Imagine, for instance, what will happen in the very near future when a man arises in Europe who, like Balladur, projects a serene but authoritative image to a world badly in need of reassurance and order. Imagine, too, that this man will also wield supernatural powers, who overcomes an apparently fatal wound, promises the world a better way and seems to be able to deliver it. Is it any wonder such a man will be accepted not only in Europe, but throughout the world?

Global Authority

The stage is also being set for this leader to exercise his global authority with the latest agreements on free trade. Very quietly in 1994, a 26,000-page treaty known as the "Final Act of the Uruguay Round" won informal approval from the representatives of 124 nations in Marrakesh, Morocco. After seven years of painstaking give-and-take, delegates from six continents marched to the podium to place their signatures on the most far-reaching trade agreement ever written. It's a document that dwarfs the controversial North American Free Trade Agreement in size and scope. But it nevertheless was approved by Congress in a bipartisan vote in early 1995.

Basically, the agreement slashes import taxes around the globe, opens markets for food and consumer goods and extends the rules of international trade to the growing business of cross-border financial services. In general, few disagree with that objective, which could grow the world economy anywhere from $100 billion to $200 billion.

That would mean a more productive world, a populace that is better educated and better fed. It would mean more services available to more people. But there is a down side to such agreements. Like NAFTA, this new agreement, which creates a worldwide governing agency called the World Trade Organization, locks nations into rules and regulations that have more authority than their own constitutions. That goes for the U.S., too. It means that signators to such an international agreement give up a certain amount of independence and autonomy for the privilege of participating in a more lively economy.

Even those directly involved in the most recent agreement were hardly enthusiastic about final approval. There was only scattered applause from participants during the ceremony in Marrakesh marking approval of the plan. The mood, according to one report, "was tempered by anxiety that the world is entering an ominous phase of tension between East and West, North and South." Indeed.

What exactly were the representatives worried about? They see a world becoming more interdependent, but, at the same time, more chaotic and disorderly. Uruguay's foreign minister, Sergio Abreau Donilla, chairman of the trade negotiations, said the common emotion at the talks was "a sense of shared dissatisfaction."

"The tensions, which have dominated discussions here," wrote one correspondent at the Marrakesh ceremony, "suggest that whereas economic struggles during the Cold War were largely along political and ideological lines, some of the most serious struggles now are between industrial and developing governments over future jobs and growth."

As grand as this latest trade pact is, the experts only suggest that, if enacted, it will merely stave off a return to "the law of the jungle" and that an even more ambitious plan is needed to reshape policies so that management of trade conflicts can help world leaders avoid future wars.

Foreshadowing World Government

"Many leaders who assembled in Morocco concurred in the view that the world is entering a new stage of uncertainty and potential upheaval as competition heats up in a global economy where capital and communications no longer respect any frontiers," reported the *San Francisco Chronicle*.

Among the most alarming aspects of the agreement for those naturally suspicious of such global pacts is the creation of the WTO that will succeed the 47-year-old General Agreement on Tariffs and Trade (GATT) and serve in a capacity similar to the International Monetary Fund and the World Bank—two of the institutions some believe are leading the world down the path toward global government.

As global trade increases and new economic powers are created, the power and influence of the U.S. is also, by necessity, diminishing. For instance, in 1947, when GATT was founded, the U.S. controlled half of the world's $25 billion in trade. Today, though the pie is much bigger—some $3.6 trillion in global trade—the U.S. controls less than 15 percent.

Much of that economic clout has shifted to the growing economies of Japan and Western Europe, which, in 1947, were still in a postwar state of shambles. In the last two decades, however, Europe and Japan have become much more assertive in standing up for their own interests against those of the United States.

Putting It All Together

What does all this mean? Where is it leading us? The Bible tells us that in the last days before the return of Jesus Christ to Earth, the world would be operating under one global economic and political system. Does the World Trade Organization create it? Hardly, but agreements like this one would be an absolutely necessary precursor to such a development. In addition, since the United States, today the lone superpower in the world, is not mentioned in that biblical scenario, one would assume that America's power and prestige would be diminished in the last days. Clearly, then, this latest mega-trade agreement, fits neatly into the pattern we should expect to see in times like these.

The 1990s have indeed seen the world moving on the fast track toward new alignments, regional coalitions and super-governments. The first day of 1993 represented a real benchmark for those with an eye on developments in Europe. That was the day Western Europe became a single economic market, linking 345 million people in 12 nations and eliminating tariffs and custom barriers. Many thought it would never come. But it did.

Later that year, on November 1, those same 345 million people became citizens of the new European Union. Here are some of the other profound developments taking place on the continent:

- The European Community created the European Monetary Institute January 1, 1994. The institute, located in Frankfurt, Germany's financial center, is scheduled to become a central bank no later than 1999, issuing a single currency.

- The EC is to forge common foreign and security policies with decisions made by consensus, unless all parties agree to vote on a joint action. Defense issues will be handled by the Western European Union, a group of nine EC states. In 1996, the states will review political cooperation and may turn the WEU into the EC defense arm and create a common defense policy.

- Majority voting replaces unanimous voting at EC meetings. The community is expanding its influence over areas including education, public health, culture, consumer protection, industry, research and development, environment, social affairs and development cooperation.

- The EC is in the midst of a massive public investment project in new roads, rail lines and communications networks that could provide a burst of economic growth and transform the continent's landscape by bringing East and West closer together.

Europe's Ambitions

For most Europeans, "the United States of Europe" is becoming more of a reality every day. And this emerging entity bears more than a striking resemblance to the revived Roman Empire—the economic and political powerhouse that, according to Bible prophecy, will dominate the world just prior to the return of Jesus Christ.

This whole movement toward a United States of Europe began for earnest in 1968 with the establishment of the Club of Rome. The Club of Rome's first report, "The Limits of Growth" issued in 1972, sold 10 million copies in thirty languages. In some ways it was the blueprint for today's brave new world of economic, military and political integration in Europe. That is precisely the direction in which Europe—or, one might call it, "the revived Roman Empire—is moving. Bigger, stronger, more tightly controlled. What is happening there has almost guaranteed the economic dominance of Western Europe in the New World Order.

The Bible shows us that the Roman Empire will be revived shortly before the return of Jesus Christ to the earth. Written before Jesus' time, Daniel Chapter 7 was known by the scribes as the greatest chapter in the Hebrew Scriptures. Jesus and His apostles referred to it many times. But still, some of it remained obscure until today.

The Biblical Case

Daniel had a dream in which he saw four great beasts come up out of the sea. The first beast was like a lion, but had eagle's wings. The second beast was like a bear; the third beast was like a leopard, but had four heads. The fourth animal was **"dreadful and terrible"**—it had iron teeth and ten horns. Angels explained to Daniel that the great beasts were "four kings, which shall arise out of the earth."

The first kingdom was Babylon, which became a world empire in 606 B.C. when it conquered Egypt. Nebuchadnezzar took over the empire from his father and made it a world kingdom. The second kingdom was the Media-Persian Empire. The Babylonian empire was conquered by the Medes and the Persians about 530 B.C. Two hundred years later, the Greeks became the third empire, when Alexander the Great conquered the Persians.

Around 68 B.C., the fourth and greatest kingdom seized world power. Rome was not given the name of any animal, but it was described as fierce. In phase one, this kingdom gained world authority, then it disappeared, and, just as the Scriptures predict, it will rise again just before Jesus returns to establish the Kingdom of God.

In phase two of the fourth kingdom, Rome will be in the form of a 10-nation confederacy. Therefore we can

expect two nations to withdraw from the EC or we can
expect to see some mergers of nations.

**"And of the ten horns that were in his head, and of
the other one which came up, and before whom three
fell; even of that horn that had eyes, and a mouth that
spake very great things, whose look was more stout than
his fellows,"** it says in Daniel 7:20.

The Future Fuhrer

And heading up this 10-nation confederacy will be a
man of such magnetism and power that he will become the
greatest dictator the world has ever known. He will be the
Antichrist. The Antichrist will be a messianic-type figure
who seems to have answers to the world's problems. He will
be extremely charismatic, attractive and beguiling. He will
dazzle the world with demonically produced miracles.

It may take a figure like this to bring Europe into its
final confederated state. And it will take this figure to lead
the world to the brink of destruction before Jesus Christ
returns to redeem the planet.

Part of the equation for this new leader is a strong
spiritual dynamic. He will not just be a political leader. He
will not just be a cultural leader. He will not just be an
economic leader. He will not just be a military leader. He
will be a combination of all three and something more. He
will also be a *religious* leader. And he will rule the world
from Rome.

Antichrist's Connection To Rome

Well, of course, throughout history, students of Bible
prophecy have naturally speculated that this leader might
have some connections with the Catholic Church, which is

headquartered in Rome. This has not gone unnoticed by the current Pope.

He has gone so far, according to those who have studied him and his writings, including author Malachi Martin, as to warn that his successor might well be a man of evil. Imagine that! Pope John Paul II has warned that the next pope might be evil personified—someone who will corrupt the church and mislead the people. Amazing that we haven't seen these warnings trumpeted in newspapers around the world, isn't it?

Opposition Within The Church

"Most frighteningly for John Paul, he had come up against irremovable presence of a malign strength in his own Vatican and in certain bishops' chanceries," writes Martin in *The Keys to This Blood*. "It was what knowledgeable churchmen called the 'superforce.' Rumors, always difficult to verify, tied its installation to the beginning of Pope Paul VI's reign in 1963.

Indeed, Paul had alluded somberly to 'the smoke of Satan which has entered the Sanctuary'—an oblique reference to an enthronement ceremony by satanists in the Vatican. Besides, the incidence of satanic pedophilia—rites and practices—was already documented among certain bishops and priests as widely dispersed as Turin, in Italy, and South Carolina, in the United States. The cultic acts of Satanic pedophilia are considered by professionals to be the culmination of the Fallen Archangel's rites."

John Paul II, by the way, at the age of 72, says he believes he will live to see the return of Jesus to save his church and redeem mankind. That's how close he believes we are. Since the Bible states clearly that this future Roman leader will make an agreement guaranteeing Israel's security, it is very interesting to note the recent rapprochement between the Vatican and the state of Israel. Israeli Prime Minister Yitzhak Rabin is, according to Joseph de Courcy, said to be considering a number of schemes for the redivision of Jerusalem under some form of international or inter-religious control, including one that would involve the Vatican. He reportedly discussed the plan with Yasser Arafat. Such an agreement would surely help facilitate the future Roman leader's change of venue.

He's Alive Today

There is a potential dictator waiting in the wings somewhere in Europe who will make Adolph Hitler and Josef Stalin look like choir boys. Right now he is preparing to take his throne, inflaming his soul with visions of what he will be able to do for mankind with his grand schemes and revolutionary ideas.

He is called by various names in the Bible: **King of Babylon, Little Horn, Man of Sin, Son of Perdition, Beast and Antichrist.** He will be the ultimate humanist, believing so passionately in mankind's ability to solve problems that it becomes part of a religious obsession. He'll believe he is doing a good thing when he brings repression on believers, and he'll be able to convince most non-believers, as well.

Daniel prophesied that there would be four major world empires. He also warned that the fourth empire—which was Rome—would go into a period of decline before reviving as a 10-nation confederacy just prior to the return of Jesus.

Daniel, Chapter 2 and Chapter 7, showed the panorama of these four great empires coming onto the scene. In

Chapter 2, it was depicted by the image of a giant man—the head of gold was Babylon, the arms and breasts of silver was Media-Persia, the torso of bronze was the Greek-Macedonian empire and the legs of iron represented the first phase of the Roman Empire. The feet and ten toes of iron mixed with clay represent the Roman Empire in phase two.

In the final phase of Gentile power, the empire is represented as a mixture of iron and brittle clay. Daniel indicates that the empire will be brittle, but it will have in it the strength of iron. That appears to be exactly the kind of situation that is arising in the European Community.

Many have tried to put together the Roman Empire since it crumbled politically in 476 AD. While it continued to exist as a religious empire—the Holy Roman Empire—others tried to reestablish the political force. Charlemagne tried and failed. Napolean tried and failed. Bismarck tried and failed. Hitler tried and failed.

Some nearly succeeded, but it wasn't God's timing. What these great conquerors could not do militarily has been done in our lifetime by economics. Jean Monnet of France is called the father of the European Common Market. His vision has always been that it would ultimately be a United States of Europe.

Clay And Steel

He knew that military force alone couldn't bring unity. And he theorized that the only way to bring the nations of Europe together was to merge their industries and monetary systems. The coal and steel pact was the very first step.

But there is still great diversity in Europe. There are different languages, customs and nationalities. Could this be represented by the clay feet and toes in Daniel? But there is also great power—that's the iron.

What Europe can produce as a unified system without hindrances is almost beyond comprehension. *Fortune* magazine said if true unity ever comes about, Europe will make Japan look like a backward nation. The economic power will be enormous. But it will also be a formidable military power as well. And it will need to be. For it will be Europe, led from Rome with its Future Fuhrer, who makes a covenant with Israel which guarantees her security, according to Daniel 9:27. Israel will need such a protector after it gives up all the land it has won in military battles and reduces itself to indefensible borders.

All that is needed to fulfill this prophecy today is a leader—a gifted visionary who will literally sell his soul to the devil for an hour of glory on the world stage. In his book, *Out of Control: Global Turmoil on the Eve of the 21st Century*, Zbigniew Brzezinski wrote that it would take some extraordinary circumstances to make Europe fully unite (especially in the way it must to live out its scriptural destiny). "To truly unify, Europe must either fashion a remarkable degree of consensus—*or be led by an acknowledged leader, guided by a clear and compelling historical vision*," he wrote. Bingo. (Emphasis mine)

Today, the man who will command this budding economic and military colossus—this phony savior of Jerusalem—is alive and well somewhere in Europe. The man who will make a pact with Satan for a few months of glory in this world is planning his ascendancy. This is the man who will lead the Western world into the Final Battle.

Chapter 9

THE
ARSENAL
FROM HELL

"For then there will be great distress, unequaled from the beginning of the world until now—and never to be equaled again. If those days had not been cut short, no one would survive, but for the sake of the elect those days will be shortened."

—**Matthew 24:21-22 NIV**

It started on a cool, crisp day—quite unexpectedly. Israelis were going about their daily routines. The Knesset was in full session, still debating the Law of Return. Arab women were selling crafts to tourists at an open-air market in East Jerusalem. Levite priests prepared their sacrifice at the newly rebuilt Temple.

Without warning, out of the clear azure skies, Scud missiles rained down on Tel Aviv and the suburbs of Jerusalem. But unlike those fired from Iraq during the Persian Gulf War, these missiles were equipped with binary chemical and biological warheads. After the first gruesome discovery of the wide swath of death left in the wake of one of those missiles, most Israelis hid in bunkers and basements and rarely removed their gas masks. The population of the entire civilized world sat riveted to television sets in horror as CNN began 24-hour live coverage within 10-minutes of the first attack.

But that was just the beginning—just a foretaste of what was to come. As Israeli combat fighters and bombers scrambled to answer the attack, they were met in the air to the north not just by Iraqi or even Syrian jets but by wave after wave of fighter squadrons from Turkey, Iran and Russia. Within twelve hours, the esteemed Israeli Air Force was blasted out of the air. Though they fought ferociously and downed many enemy aircraft, they were overwhelmed by the sheer numbers of attacking aircraft.

At the same time, reports from the Persian Gulf indicated that a fleet of 20 U.S. warships, including the aircraft carrier USS George Washington and the USS Tripoli were attacked without provocation by Iranian Kilo submarines, missile boats and land-based Silkworm missiles.

Within minutes, cruise missiles are fired from Syria on commercial and military targets in Israel: a desalination plant in Eilat, government offices in Jerusalem, a naval installation at the port of Haifa, a military air base in Dimona. It's clear this is an all-out attack—and not one orchestrated in Damascus or Cairo or even Tehran. On this one, Moscow called the shots. But before the gravity of the situation has even been realized in Washington or Jerusalem, the Russians launch a full-blown pre-emptive nuclear first-strike against the United States.

Then the Russians, under the command of an ultra-nationalist leader the world simply didn't take seriously, began what they called their "final dash to the South"—in a desperate gamble to recapture their place as a world superpower and to gain back their national pride. They felt that if they could capture and control the oil reserves of the Middle East, as well as the strategic land bridge that connected the continents of Europe, Asia and Africa, they could reenter the game as a true player.

Fact And Fiction Draw Closer

This is not a prophecy. This is not a prediction of future events. It is, however, one possible scenario of how World War III could begin—not 100 years from now, not even twenty or thirty. This could happen very soon—almost anytime. You know, you don't have to be a student of Bible prophecy to see it coming. I have heard similar scenarios from secular international intelligence experts, military leaders and even novelists and Hollywood screenwriters.

It's not fantasy; it's the future. The script has already been written. It was written thousands of years ago by men who were permitted by God to see this Final Battle. While much of what they saw in this high-tech, Star Wars age was beyond their comprehension, they did a remarkable job of recreating it in Holy Spirit-inspired word pictures.

How The Battle Is Shaping Up

Let's take a look at how mankind's Final Battle is shaping up in today's world. As I have mentioned earlier, our friends in the intelligence community tell us that with the failure of Soviet Communism, the most destabilizing conflict in the world is the one between Islam and the West. And one of the things I have desperately tried to demonstrate in this book is that all we need to do is listen to the actual words of radical Islamic leaders to understand their true intentions.

Every once in a while an important Arab leader will let his hair down and tell the press and public what he really believes. When they do, it's important to be listening and comprehending. Syrian President Hafez Assad did just that, when, in a very far-reaching address he gave to visitors from Kuwait, he outlined his long-range policies and what he calls his "100 years war" to liberate Jerusalem and Palestine.

Wars may be interrupted for hundreds of years, but Syria will never give up as long as one Syrian village remains under occupation," he told the audience in a speech reported by Joseph de Courcy's *Intelligence Digest*. He explained that he joined the Madrid peace process because Syria believes the Bush administration may represent a one-in-a-lifetime opportunity to force territorial concessions from Israel.

However, Assad made it clear that if he does not get everything he wants unconditionally—namely all of the territory occupied by Israel on the Golan Heights—then war can easily be resumed. He also made it clear he does not believe long-term peaceful co-existence with Israel is possible, even if those territorial concessions are made.

What Assad is saying is that there are all kinds of maneuvers that can be made within the political and diplomatic arena. But Syria, along with its allies in Iran, remains committed to the complete destruction of the nation of Israel and the denial of all Western influence in the Middle East. Damascus is in this game for the long haul. And it is not alone.

While Assad has used his cunning to win over support from Western leaders, his closest ally in the Middle East, the nation of Iran, has remained its old bellicose self, relying not so much on diplomacy for a leading role in the Islamic world, but on raw power.

The Role Of Iran

Iran's radical fundamentalist Islamic regime is directly challenging U.S. military supremacy with some of the most provocative maneuvers in the Persian Gulf since the invasion of Kuwait by Saddam Hussein's Iraq. Iranian President Hashemi Rafsanjani, obviously testing the U.S., has been launching air attacks against armed Iranian expatriates in neighboring Iraq.

Some analysts suggest the attacks might be motivated in part to divert attention within Iran from the rising discontent with the regime of Iranian President Akbar Hashemi Rafsanjani. Even more revealing of his broader military aims in the region, Rafsanjani has quietly purchased 400 Russian T-72 tanks worth $1 billion. Iran is also flexing its muscles with its growing naval forces. In recent war games, Iran's navy performed mock exercises in an area encompassing 10,000 square miles.

The government-controlled press reported that the maneuvers proved Iran has authority over all sea traffic "in the crystal blue waters of the Gulf" and can prevent an enemy from "penetrating into the strategic Strait of Hormuz." The only enemy Iran is thinking about in this context is the United States of America.

"Iran is Washington's focus today," state syndicated columnists Rowland Evans and Robert Novak. "It has now become clear that the new rulers in Tehran differ from the Shah in every respect but one: The insistence that Iran be treated as a major South Asia regional power with hegemony over the Persian Gulf and an important voice in lands adjacent to Iran, whatever Saudi Arabia or any other Arab state says."

Iran seeks to exert its military authority in the region at the very time it is exerting its spiritual authority over the entire Islamic world. The biggest opportunity in that respect is in Central Asia where, the *New York Times* reports, "Islam, as an enduring means of ordering spiritual and social life, is taking over from the failed ideology of Soviet Communism."

"After more than 70 years of official atheism, dispersal of nationalities and harsh suppression of Islam, the very ideas of independence and democracy in the region have taken on an Islamic coloration," the report said.

The Sword Of Islam

Most people in the West still do not understand the extent of the threat Islam poses to the Judeo-Christian world order. A British TV documentary, "The Sword of Islam," presents the alarming picture and shows how Islamic fundamentalism represents a threat to the West more grave than Nazism or Communism.

"Were Franklin D. Roosevelt around to see this report," said Greg Dawson of the *Orlando Sentinel,* "He would amend his most famous words 'We have nothing to fear, but fear itself and Islamic fundamentalism.'"

When the zealots leading Iran and the Islamic world tell us quite openly that their intent is to topple the Judeo-Christian world order, it is not just fiery rhetoric. As we have reported before in *Countdown Magazine,* Rafsanjani says Islam's goal is to unite all of the Islamic nations under the leadership of a coalition led by Iran and Syria in a jihad against Israel. But that's only the first part of the goal—"liberating Palestine." The second goal of this unholy alliance is to replace the Judeo-Christian world order with an Islamic world order. And they will use any means necessary to achieve these goals—including nuclear terrorism and war.

"But, Hal," you say, "even if Iran were able to deploy a handful of nuclear weapons, how could they hope to take on the whole world?"

Good question. The answer, as I have suggested earlier, is that Iran will procure the help of some major allies, notably Russia, which certainly has the nuclear and conventional military might to engulf the entire world in conflict.

The Fall Of The Soviet Union

Let's review some of what has happened in the world since 1990. The Soviet Union very quickly fell apart. It shocked everyone. After the disintegration of the Soviet Union some amazing things began to happen. The Russians needed hard currency to repair their fractured economy. They realized that seventy-two years of Communism had never produced an industrial base that can manufacture peacetime goods. In other words, they could not make washing machines or find one that works. What had they been doing all those years? They were developing a formidable military machine. The products that they learned to make on a world-class scale were combat aircraft, nuclear weapons, ballistic missiles, artillery, tanks and so on.

So when the Soviet Union broke apart, the Russians, and some of the other republics that had made up the old Soviet empire, were left with an enormous military arsenal. They found one sure way to raise the money they needed was to sell off part of their inventory. The Islamic nations—notably Iran, Iraq and Syria—went on a buying spree.

Keep in mind that there are five former Soviet republics to the south that are considered a threat to Russia. Moscow was concerned that Iran might evangelize and radicalize these Central Asian nations that have been historically so important to Russia. Three of those five were left with large storehouses of nuclear weapons. So, in February 1991, the Russians made a secret agreement with Iran. Rafsanjani pledged to Boris Yeltsin that Iran would stay out of Central Asia if Russia would sell its best arms and nuclear technology to Tehran. Another part of the agreement was that Russia would be bound to fight alongside Iran and the rest of the Islamic forces in a showdown with Israel and the West. In addition, Iran also purchased three fully built and

ready-to-deploy nuclear warheads from one of those ex-
Soviet republics—Kazakhstan.

The Arms Race

These deals began a timetable and a countdown to the
fulfillment of Ezekiel 38 and 39, the two biblical
prophecies that best describe Russia's last dash to the
South and the beginning of the world's Final Battle. Now
let's examine some of the developments that have occurred
since these deals:

- Remember during the Persian Gulf War how we held
  our breath waiting to find out whether Iraq's chemical
  weapons arsenal constituted a real threat to Israel and
  other nations of the Middle East? While Saddam
  Hussein never launched any warheads of mass
  destruction, we now know that he had the capability.
  United Nations inspection teams have found a
  stockpile of some 46,000 chemical munitions of
  various kinds. Iraq, which has almost completely
  rebuilt its military infrastructure since the war, had at
  least 30 chemical-filled warheads for Scud ballistic
  missiles. He still has them. He's building more. And
  he's not building them for fun. He plans to use them
  someday soon—against Israel.

- **Iraq** has also secretly developed biological weapons
  designed to spread cholera, tuberculosis and the plague.

- Iraqi officials have now acknowledged time that they
  have a sophisticated system to enrich uranium for
  nuclear bombs.

- Iraq's neighbor Iran has embarked upon a massive
  military modernization campaign emphasizing a large

force based on three components —tanks, Soviet-supplied MiG-29s and Sukhoi-24s and, most importantly, surface-to-air missiles capable of hitting targets 1,000 kilometers away.

* **Iran** will soon have a small, but fully deployed, nuclear arsenal with several delivery systems—including missiles and bombers.

* The Iranian navy can control the Persian Gulf and the strategic Straits of Hormuz with its Russian-built Kilo submarines, Hawk anti-aircraft missiles, Silkworm missiles and anti-ship cruise missiles.

* **Libya**, too, has attempted to hire Russian nuclear experts. No one seems certain whether they were successful.

* Because **Russia** is in a relatively weakened state—economically, militarily and in terms of morale—Islamic influence on Moscow is at an all-time high.

* There is a serious threat of another coup in Moscow—most likely by the military. In addition, even if Yeltsin lasts until the next election, chances are an adventurous hard-liner, much less inclined toward democracy and reform, will replace him.

* The Russians have not forsaken intercontinental ballistic missiles. In fact, they are preparing three new models of ICBMs.

* The Russians have also built up their navy and plan to have a force of 24 (Red October style) Typhoon-class SSBNs equipped with upgraded SS-N-20 ballistic missiles by the year 2000.

- Despite their assurances to the contrary, Russia continues to develop and manufacture the most deadly binary chemical agents and warheads known to man, according to intelligence experts. One is called *Novichok,* which is reportedly *10 times more toxic to humans than any nerve gas.*

- A growing number of renegade nations are nearing the point where they will be able to deliver nuclear, chemical and biological warheads by missile at selected targets. This poses immediate problems for Israel, but it will eventually be a major concern for Americans as well.

- **Muslim zealots** are gaining power around the globe. From the Persian Gulf to Morocco, Islamic die-hards are using any means necessary—from ballots to bullets—to take over nations. Lebanon, Algeria, Egypt, Jordan, Tunisia, Sudan—and even in Israel—Islamic fundamentalists are clamoring for power.

- Five former Soviet republics formed an economic bloc with Iran. The vastly expanded regional grouping will cover 600 million square km (372 million square miles) and include about 300 million people.

- Iran and **Turkey**, two of Islam's most powerful and divergent nations, have decided to put many of their differences aside. Turkish and Iranian leaders met toward the end of 1992 and said it was better to cooperate in central Asia than to compete for influence in the Moslem republics in what was once the Soviet Union.

- **Syria** has stockpiled hundreds of Soviet-made Scud, SS-21 and shorter-range Frog 7 missiles and has won help from North Korea and China in improving their range and accuracy.

- Syria is also known to have an active biological warfare program and has gained technical help from North Korea.
- Libya has a major chemical weapons complex just 50 miles from Tripoli.
- The U.S. has shipped hundreds of M-60 A1 tanks no longer needed in Europe to Egypt and is selling 576 Hellfire anti-tank missiles to Jordan.

The Role Of Egypt

Now, you might ask, "Hal, why are you worried about Egypt? Cairo is friendly to the United States and has had a long-standing peace agreement with Israel?"

I have talked to military and intelligence experts in Israel. I have also studied this issue—both biblically and geo-strategically—and have come to the conclusion that the most dangerous nation in the Middle East may well be Egypt. While it is true that there is a peace accord between Israel and Egypt, the latter has been moving rapidly toward a state of belligerency toward Jerusalem. They have never really been at peace, as I mentioned earlier in this book. It has been, at best, a "cold peace."

Egypt alone has a tremendous arsenal supplied by the United States. And Egypt clearly will be a part of this Armageddon coalition against Israel in the last days, according to scripture.

"Egypt signed a peace treaty with Israel in 1979, yet the scale of its armaments procurement since then does not give the impression of a peaceful intention," says de Courcy. "For instance, Egypt's stock of main battle tanks has gone up from 1,600 in 1979 to over 3,300 today. This increase has largely been achieved with U.S. tanks, including 147 M1A1 Abrams tanks assembled in Egypt.

Egypt's inventory of combat aircraft has not shown a comparable increase in numbers (551 in 1994 against 561 in 1979), but the quality has increased dramatically from the Soviet-supplied air force of the 1970s to today's air force consisting largely of American and French combat aircraft. The dramatic increase in anti-tank guided weapons (from 1,000 in 1979 to 2,340 today) is particularly worrying for Israel as Israel's is the only armored force large enough to justify such an inventory of anti-tank weapons."

How has Egypt, a poor, oil-less Arab nation, achieved this military capability? With huge amounts of U.S. aid. Since the Camp David peace agreement, American taxpayers have transferred about $30 billion to Egypt. About $17 billion of that aid was in direct military assistance.

Syria's New Might

Syria, another front-line Arab state involved in every single war against Israel, does not need American aid to arm itself. It received massive Soviet backing through the 1980s and has recently renewed its military ties with Moscow. As of 1994, the total strength of the Syrian Armed forces was 808,000, including 408,000 on active duty. It has 4,500 main battle tanks and 591 combat aircraft, according to de Courcy.

"Before the end of the Cold War, it was Syria's intention to achieve strategic parity with Israel through the help of the Soviet Union," explains de Courcy. "This effort ended with the change in Moscow's policy towards supplying arms to non-paying client states and with the demise of the Soviet Union. But since the Gulf War, and more particularly since

Russian Deputy Prime Minister Oleg Soskovets' visit to Damascus in April 1994, there has been a noticeable improvement in Syria's strategic position."

De Courcy's sources say that Moscow has agreed to write off up to 90 percent of Syria's debt, which by the year 2010 would be between $10 billion and $11 billion. The only requirement is that Syria now become a cash arms client.

The Modern Saudi Army

Israel is by no means preoccupied with the military threat posed by Saudi Arabia. Yet, the huge amount of sophisticated weaponry the oil-rich state has purchased in recent years must be factored into any calculations of military balance.

"Riyadh's arms shopping spree since the end of the Gulf War has been extraordinary," reports de Courcy. "It has bought some $30 billion of arms. But this just represents an acceleration of a trend that has been present for a quarter of a century. During this time, the desert kingdom has transformed its army, air force and navy, spending $250 billion in the last ten years alone. The quality of the purchases has been notable, with Riyadh trying to make up for its lack of manpower with high-tech weaponry, particularly for its air force."

The Saudi air force has been reoriented, de Courcy says, from a predominantly defensive force into a formidable offensive threat with the coming of the Tornado and F-15 strike aircraft. It now has a force of some 292 combat aircraft. The Saudis also can deploy 770 main battle tanks.

Iran's Military Clout

Iran, meanwhile, has an armed forces numbering 863,000 with more than a half-million on active duty. The country has 1,245 main battle tanks and 295 combat aircraft. Iran, however, is in the midst of a major rearmament program that will include a $15 billion deal for new MiGs and T-72 tanks from Russia.

Another strategically important nation that will join this unholy alliance is Turkey. Earlier, I showed how Turkey is moving into a closer relationship with Iran and Syria and how it has been shut out of the European Union. I know from my study of the Bible that the final great war includes Turkey as part of the Islamic grouping allied with Russia.

Just imagine this overwhelming force! How could Israel ever defend itself against such an onslaught? Here is the arsenal from Hell that will soon be headed toward Jerusalem:

- Even without factoring in Turkey's army or Russia's, the combined troop strength of Syria, Lebanon, Egypt, Saudi Arabia. Jordan, Yemen, Libya, Iraq and Iran comes to *more than 5 million.*

- These armies could field *19,269 main battle tanks,* including T-72s, M1A1 Abrams and Britain's Chieftains. That is more than the United States can mobilize!

- They could scramble *3,325 first-rate combat aircraft,* including F-16s, MIG 29s, MIG 31s and Mirage F-1s. Iran will soon have the backfire bomber that can go to Mach2 and attack targets as far as 3,000 miles away.

The Global March

This is the sort of impossible odds Israel will face in the coming war. But there's really much more. If we add Turkey to the total, the troop level increases to *6.4 million men,* the tank total to more than *24,000* and the combat aircraft to *3,880.* When we factor Russia into the equation, we see that this coalition can march *10 million men* toward Jerusalem. You don't hear much about some of the most awesome parts of the Russian arsenal anymore. But it hasn't been destroyed. It hasn't fallen off the face of the Earth. These weapons are still around, but where? For instance, where are those 18 Red October-style Typhoon submarines right now? Each one carries 200 nuclear weapons, each capable of ionizing a major city. Multiply 200 by 18 and you have some idea of the destructive capacity of those subs. Add to that the backfire bombers that were built. They are fast enough to outrun most of our interceptors. They are all under Boris Yeltsin's control. And, despite recent disarmament agreements, they still have much of their intercontinental ballistic missile arsenal.

Just statistics, you say? I know they are dry numbers, but, believe me, the fate of the world turns on them. So don't tune out. Now, what does Israel have to counter this force? Well, Israel is a tiny nation of just 5 million people, of whom 14 percent are Arabs. It has 172,000 active members of the armed forces with another 430,000 reservists giving it a total armed manpower of 602,000. In its 1994-95 report, the International Institute for Strategic Studies records an Israeli force of 3,895 main battle tanks and 478 combat aircraft.

It Will Take A Miracle To Save Israel—*Intelligence Digest*

A miracle is just what Zechariah Chapters 12 through 14 predict and promise will save Israel. God has promised in several passages that their nation will never, ever again be destroyed. All the weapons in the world won't overturn that promise. But Israel is in for a very rough time. The

Jewish state will be brought to the brink of destruction. Of course, the Israelis have one other no-so-secret weapon to help equalize matters—approximately 300 nuclear warheads produced at their Dimona facility.

The real purpose for God allowing this near holocaust is to bring the Israelites to such desperation that they will turn in faith to their true Messiah, the Lord Jesus. Zechariah predicted, **"On that day I will set out to destroy all the nations that attack Jerusalem. And I will pour out on the house of David and the inhabitants of Jerusalem a spirit of grace and supplication. They will look on me, THE ONE THEY HAVE PIERCED, and they will mourn for him as one mourns for an only child, and grieve bitterly for him as one grieves for a firstborn son."** (Zechariah 12:9-10)

With its back to the wall—and that is surely where Israel will be after making more land concessions for peace agreements—the Jewish state will not and cannot hesitate to arm the doomsday weapon, to go nuclear. But it is far from alone in the Middle East as a nation armed with non-conventional weapons.

"Israel's potential enemies have been making rapid progress in all three key areas: the acquisition of missiles, the development of chemical and biological weapons and the development of a nuclear capability," says de Courcy.

Missiles, Missiles Everywhere

China and North Korea have been especially active in selling ballistic missiles to the Islamic nations of the Middle East. There are four reasons they are so popular, says de Courcy:

- They are the new prestige weapon of the Middle East. If you don't have them, you simply don't rate as a real terrorist state and enemy of Zionism.
- Deterrence against attack. Keep in mind, the Muslim states have warred against each other more than they have warred against Israel.
- The ability to attack an enemy from afar and in the rear.
- The terror factor. Hitting civilian targets gives them their biggest kick.

"For the Arabs," de Courcy says, "ballistic missiles are particularly attractive because of the poor historical performance of Arab air forces against Israel. In the 1982 Lebanon war, Syria lost 82 aircraft in 266 sorties. In other words, its aircraft (and pilots) had a life expectancy of 3.25 missions. To an extent, ballistic missiles overcome this problem in that there is no effective defense against incoming ballistic missiles. (Even the Patriot anti-missile system is ineffective and was credited, for propaganda reasons, with far more interceptions in the Gulf War than it actually achieved). Ballistic missiles are relatively fast, more or less unstoppable, and give an element of surprise."

Missile warfare takes an emotional toll on a civilian population, as we saw in the Gulf War. That was even more dramatically witnessed in the Iran-Iraq war, when Iraq bombarded Iran's cities with 190 missiles. Egypt, Iran, Syria, Yemen, Saudi Arabia, Iraq and Libya all have ballistic missiles of one kind of another.

Chemical Weapons

But it's not the missiles themselves that frighten Israel. It's what they are armed with—nuclear, chemical or biological warheads. While none of the Arab nations has a nuclear warhead that can be delivered by missile, at least twenty-four countries now have chemical-weapons capability, including Iraq, Iran, Syria, Libya and Egypt.

"The mainstays of the chemical-weapons arsenals of these states are mustard gas and nerve agents, but there have been some reports from remote corners of the Middle East of agents so virulent that they can kill instantaneously," says de Courcy. "This would have to be a nerve agent carried on fine particles, along the lines of the so-called 'dusty mustard' which is a highly refined and potent version of mustard gas. Agents carried on very fine particles are capable of penetrating some filter systems."

When the United Nations inspectors began poking around Iraq after the Gulf War, they were shocked at the extent of Baghdad's commitment to chemical weapons. They found 50 chemical-filled ballistic missile warheads, 12,694 mustard gas-filled 155mm artillery shells and over 10,000 sarin-filled 122mm artillery and rocket warheads. They also discovered 300 tons of bulk agent ready for use. And, keep in mind, this is just what Iraq was unable to hide!

Libya is also very determined to acquire a chemical weapons arsenal, despite the destruction of its production facility at Rabta several years ago. De Courcy cites a report of a new facility near Tarhuna, 40 miles southeast of Tripoli, where tunnels have been bored into a remote hillside apparently for the production and storage of mustard gas.

Syria, de Courcy says, has scores of chemical warheads filled with the nerve agent sarin for its Scud-B and Scud-C missiles. Damascus, he says, has stockpiled thousands of bombs filled with sarin and the VX nerve agent for delivery by its SU-24, MiG-23BN and SU-20/22 aircraft.

Biological Warheads

"Perhaps even more frightening than the chemical-weapons arsenals is the fact that Syria, Libya, Iran, Egypt and Iraq have all been involved in the research into and probably production of biological weapons," says de Courcy. "Biological warfare is at least as old as the Middle Ages when besieging armies would catapult corpses infected with the plague into the besieged towns. It involves the use of microorganisms or toxins derived from living organisms to spread death and disease. Past plagues, the introduction of myxomatosis to reduce the rabbit population and the AIDS epidemic all illustrate the devastating capacity of natural agents. In 1970, a World Health Organization report said that if anthrax were to be sprayed over a city of 5 million in a developed country, it would kill 100,000 and incapacitate 150,000 more. The same report said that if botulism were introduced into the water supply of an average town of 50,000, nearly 30,000 would die. Animals are also very vulnerable, and the only way to control an epidemic amongst livestock would be wholesale slaughter which would have implications for food supply in time of war."

Interesting, isn't it? Biological warfare induces plagues. The Bible predicts that this same time period—in which we see this cataclysmic war taking place—will witness the worst plagues the world has ever seen.

The Islamic Bomb

There already is an Islamic bomb, de Courcy points out. It is wielded by Pakistan. While Pakistan is not itself a party to the Arab-Israeli dispute, it is a close ally of many of the Arab states and Iran.

"Iran also has close ties with China, North Korea and Russia, all of which are capable of passing nuclear technology to Tehran," says de Courcy. "Both China and Russia have undertaken to help Tehran with its nuclear energy program despite strong opposition from the United States."
Israeli intelligence predicts Iran will be able to manufacture its own nuclear weapons by the year 2002. But, of course, as I have pointed out, Iran already has several bombs which it purchased from Kazakhstan. Iraq, it has been said, was only six months away from producing its own nuclear weapon when it invaded Kuwait. Despite the setback that program received in Iraq's defeat, it may still be closer to production than any other Arab nation.

"The Middle East, and the world, had a lucky let-off with Iraq," says de Courcy, "but no one doubts that nuclear proliferation is something that can only be delayed, not halted. Apart from the long-established nuclear powers (America, Britain, France, Russia and China), Israel, India and Pakistan have already achieved nuclear status. Five other countries are on the verge of nuclear capability (if they have not already achieved it), namely North Korea, Iran, Iraq, Libya and Algeria. Of these five, four have a direct impact on Israel's security. Other than these, South Korea, South Africa, Taiwan, Argentina and Brazil are all known to have quiescent nuclear programs. More importantly for Israel, Egypt is also thought to harbor nuclear ambitions, as does Indonesia, the Far East's largest Muslim state."

Russian Aid
Here's something I don't think you have read anywhere else, folks. But it should be on the front page of every newspaper in the United States: As President Clinton and

the European powers offer Russian President Boris Yeltsin a virtual blank check to help revitalize his suffering economy, Moscow continues to spend billions modernizing its strategic nuclear arsenal.

Yes, I know. You've been told that the Russians are scrapping their nuclear weapons and that's why we need to encourage them with foreign aid. Well, let me tell you, Russia's nuclear weapons are as well-positioned to destroy the United States in a first strike as they have ever been. And it is the United States, not Russia, that is unilaterally disarming at a dangerous pace.

Let me be clear about something: I am not suggesting Yeltsin is the type of man who would launch a nuclear first strike against the United States or anyone else. However, he is one man. He may not even have total control over the military in Russia. And he is literally surrounded by men who more closely resemble the hard-line, Communist totalitarian leaders of the old Soviet Union.

Once before the United States made the mistake of betting on one man's ability to reform Russia. Mikhail Gorbachev was then ousted in a coup. Isn't it possible the same thing could happen to Yeltsin? Isn't it likely? And who will follow him? The alternatives are not very encouraging.

Take Vice President Alexander Rutskoi, for instance. He is calling for reinstating state control of the economy and disagrees with Yeltsin on moves toward widening freedoms for average Russians. This man is one bullet away from taking over the reins of power in a nation that still has a gun to our head—a nuclear gun.

The Russian Buildup

The way the nuclear weapons modernization program continues at full speed in Russia should, therefore, give every American reason to be alarmed. With the MIRV (Multiple Independently-targeted Reentry Vehicle) ICBMs due to be eliminated under the terms of START and START II, Russian modernization efforts are concentrated on single warhead missile systems like the SS-25. Intelligence reports suggest that by the end of this decade the Russians will deploy three new strategic systems, an SS-25 mobile, a silo-based version of the SS-25 and a new missile to replace the SSN-20 on the Typhoon class submarine.

Reports also indicate that the modernized versions of the SS-25 will have larger throw-weights and much greater accuracy.

This is being done by the Russian republic at the very time that the U.S. has basically halted much of our own strategic modernization program and is proceeding unilaterally in many respects to dismantle the existing strategic systems in advance of entry into force of either START I or START II treaties.

The modernization effort is not a violation of any treaty with the United States. START restricts the size of the strategic forces but not their capabilities. So the Russians are accomplishing more with less.

"The continued deployment of Soviet mobile ICBMs (such as the SS-25) will give the (Russians) a monopoly on a survivable, land-based strategic reserve," says Lawrence Fink, a Soviet and defense analyst writing in *Defense News*.

The modernization effort began long before the Soviet Union collapsed. U.S. intelligence experts have been predicting it would come to a halt for several years, but it continues unabated.

"The SS-25's modernization has been ignored by the media, while aid to Russia has dominated the headlines, as well as the administration's policy," stated *Defense Media Review*.

The most disturbing part of this revelation, however, is the fact that the U.S. is leaving itself totally vulnerable to whatever fate dictates for Russia. After spending $32 billion developing a strategic defense, the U.S. program has been virtually abandoned by the Clinton administration. No strategic defense. No modernization effort. Combine that with the massive military cutbacks and you have a prescription for disaster.

Has The Bear Really Changed?

I was among those who warned about the dangers posed by the old Soviet Union for years. Were we right? According to documents discovered in East Germany, were we ever. The *Washington Post* reported that the Soviet Union and East Germany were planning a full-scale invasion of West Germany "so detailed and advanced that the Communists had already made street signs for western cities, printed cash for their occupation government and built equipment to run eastern trains on western tracks."

When western officers took over eastern bases after the reunification of Germany in 1990, they found more ammunition for the 160,000-man East German army than the West Germans had for their 500,000-man force.

"The operational planning was far more advanced than anything our intelligence had envisioned," said Vice Admiral Ulrich Weisser, chief of the planning staff for the German *Bundeswehr*, or armed forces.

Keep in mind, these grand plans and preparations were made in total secret! Could it be that plans for a dash to the South are already drawn up? The Bible tells us that Russia will play an important military role in the last days. Though all of the talk these days is about Russia disarming, it is clear she is still well-equipped to play out that final endtimes role scripted for her in prophecy.

Chapter 10

200 MILLION ASIANS ATTACK

"And the sixth angel poured out his bowl upon the great river, the Euphrates; and its water was dried up, that the way might be prepared for the kings from the east."

—Revelation 16:12

In the early morning hours of a rainy Sunday in June of 1950, North Korea's Kim Il Sung sent his elite advance guard across the 38th parallel to invade the south. The war that ensued lasted three years, involved twenty nations and resulted in the deaths of some four million people, most of them civilians.

The capital of North Korea, Pyongyang, changed hands twice. The capital of South Korea, Seoul, changed hands four times. When the war was over, not a single major building was left standing in Seoul. Both halves of the Korean Peninsula were in ruins. It took 30 years for the Koreas to recover from the devastation.

In June 1994, Korea was back in the news. All over the world, people held their breath in dire fear that another Korean war might be on the horizon—this time, however, fought not only with conventional weapons but possibly nuclear as well.

Most Dangerous Place On Earth

U. S. News and World Report offered a cover story that month calling North Korea "The Most Dangerous Place on Earth." North Korea was dominating the news because its totalitarian regime defied the United States and the United Nations by refusing to halt its effort to develop nuclear weapons.

The world seemed braced for the worst for several weeks until Pyongyang's "Great Leader," Kim Il Sung, died suddenly at the age of 82. The quiet and orderly succession of leadership that saw Kim's son, Kim Jong Il, assume power over the secretive, isolated and thoroughly unstable Communist nation served to let some steam out of the international pressure cooker. As with any global hotspot, once they move to the back burner, the media and Western leaders tend to lose focus on potential crises. But it's not difficult to imagine how Korea could serve as a lightning rod for the world's Final Battle.

North Korea has the world's fourth or fifth largest standing army—with 1.2 million men backed by 8,400 artillery pieces and 2,400 mobile rocket launchers. As the world learned in December 1993, from a chilling front-page *New York Times* article, the Central Intelligence Agency has concluded that North Korea has already developed at least one or two nuclear bombs.

"Most of the intelligence analysts agree," reported the *Times*, "that North Korea is investing significant amounts of spare cash in a program to obtain plutonium, develop the high-explosive trigger needed for a nuclear detonation and build a medium-range missile that can reach Japan."

West Pays For Nukes

North Korea may be preparing to expand its production of plutonium by shutting down one reactor and reprocessing all of the fuel. In addition, a second larger reactor is scheduled to be completed soon. Perhaps the most amazing thing about all this is that President Clinton has offered to raise $4 billion to help pay for new nuclear reactors in

North Korea—this, in an effort to stop the nuclear proliferation!

While the biggest fear of a nuclear-armed North Korea was the immediate threat it posed to the south and to nearby Japan, the real effect of this revelation has been to touch off an arms race throughout Asia. Secondly, it has caused Japan to reevaluate the importance of its own Western alliances, prompting a more Asian-oriented foreign policy for Tokyo.

Asia Comes Together

Certainly, bringing the Asian powers together, as North Korea has managed to do, is a major development in world politics. It will have profound importance, as I will show in this chapter. But the real threat of North Korea is in the renegade nation's willingness to produce nuclear bombs and missiles that can and will be traded for oil and hard currency—traded to nations like Iran and Syria. In addition, North Korea has long been producing chemical and biological weapons for use on the south. Those weapons, too, could be sold to the Middle East as part of the biggest regional arms buildup in the history of the world.

North Korea is already the world's largest proliferator of ballistic missiles. Iran is expected to procure the new Nodong missile, which has a range of about 600 miles. That would double the range of any weapon in Iran's current inventory. A longer-range version of the Nodong is still in the development stage. Reportedly, it could threaten Europe from Iran with a range of 800 miles. But we know Iran's real target is Israel. North Korea has also been negotiating with Libya for the sale of Nodongs

How desperate is North Korea for money? A report in the *Washington Times* in February 1995 disclosed that the government itself has entered the drug-smuggling business. The operation came to light when two North Koreans were arrested in Russia trying to unload eight tons of heroin. Earlier, two other North Koreans were arrested in Shanghai trying to sell six kilograms of opium. One of them carried a diplomatic passport.

North Korea's Big Buddy

While North Korea was an international outlaw nation for many years, one powerful ally has consistently remained in its corner—China. China stood by North Korea during the war nearly a half-century ago, and it stood by Pyongyang again through the tense hours of standoff with the United States over the nuclear weapons issue in 1994. When one talks about the new power in the East, these days, one is talking about China.

No nation in the world—not the United States or anyone else in the West—has any real effective force to counter the awesome size and population of China.

"The sheer size of the country and its population, coupled with the astonishing speed of its economic development, ensures that the West will do nothing to harm its economic interests in China if it can possibly be avoided," explains Joseph de Courcy. "President Clinton's behavior over the renewal of China's most-favored-nation trading status is a case in point. He made much in his presidential election campaign about former President Bush hobnobbing with the "tyrants of Beijing," but when the pressure was on to renew MFN because of the potential trading benefits to American companies, Clinton had no option but to concede."

The Sleeping Giant Awakes

Think of the magnitude of what's at stake in China: a 1.2 *billion*-strong population that is growing at 13 percent a year. The country's population is growing at somewhere between 16 million and 20 million a year at a time when agricultural land is diminishing. By 2000, the population will be 1.3 billion. Those unemployed or underemployed today number between 120 million and 150 million. This is why today, Beijing, once a closed country, is willing to encourage emigration.

"This all terrifies the West (and Russia) as the likely outflow of Chinese, given the freedom to emigrate and a welcoming destination, would be several hundred million, a point that was made to former U.S. President Jimmy Carter when, during a meeting in the late 1970s, he urged China's paramount leader, Deng Xiaoping, to allow free emigration," recalls de Courcy. "Deng, straight-faced, asked Carter in return: "How many millions do you want?""

Approximately 100,000 Chinese immigrate illegally to the United States every year, according to the best estimates. Most arrive from staging posts in Central and South America. Other Western nations—even Japan—are being forced to watch their borders.

"When coupled with the promise of untold riches from participation in the Chinese economic miracle, the migration threat enables Beijing to run a classic carrot-and-stick diplomacy whenever the West tries to act tough," says de Courcy. "President Clinton could not resist this when it came to renewing China's MFN trade status, and it is unlikely in the extreme that the West will risk much in any attempt to stop China supplying weapons and sophisticated technology to the post-Madrid Middle East. If it continues to suit it to do so (and there is no reason why it should not), China will continue to sell sophisticated weaponry to the Middle East with impunity."

Why Would China Attack?

But I have my own theories about why—no matter what—China will be unable to resist the notion of someday soon marching its 200-million-strong army off to war. I have always believed—and science and sociology have helped confirm this in recent years—that women are a civilizing influence on men and society. George Gilder has written eloquently about this. Well, my friends, China doesn't have a shortage of very many things but it does have a shortage of women.

Why? The forced-abortion program has had the unwitting effect of drastically diminishing the number of baby girls born in the country. According to the 1990 census, for instance, 114 boys are born for every 100 girls.

"A bias toward male children, and the loss of female children due to infanticide and neglect, have continued in some countries for millennia," explains population biologist Marcus Feldman, director of Stanford's Morrison Institute for Population and Resource Studies. "It is exacerbated now by advanced technologies that permit sex selection before birth. China's one-child-per-family policy intensifies the pressure, with fewer chances per couple to produce a male heir."

A *New York Times* article on the subject in 1994 was even more brutally frank: "The preference for boys has meant that millions of Chinese girls have not survived to adulthood because of poor nutrition, inadequate medical care, desertion and even murder at the hands of their parents."

What all this means in the geo-strategic sense is that China will soon have a "marriage gap." By the year 2000, men of marriageable age, 22 to 31, will outnumber their female counterparts so that 6 men of every 100 will be left partnerless.

"By early in the next century, the missing girls and extra boys will mean tens of millions of young men without the social ties of wives and children," explains Feldman. "They pose a threat of social disruption and national instability and may result in a new wave of migration patterns around the world."

To that let me just add that this problem won't just cause national instability, but *international,* as well. Just consider how bad the situation is already. The 1990 census figures showed that there are 205 million single Chinese over the age of 15. Of those, men outnumber women by 3 to 2. It gets worse: Of the 8 million people in their 30s who are still single, men outnumber women by nearly 10 to 1.

The Great Danger

All of this means China will represent a great danger to the world in the coming years. Here's how Joseph Nye Jr., assistant secretary of defense for international security affairs, puts it: "We do not want to see China as an enemy. Secretary (of Defense William) Perry has made this clear a number of times. He made it clear again during his trip to China last October (1994). China is a very large and rapidly growing economy, and its defense expenditure grew by 40 percent in real terms over the last five years, albeit from a low base. What the secretary said to his Chinese interlocutors during the trip was, "We urge upon the Chinese that they enter into discussions with their neighbors to increase transparency and confidence in the region so that the worst-case assumptions will not be made." I fully expect China to do just that over the next few years: Reach out to its neighbors in Asia—especially Japan—to form a regional trading and, eventually, political-military alliance throughout the continent. When that happens, it will be an awesome power, perhaps rivaled only by the Western alliance and existing in a kind of shaky world balance of power.

Japan And China

Japan? Aligned with China? Seems a little far-fetched, huh? But that is exactly the scenario Far East experts see developing in the next few years. America's relative economic importance to Japan is dwindling in proportion to growth in Asia, where Japan's trade surplus now exceeds its black ink with the United States. The threat of a trade war with the United States caused remarkably little fuss in Tokyo.

"The 21st century will be China's century—and Japan's foreign policy will revolve on the dual axis of Japan-U.S. relations and Japan-China relations," says Kosuke Ito, a member of the Liberal Democrats' policy board. In an earlier era, the U.S.-Japan axis was the *only* one of importance to Tokyo.

If you needed it spelled out even more clearly for you, consider this late 1994 report from the *Los Angeles Times*: "From Japan's government ministries to Tokyo's trendy youth districts, the scent of change is unmistakable: Japan—an unquestioned ally of the United States for half a century and a passionate student of Western learning—is looking to its Asian neighbors, the East."

The end of the Cold War and the threat of Soviet expansionism once again change the dynamic at work in the Far East. Japan's only military threats are now local. But, more importantly, Tokyo understands the unprecedented economic ascent that is taking place in Asia—particularly in China.

The Declining United States

"Trade is exploding, growing twice as fast within the region as with the United States in the last five years," the *L. A. Times* report said. "Government officials are voicing a growing desire to play a more active political role in the region and are being exhorted to do so by leaders such as Malaysian Prime Minister Mahathir Mohammed and Lee Kuan Yew, the former Sinaporean leader. As a result, more Japanese are beginning to assert an agenda of 'Asian values' that could lead to differences with the West over human rights, labor relations and other issues."

Japan is even reviewing its security relationship with the United States. Defense experts recently reported to the prime minister's office that new military ties with Asian neighbors would supplement Japan's heavy reliance on the United States.

"Asia's ascent as an economic superstar and China's emergence as an even more formidable military and political power of the future contrast with the growing image of the United States as a declining power saddled with criminals, drug addicts and lazy workers," said the *Times* report. "One of Japan's time-honored proverbs advises to 'move with the powerful,' and that, to some, spells Asia."

Chalmers Johnson, president of the Japan Policy Research Institute, is more blunt: "I believe Japanese officials and the mass media are preparing the public for a disengagement from he United States in favor of the United Nations and Asia." It's no wonder. Look in any department store or toy shop. Notice where products are being manufactured these days—everything from clothing to sporting goods. Remember back in the 1960s, when all the inexpensive merchandise was made in Japan. It was kind of a running joke at the time. "Made in Japan" was synonymous with shoddy merchandise or cheaply made goods for a long time. That all changed in the 1970s as Japan became a leading world economic power. Today, we see a similar pattern emerging.

China's Untapped Labor Pool

In the 1990s, it's no longer Japan churning out the inexpensive merchandise so popular with American and Western European consumers; it's China. And, like Japan before it, it's China that is quickly emerging as a world economic power. What makes China able to produce so much and usurp such a big part of the western markets? The No. 1 answer, of course, is cheap labor—in some cases, free, or slave labor.

Recently, the West learned that not only does China exploit the labor of prisoners, who are often held on political charges. China is also putting to work its massive military machine. China, of course, has the largest standing army in the world. And in recent years, news reports are now detailing, China's totalitarian leadership has put its soldiers to work producing many of the goods Americans find on their store shelves today.

And where does that money go? Right back into building the increasingly powerful Chinese military machine. In addition, new details are filtering out of China on another source of inexpensive labor. Some 80 million peasants—most of them young and striving for a better way of life—have been uprooted from their rural villages and flocked to the major cities in search of manufacturing work.

Their cheap labor has become a major factor in keeping China's economic growth at 13 percent annually for the last several years. When you pick out a pair of sneakers or a shirt or a toy from the shelves of America's stores today, chances are you picked up something made by this peasant army. In addition, they are building the office towers, hotels and highways that are transforming Beijing, Shanghai and Canton into modern-day metropolises.

How cheap is the labor? In Liujiaguanfang Village in Shandong province in eastern China, a survey found the average income was equivalent to $50 a year for families without migrant members and $147 for those with someone working in the city.

This trend represents a real break from the past. For the first three decades of Communist rule, people in China basically stayed where they grew up, bound not only by tradition but by strict population registration systems and travel controls. When the government began relaxing the controls in the 1980s, Beijing wasn't quite sure what to expect. At first, most of the travel out of the agricultural areas and into the cities occurred in the winter when farming was impossible. Later, however, the peasant army invasions of the city became a year-round phenomenon.

Why all the permanent dislocation in China? Because there are few jobs in the rural areas and many young people are searching for a life free of the tyrannies of flood, drought and government grain quotas. But this refugee crisis seems to work to China's advantage. The cheap labor that it creates in the manufacturing zones is helping to turn the country into an economic powerhouse. And, as the economy grows, so does China's military capabilities.

Picture This Scenario

OK, let's use our imaginations a little. To this point, I have described the players in the coming future battle—the Muslim nations, aligned with Russia, invading Israel. Defending Israel, and its own power in the world, will be the European bloc, headed by a Roman dictator with extraordinary personal, religious, political and economic power. Suppose such a conflagration took place in the word in the next few years. And the Asian nations, headed by a coalition between China and Japan, were simply waiting in the wings to see how things worked out. Following the unprecedented destruction they witnessed, could the Asians powers afford not to get involved? Could they afford not to try to collect the spoils of war for themselves at the expense of the depleted power of Russia and the West? I don't think so, especially when you consider the kinds of internal pressures that will be building within China.

In effect, China will have an excess population of men—a "disposable" wealth that could be invested in a desperate and opportunistic grab for total world power.

Reading The Tea Leaves

Let me tell you how the Bible describes this event. Revelation 9:13-16 states: **"And the sixth angel sounded,**

and I heard a voice from the four horns of the golden altar which is before God, one saying to the sixth angel who had the trumpet, 'Release the four angels who are bound at the great river Euphrates.' And the four angels, who had been prepared for the hour and day and month and year, were released, so that they might kill a third of mankind. And the number of the armies and of the horsemen was two hundred million; I heard the number of them."

Besides 20th century China, no other nation in the history of the world could ever assemble an army of that size. Yet the Bible foretold this development twenty centuries ago. There's only one specific reference to the nations of Asia in the prophetic word. But it is a very important one that shows they will play a momentous role in the Final Battle. It's found in Revelation 16:12. It's a clear reference to the nations of Asia, because in the Greek, "east" is literally translated as **"Kings of the rising sun."**

Let me tell you about the significance of the Euphrates River, too. This body of water has long been the dividing line between Asia Minor—what we call today the Middle East—and Asia, or the Far East. Asia, to the people of the Middle East in the biblical times was a vast unknown world. Asia has always been something of a mystery to the Western mind, though China was one of the first great civilizations.

Asia's False Religions

What caused them to falter? Why have they been inhibited in modern times from prospering further and dominating the world? I believe part of the answer is their false religion. Paganism found its deepest roots in Asia. So, even though the Chinese invented gunpowder, rocketry and other great breakthroughs that could have allowed them to become a world power, they still only went so far. The Japanese, too, remained a separate society until Admiral Perry sailed in and persuaded them to open up for trade. India, the world's largest democracy, has been held back by a religiously imposed caste system and the worshipping of many gods and idols.

In the Book of Acts, the apostle Paul writes about how he tried relentlessly to take the gospel into Asia, but the Holy Spirit wouldn't let him. The apostles Thomas and Matthew went and both died as martyrs there. I think there's a reason for that. Behind the scenes in this world, there's a spiritual battle taking place. Angels are the foot soldiers in that war. They play a vital role in history, too. In Revelation, the Bible tells us that one angel, apparently loyal to God, is ordered to release four other fallen angels, or demons, who are bound at the Euphrates River.

Unleashing The Demons

These four demons are very powerful. At some point in history, they were bound and their authority limited to the Eastern side of the river. For centuries since, they have apparently been restricted from exercising their influence on the western side. God just hasn't permitted it. But at some time in the future—and I believe that time is coming soon—the four demons will be unshackled and permitted to fulfill their own destiny of torment and destruction beyond the Euphrates. Specifically, the Bible says, they will help kill *one-third of mankind!*

Revelation 16:12 also predicts **that the Euphrates River will be dried up to prepare the way for the kings of the East to invade the Middle East.** Such a phenomenon must have been virtually unthinkable at the time of the Bible. How could such a great river be dried up? Surely only God could perform such a miracle. But, again, it has become possible to do just that in the 1990s—at the very time we see so many other Bible prophecies being fulfilled before our very eyes!

Drying Up The Euphrates

Back in 1990, Turkey cut off the flow of the Euphrates at its source for a period of 30 days, so that a huge concrete plug for a diversion channel could be built. Turkey used the water flow to fill up a huge reservoir. It was done once. It can be done again. And it will be.

The Asian nations will make a tactical decision to swoop in and invade the Middle East. It seems to be an opportunistic decision. By process of elimination, they will have become the most powerful force on Earth. And without a presence in the Middle East, they run the risk of losing their access to the lifeline of industrialized life—oil.

This is not, contrary to popular opinion, the **"battle of Armageddon."** But this isn't a battle—it's a war. The Bible never actually talks about a "battle" of Armageddon. There are several huge battles that take place. And the reason that Armageddon, or the "hill of megiddo," is at the center of things in this huge Final Battle is simply because it is the geographical, strategic center of the land bridge between three continents and a vital link for Asia to the oil reserves of the Persian Gulf.

In this phase of the war, Asia finishes off the Russian coalition forces and marches in to claim its spoils. But they are confronted by the remains of the Western forces. It's an ugly and unimaginable clash in which, the Bible says, the blood will run as deep as the horse's bridle in a valley 200 miles long. Interestingly, in Israel there is only one valley that long—the Jordan River Valley, which starts north of the Sea of Galilee and comes down south along the Jordanian border to the Gulf of Eilat.

What we're talking about here is a real-life horror movie—the greatest holocaust ever. For the first and last time, man will be released from God's restraint to do what he has always wanted to do in his heart.

Fire And Brimstone

Revelation also mentions "fire and smoke and brimstone" in connection with this deadly battle. I will elaborate on this later, but I believe this is a reference to tactical nuclear war. Interestingly, China and India are both capable of deploying tactical nuclear weapons. North Korea and Japan may soon be able to as well. The West is also preparing for a defensive system of theater ballistic missiles in Asia.

"We believe that theater ballistic missile defenses are going to be an important part of defenses in East Asia in the future," says Nye. "As we face the prospects of proliferation, this type of defense will be important in East Asia and in other regions as well."

The Bible tells us that in the last days, those in the East will become a great and formidable people. As we look at how things have developed in the 20th century, China has been a real sleeping giant. For centuries it had been in decline. But when Communism took root there in the 1920s, it wiped out the feudal system and the warlords and united the people past the barriers of religion and culture. As brutal as it has been, central control has really turned

China into a nation again and brought the people into the industrial age. The sleeping giant has awakened.

In recent years, the Chinese leaders realized they could never feed 1.2 billion people with a centrally controlled economy. China is, thus, moving against its will toward a market economy. It's really a natural for the Chinese. They may be the most naturally capitalist people in the world.

China has barely begun to scrap its Communist bureaucracy and apparatus, but already it is experiencing boom times financially. Last year, for instance, the International Monetary Fund and the World Bank announced that China's gross domestic product was between four and five times greater in 1992 than it had previously been estimated to be.

According to the new estimates, China is now the third largest economy in the world after the U.S. and Japan. At its current rate of growth, China will surpass Japan in size later this decade. In addition, China is continuing to build its already awesome military machine and modernize its nuclear arsenal for better targeting against the West.

Yes indeed, the kings of the East are gearing up for the Final Battle.

Chapter 11

THE
LATE GREAT
UNITED STATES

"Woe to the land shadowing with wings, which is beyond the rivers of Ethiopia: That sends ambassadors by the sea...."

—Isaiah 18:1-2

"The first angel sounded his trumpet, and there came hail and fire mixed with blood, and it was hurled down upon the earth. A third of the earth was burned up, a third of the trees were burned up, and all the green grass was burned up."

—Revelation 8:7

Revelation Chapter 8 describes in detail the devastation of the second stage of escalation in the Final Battle. It indicates that one third of the Earth will experience utter destruction—the kind of devastation that, by human hand, could only be accomplished through thermonuclear attack.

I know many of my fellow Americans are probably wondering: "Will the United States survive?" There is very little scriptural evidence to indicate one way or the other. Though I think we can make some educated guesses.

"To Whom Much Is Given, Much Is Required"

First, I've said it before and I'll say it again: America has been inviting judgment on itself for a long time. Most of the world has, for that matter. But the United States of America, founded as one nation under God, has truly betrayed its heritage in many ways. We have become a nihilistic, hedonistic, self-centered, humanistic nation. The Lord has blessed this nation so greatly, and because of those blessings, we have a profound responsibility. If we continue to push God out of our public life, He is going to withdraw His blessings.

We've seen that pattern over and over in the Bible. We've been warned. We should know better. I think the fate of America is still open if we would make some right choices. If we as a nation were to repent and re-commit ourselves to Godly principles, the future of the land could be considerably brighter.

But my gut reaction is that America will continue to decline in power and influence in the coming years. Clearly, America does not appear to play an extraordinary role in the endtimes events. If she did, there would be more scriptural evidence for it. When you examine the scriptures dealing with the last days, there are some obtuse allusions to other nations, which play supporting roles before the final curtain falls. But I can find no direct references to a nation that is unmistakably America.

The Last Days Of Western Power

But there is no question as to the great power of the western world will be in the days that lead up to the climactic final battle and the end of history as we know it. It is unmistakably the revived form of the old Roman culture and people united together in a 10-nation confederacy.

It's possible that America could be in an alliance with this reborn form of the old Roman Empire of Europe, but only as some kind of lesser power. It appears that we will simply be reduced to military and economic irrelevance. Why would God allow such judgment upon America? Well, no other nation has been so blessed, yet, like the ancient Israelites, we have become proud and haughty. We don't thank God for our blessings. We take them for granted. That, my friends, is always a sure recipe for disaster with God.

Man Learns Nothing From History

I'm reminded of how Rome fell. It was sudden destruction that brought down the greatest empire the world had ever known. The real death knell came on December

29, 406 A.D. It was an exceptionally cold winter. So cold, in fact, the Rhine River froze that day, allowing, for the first time in anyone's memory, people on one side to cross over to the other side on the ice.

By this time, the Roman army had been reduced to something much less glorious than in its days of glory. The leadership wasn't as strong. The discipline wasn't as strict. It was made up of largely mercenaries, hired by the nobility in place of their over-indulged sons. So, when the barbarians from the other side of the Rhine stormed across the frozen river, the Roman army was only a shadow of its vaunted legions of the earlier days. The barbarians came by the hundreds of thousands, according to Thomas Cahill, author of *How the Irish Saved Civilization.* They decimated the Romans and totally defeated them.

In any case, once that river was breached, the cultural identity of Rome was also breached. And the decline of an empire was put on fast-forward.

Are there any parallels here for America to ponder? No, it's not just the failure of America to control illegal immigration to which I am alluding—though that, too, is a serious problem for our country. What I am talking about is the devolution of the American culture.

America's 30-Year Record

I warned in both *The Late Great Planet Earth* and again in *Planet Earth—2000 AD* that the West was in the midst of a 30-year cultural meltdown. Consider how conditions have deteriorated in that period:

- There has been a 560 percent increase in violent crime.
- Illegitimate births have increased 419 percent.

- Divorce rates have tripled.

- The number of children living in single-parent homes has tripled.

- The teen-age suicide rate has increased 200 percent.

- Student Achievement Test scores have plummeted 80 points.

"The West," explained Alexander Solzhenitsyn, "has been undergoing an erosion and obscuring of high moral and ethical ideals. The spiritual axis of life has grown dim."

America today is caught in the cross-fire of a "culture war" that literally threatens to destroy the nation's political heritage. The Founding Fathers understood that democratic rule and the principles of justice and freedom depended on a population influenced by the ethic of a Christian conscience of thought. That view is now under siege from those who contend the nation is not bound to any fixed truths.

Ultimately, this war of values could bring about the collapse of democracy and the rule of law. After all, if people are not accountable to God for their actions—or at least some absolute standard of morality, there is no way to make them accountable to society except by coercion and terror. Government's job becomes much bigger in a nation whose inhabitants believe they answer only to themselves. This is why once the totalitarian rule of terror in the old Soviet Union was removed, the republics have gone into moral chaos.

My Regretful Warning

As difficult as it is for me to admit it, America is very much on the decline. And this is exactly what I have foreseen and predicted for this country for over thirty-five years.

I presented this conviction in 1969 in the *Late Great Planet Earth,* "The United States will not hold its present position of leadership in the western world," I wrote then. "Lack of moral principle by citizens and leaders will so weaken law and order that a state of anarchy will finally result. The military capability of the United States, though it is at present the most powerful in the world, has already been neutralized because no one has the courage to use it decisively. When the economy collapses, so will the military."

Remember, folks, these words were written in 1969, not the 1990s! Today, more than ever, we understand their significance. I added, "The only chance of slowing up this decline in America is a widespread spiritual awakening." That's still true, but our hope for the kind of major spiritual revival that would be required to shake America out of its occultic and New Age induced doldrums is growing dimmer by the day.

In the late 1960s, I could already see the devastating effects of drug abuse on an entire generation. But today, in the 1990s, drug abuse knows no generational boundaries. From the very young to the very old, drug use has reached epidemic proportions. I know businessmen who routinely test potential new employees for drugs who say they have trouble finding anyone not using marijuana, cocaine, psychedelics or the even more dangerous new synthetic narcotics. This is so common that it's no longer considered "newsworthy."

New Morality's Legacy

With the "new morality" of the '60s came the "sexual revolution." Out went the old taboos about multiple sex partners, same-sex partners and promiscuity of all forms. With that, of course, came the judgment of AIDs and a whole host of other sexually transmitted diseases. The liberal social engineers told us that would be enough to discourage these "unsafe sex practices." But, despite all the publicity about AIDs, the latest statistics show people are more sexually active outside of marriage than ever.

"The enormous tensions and backlash generated by these devastating sexually transmitted diseases made the practitioners of casual sex pause," wrote the research team of Samuel and Cynthia Janus who studied 8,000 people over a nine-year period. "In a sense, it was a time of national reassessment. Rather than lapsing into the sexual 'dark ages' however, Americans as a whole decided to move forward. This really marked the beginning of the 'Second Sexual Revolution' . . . an overall willingness to engage in a variety of sexual practices, some of which may once have been considered 'deviant' or at least 'unacceptable' by society."

Well, so much for that kind of closemindedness, right? On with the revolution. Forget the taboos. Who's to say what's right or wrong? If it feels good, do it. The spirit of the '60s—I am convinced inspired by demons—is alive and well as we hurtle toward the second millennium. You have to wonder: How long will God tolerate this kind of behavior? As Billy Graham so aptly put it, "If God doesn't judge America, He'll have to apologize to Sodom and Gomorrah."

The New Sexual Hedonism

God warned that the very fabric of society would break down in the last days, just shortly before Jesus the Messiah would return, **"But mark this: There will be terrible times in the last days. People will be lovers of themselves, lovers of money, boastful, proud, abusive, disobedient to their parents, ungrateful, unholy, without love [natural affection], unforgiving, slanderous, without self-control,**

brutal, not lovers of the good, treacherous, rash, conceited, lovers of pleasure rather than lovers of God— having a form of godliness but denying its power. Have nothing to do with them." (2 Timothy 3:1-5 NIV)

Back in the late '60s, heterosexual promiscuity, open marriages and group sex were considered *avant garde*. Today, that stuff is considered child's play among the social crusaders. Even homosexuality and lesbianism are considered mainstream. On the cutting edge now are such bizarre practices as sado-masochism, pedophilia and bestiality.

Anyone who opposes such behavior better watch out. In the name of "tolerance" and "diversity" even the Boy Scouts of America will be shut out of funding, picketed, sued and boycotted in this new wacky, upside-down world of ours. I knew things were going to get strange, but even I'm amazed by how far it's gone.

And now, in addition to AIDs, we have super strains of all the old venereal diseases that have developed immunity to almost every known antibiotic.

"Without Natural Affection . . ."

The whole nation was shocked when a young mother drove her two infant sons into a lake and drowned them in cold blood, still strapped to their infant car seats. She did this because her boyfriend didn't want kids around. Then the news of a whole rash of mothers and fathers murdering their children came out. It's exactly what God predicted would happen when the family unit would break down and children would become disobedient and rebellious to the point that their whole nature would be twisted morally. Today we see the results: We have young people with no conscience and no feeling or sense of the pain they inflict. Cold blooded killers are now as young as 12 years old.

God is speaking to this generation through these wake-up calls and serving notice that His day of judgment is very near, and that we should turn to Him and receive forgiveness and a new birth that will give us God's desires and His power to be good people.

Look what else I wrote about this subject in *Late Great:* "Look for the present sociological problems such as crime, riots, lack of employment, poverty, illiteracy, mental illness, illegitimacy, etc., to increase as the population explosion begins to multiply geometrically. . . . Look for drug addiction to further permeate the U.S. and other free-world countries. Drug addicts will run for high political offices and win through support of young adults."

Whatever Happened To Moral Convictions?

Newsweek published a surprising article in early 1995 called "The Return of Shame." It pointed to such national embarrassments as the reelection of Marion Barry. Barry was arrested with a prostitute in a hotel room while smoking crack cocaine. His illegal actions and the arrest itself were captured on video tape and played on national television. Barry claimed the arrest was racially motivated, rather than accepting responsibility for his own actions. He parlayed his 'victimization' into political support from the predominantly black electorate and took back his seat as mayor of the capital city of the United States of America.

The president of the United States has embarrassed the country with his activities, from his highly questionable tactics to avoid combat during the Vietnam War, to Whitewater, to his marital infidelities, and beyond.

Nonetheless, our own "Teflon king"—consummate politician that he is—is beginning to recognize the shift in public mood. In a reversal of his campaign rhetoric, he is suddenly the champion of morality. *Newsweek* looks back to the "Murphy Brown Affair" in which Vice President Dan Quayle condemned Hollywood for promoting single motherhood as courageous and morally acceptable. President Clinton defended Hollywood back then, but sensing the outrage of Americans, *has reversed himself again.* He has backed away from supporting homosexuals, single-parent families, and the "Hollywood elite," and has become a Puritan. Recently he made a public statement that since taking office, he has read the entire Book of Psalms seeking comfort from his political enemies. Of his newly found religiosity he says, "The people who don't believe it is real are those who disagree with me politically."

Suddenly, we are collectively embarrassed! Who could have imagined only three short years ago that a national secular magazine like *Newsweek* would have said, "Obviously shame cannot be legislated. It must arise from what UCLA public policy professor James Q. Wilson calls the 'moral sense' in all humans. The theologian Richard John Neuhaus thinks that shame faded away not in the moral relativism of the 1960s as is usually argued, but in the Pollyannish '50s when spiritual leaders like Norman Vincent Peale argued that you could have the positive side without the negative, which is philosophically and practically negative. After all, adds Neuhaus, we should dislike ourselves because there is much about ourselves that is not only profoundly dislikeable, but odious. It's not for nothing that the Ten Commandments are put in the negative."

"The Down Right Reverend" Bill Clinton

Even more astonishing was this quote from the same magazine. "If religious congregations are to be of service to society—as President Clinton asked in his state of the Union address—they must first deal with the sinners in their midst. All religions remind us that actions have consequences for which guilt can and must be acknowledged, forgiveness humbly begged, reconciliation sought. Sin is evil." Physician, heal thyself!

The courts are beginning to see the value of shame as an effective deterrent to crime. A judge in Memphis sometimes sentences burglars to probation with the condition that they permit their victims to enter their homes, in front of all their neighbors, and take something they want. A Maryland experiment requires offenders to get down on their knees and apologize to victims in public. In one study, Maryland reports an astonishing 97 percent of those offenders never repeat the crime.

The public is also recognizing the value of shame. In residential areas plagued by drugs and prostitution, residents have begun photographing clients of prostitutes and drug dealers, and publishing their pictures. La Mesa, California, published the photographs of convicted "johns" in the local paper. Many major newspapers list the names of fathers who are behind on their child support payments. Some states issue specially marked license plates to convicted drunk drivers.

It's Easy To Condemn What Will Not Alter You

Shame means being intolerant of behavior illegal or destructive to the social contract. We are cheerfully intolerant of cigarette smoking or wearing fur coats. On the other hand, on issues of morality, of sex, reproduction, family and honor, we are considerably less judgmental. Hypocrisy is alive and well in this country. Like the old maxim that says we get what we deserve, this truism is reflected in our children, our marriages—and our national leaders.

The United States is learning from experience what the Christian learned from the pages of scripture. Romans 6:23 tells us, "The wages of sin is death." We are witnessing the death of our culture, our international reputation, our internal security, and in far too many cases, even the death of our children.

Soon, very soon, I am afraid, if we do not return to the principles upon which our country was founded, we will bear witness to the most tragic death of all, the death of our greatly blessed nation.

I wish I were wrong, but I am expecting America to slip into a secondary role as a world power in the coming days. Then we will look back at the silly little social experiments this country is conducting with our military preparedness— gay troops, women in combat, radical defense cuts. Foolishly, the White House has even abandoned the Strategic Defense Initiative and the idea of a shield against incoming intercontinental ballistic missiles. This decision alone could prove to be our national undoing.

On February 15, 1995, a vote took place in the U.S. House of Representatives that could have profound ramifications on the survival of the United States. Rep. John M. Spratt Jr., D-South Carolina, offered an amendment to the "National Security Revitalization Act" that was approved by a 218-212 vote. The amendment eliminated the requirement for the White House to put forward a plan within 60 days for a national missile defense system.

Spratt's amendment effectively made the top priority of the U.S. Defense Department "operational readiness of the armed forces," followed by the promotion of theater missile defenses and lastly the development of a *ground-based* interceptor system capable of destroying ballistic missiles launched against the United States. The trouble with all this—aside from the low priority given defense of U.S. citizens—is the requirement that any such system be "ground-based." Lt. Gen. Daniel Graham, the pioneer behind the High Frontier concept of missile defense insists that a space-based system would be cheaper, easier to build and quicker to deploy than a ground-based system. It's a little odd that Congress would want to micromanage the defense system in such a way that makes a space-based system off-limits.

The key for the liberals—Democrats and Republicans—who voted for this concept was the desire to take "Star Wars" off the table all together.

In these days of rogue Islamic nations acquiring nuclear missile capabilities, such short-sightedness is close to national suicide. When you add the ingredient of nuclear suicide bombers, the picture gets truly frightening.

Disrespect For Military

Does any of this sound familiar? All of the problems I listed have evolved into "crises." Now we have had a president of the United States who smoked marijuana but "didn't inhale." The American military is completely demoralized. Its mission has been radically altered from fighting force to "humanitarian" force. And as the defense budget is hacked away mercilessly, America's naive political leadership keeps finding more remote parts of the world in which to commit our confused young troops.

I read in amazement that the United States, under orders of President Clinton, is cutting the American arsenal of bombers and submarines *in hopes* that Russia will follow suit. The administration is cutting the number of Trident submarines in the Navy's fleet from 18 to 14 and the number of B-52 strategic bombers from 94 to 66.

"The way we want to go is to point out steps that we are taking to lower our dependence on nuclear weapons," explained Deputy Defense Secretary John Deutch. "We would hope that each side taking unilateral steps will also improve the stability in the world."

Congress' "Down-sizing" Of Security

The down-sizing generally of the U.S. military has reduced combat units to a level wholly inadequate to defend the nation's vital interests. I've said it before: I don't think the U.S. is capable of mounting another "Desert Storm" operation in the Middle East or anywhere else. That's how far we've come, so fast. In the Gulf War, the Army deployed eight divisions. The Army's current authorized level is only 10 active divisions, down from 18 in 1989. What if we had to fight on two fronts?

The army's troop strength level has been reduced from 790,000 in 1989 to 510,000 in 1995 and going down to 495,000 by 1997. In addition, only five Army divisions are assigned to Force Package 1, the group kept at full readiness for immediate commitment in time of crisis. Facilities repair and maintenance funding have been reduced by a third. Maintenance and supply per division have fallen by 22 percent. Depot maintenance per division has been cut by 38 percent.

Hundreds fewer helicopter pilots are being trained—far less than are needed, according to top military analysts. Maintenance crews in the Air Force are struggling to keep operational adequate numbers of jet engines. Budget constraints have limited the availability of spare parts. The once vaunted carrier force is being reduced from 15 to 11. Inadequate logistics have pushed the F-117 stealth fighter below Air Force standards in its mission-capable rate. The AWACs and the F-15E and F-111 fighter-bombers have similar problems.

Who's Kidding Who?

Have we learned nothing from history? We live in a world that is governed by the aggressive use of force. Appeasement has never led to anything but disaster. Peace is always and only achieved through strength.

There is one other major concern I have regarding the fate of the United States. I have always believed and stated quite plainly that the fate of America is, to a great extent, determined by how it treats Israel. Why? Because God promised to bless those nations that were a blessing to Israel and curse those that were a curse upon the Jewish state. I won't go so far as to suggest that America has been a curse upon Israel of late, but it has been far from a blessing either. The United States has been responsible for pushing Israel into the militarily untenable position I described earlier in this book.

In a recent interview, Joseph de Courcy revealed, "There is a widespread belief that the United States is a staunch and unshakable ally of Israel. However, current strategic and domestic developments are working to weaken America's commitment to the Jewish state, and even the historical record of U.S. support for Israel is not as convincing as popular opinion would have it."

De Courcy pointed out that it was only after Israel's decisive military victory of June 1967 that the U.S. began to see the Jewish state as a useful strategic ally in the Cold War. It was only then that the U.S. became Israel's main supplier of arms.

Egypt, Exhibit No. 1

"But this phase lasted just three years, until the death of Nasser in 1979, after which the prime U.S. objective in the Middle East came to be the severance of Egypt's ties with the Soviet Union," says de Courcy. "This policy was maintained despite President Sadat's clear intention of attacking Israel (his expulsion of the Soviets from Egypt in 1972 was because Moscow would not supply Egypt with the offensive weapons it needed to wage a successful war against the Jewish state); and it continued after Sadat had launched the October 1973 war when Washington prevented Israel from reaping the fruits of a counterattack which took it to within 60 miles of Cairo."

After Jimmy Carter was elected president in 1976, America took a more strongly pro-Cairo line, says de Courcy, even pressuring Israel to return the captured Sinai. Under President Bush, things deteriorated even further. I remember oh so clearly Secretary of State James Baker III telling the Israelis to call him when they were "serious about peace."

George Bush's administration represented the most anti-Israel U.S. presidency ever. But that was then, and this is now. The current administration and, particularly, the new leadership emerging within the State Department, may make the Bush years look good by comparison.

U.S. Policy Turns Against Israel

Strobe Talbott, the No. 2 man in State—and, most agree, the next secretary of state—has left a viciously anti-Israel paper trail over the years in his writings for *Time* magazine. In 1990, just a few short years ago, Talbott likened Israel to Iraq—at the time, remember, our chief adversary in the world. In an essay titled, "How Israel is like Iraq," he wrote: "So Israel's policy today does indeed have something in common with Iraq's. Saddam says that since Kuwait and Iraq were part of the same province under the control of the Ottoman Turks, they should be rejoined now. For their part, many Likud leaders believe that since the West Bank was ruled by Israelites in biblical times, not one square inch should be traded away as part of an Arab-Israeli settlement."

Talbott has also labeled a "delusion" the idea "that Israel is, or ever has been, primarily a strategic ally." And listen to this essay, "What to do about Israel," from a 1981 issue of *Time,* "Israel sometimes seems to have taken a visage and tone of a rather nasty (and) bitter nation, even a violent one. . . . Israel in the past has managed to convey more sorrow than anger when it wielded its terrible swift sword. Now there seems to be only anger, and it is too often shrill, self-righteous and even a bit frightening—more so to those who love Israel than to those who hate her."

He added that "Israel is well on its way to becoming not just a dubious asset but outright liability to American security interests, both in the Middle East and worldwide." Talbott suggested cutting military aid to Israel would be a good way for the U.S. to punish the Jewish state.

He also suggested it was time for the U.S. to interfere in internal Israeli politics if necessary. "It is high time for the

U.S. to engage Israel in a debate over the fundamental nature of their relationship. If that means interfering in Israeli internal politics, then so be it."

What was Talbott's explanation of these anti-Israel diatribes? "I have simply changed my opinion," he said. It sure doesn't seem that way—not with all the pressure the United States is placing on Israel to make land-for-peace concessions.

"In order to further this policy, the U.S. has put immense pressure on Israel," says de Courcy. "It has also continued its huge military assistance to Egypt; played the decisive role in securing the write-off of 50 percent of Egypt's foreign debt; and followed a conciliatory policy toward Damascus despite the evidence of Syria's continuing involvement in international terrorism, including the bombing of the Israeli embassy in Buenos Aires in 1992. Washington believes the ultimate reward of peace in the Middle East justifies these risks, and that in any event it will lessen the risk to Israel by providing it with a post-settlement security guarantee. But it is precisely the value of this guarantee that is in doubt."

Amazingly, the majority of the 6 million Jews in America seem to favor the kind of territorial concessions Israel is being forced to make —the kind that, in my opinion, are jeopardizing Israel's security. This means there will be very little pressure bought to bear on the U. S. to fulfill the guarantees that are being offered to Israel.

At the same time, de Courcy points out that Muslim influence is increasing in the U.S. There are now more than 1,100 mosques in the country, 80 percent of which have been built in the last dozen years. There are at least 3 million Muslims currently residing in the U.S. and the

number is growing fast. One-third of America's Muslims
are black Americans who are converting to Islam in record
numbers. Some are responding to the calls of extremists
like Louis Farrakhan, who has referred to Judaism as a
"gutter religion."

"Even if these changing electoral realities in America
do not turn the United States overtly anti-Israel they are
likely to make the nation's commitment to the defense of
the Jewish state less determined," says de Courcy. "The
American public . . . does not like its soldiers dying in
foreign causes. One highly destructive car bomb in 1983
(killing 241 Marines) was all the thanks the United States
received for trying to bring peace to Lebanon. The
Marines were withdrawn. Ten years later in Somalia,
where the U.S. launched a humanitarian mission to halt
anarchy-induced famine, the American public liked it no
better when 17 Marines were killed in one engagement
with hoodlums in pickup trucks. The president ordered a
withdrawal. The Yugoslav civil war, on the other hand, was
considered too dangerous from the outset for any kind of
American ground deployment, given that it was primarily
a European problem."

**I will bless those who bless you, and I will curse him
who curses you** —The God Of Abraham, Isaac and Jacob
(Genesis 12:3 NKJV)

I presented the above evidence to show one basic thing.
The U.S. has been protected by God because it has been a
haven for Israelites and an ally for their survival. It has been
one of those great factors in our protection. Now that we are
turning away, look for the "Late Great United States."

All of this represents a depressing picture for
America—but it is doubly serious for Israel if it is

expecting to rely on a US guarantee for its security once it has traded territory for peace treaties. It's understandable why America may be all but irrelevant by the time of the Final Battle.

Chapter 12

THE LAST WAR AND FINAL BATTLE

"Behold, the Lord lays the Earth waste, devastates it, distorts its surface, and scatters its inhabitants. . . . a curse devours the Earth, and those who live in it are held guilty. Therefore, the inhabitants of the Earth are burned, and few men are left."

—Isaiah 24:1, 6

Let me begin this chapter with a warning. If this were a Hollywood movie, it would be rated "R" because of excessive violence. It's not a chapter I would recommend for children or for adults with weak stomachs. What I am about to describe, in as much detail as I can, is the terrible destruction and devastation that will be wrought on man and Earth by the Final Battle. This is the main event before the final curtain of history as we know it—the *piece de resistance*. After this will come the *true* new world order.

But there's often misunderstanding about "Armageddon." It is vastly understating it to describe it only as a "battle." Actually, *Armageddon* is the fiercest battle of the greater **war of the great day of God Almighty** it describes. The word translated battle in the original Greek is πολεμον, which means *an armed conflict or war.* The context says, **"They are spirits of demons performing miraculous signs, and they go out to the kings of the whole world, to gather them for *the war* [πολεμον] *of the great day of God Almighty* . . . Then they gathered the kings together to the place that in Hebrew is called Armageddon."** (Rev 16:14, 16)

A war—along escalating war, an intense war which will trigger an ultimate global nuclear holocaust—will be fought in and around the Valley of Jezreel which lies beneath the ancient fortress of Megiddo. The fortress city of Megiddo guarded the entrance to this Valley via the ancient trade route from Egypt to Damascus and the Far East called the Via Maris.

I don't believe any author has devoted as much time, space, attention and study to the particulars of this clash. The reason I do it is clear: *I want to shock you.* Not with speculation, not with sensationalism, mind you—but with the naked truth of what is going to happen to the world in the very near future.

But first, a preamble: Our world today is rapidly falling apart. This was vividly depicted in a February 1994 *Atlantic Report* report entitled "The Coming Anarchy." It detailed a planetary state of affairs we don't hear much about from the people intent on ringing in a millennium of peace and harmony through their New World Order. The report explained "how scarcity, crime, overpopulation, tribalism and disease are rapidly destroying the social fabric of our planet."

"Nations break up under the tidal flow of refugees from environmental and social disaster," the article began. "As borders crumble, another type of boundary is erected—a wall of disease. Wars are fought over scarce resources, especially water, and war itself becomes continuous with crime, as armed bands of stateless marauders clash with the private security forces of the elites."

This, the magazine promised, would be a glimpse of the world in the first few decades of the 21st century.

"In forty-five years I have never seen things so bad," complains a minister in the West African nation of Sierra Leone. "We did not manage ourselves well after the British departed. But what we have now is something worse—the revenge of the poor, of the social failures, of the people least able to bring up children in a modern society."

And how bad is it? "The cities of West Africa at night are some of the unsafest in the world," the *Atlantic* report explained. "Streets are unlit; the police often lack gasoline for their vehicles; armed burglars, carjackers and muggers proliferate."

Crime is so rampant that the airport is indefinitely embargoed by the U.S. State Department. Restaurants in the cities have stick-and-gun-wielding guards who walk customers to their cars and the entrance. Even diplomatic staff members and their families are victimized almost routinely by the criminal element.

But what I found so riveting about the report is the premise—worse—the revenge of the poor, of the social failures, of the people least able to bring up children in a modern society."

And how bad is it? "The cities of West Africa at night are some of the unsafest in the world," the *Atlantic* report explained. "Streets are unlit; the police often lack gasoline for their vehicles; armed burglars, carjackers and muggers proliferate."

Crime is so rampant that the airport is indefinitely embargoed by the U.S. State Department. Restaurants in the cities have stick-and-gun-wielding guards who walk customers to their cars and the entrance. Even diplomatic staff members and their families are victimized almost routinely by the criminal element.

But what I found so riveting about the report is the premise—a correct one, I believe—that this is the direction much of the world is going in as we approach the 21st century. This will not be the exception but the rule in a few short years. Author Robert Kaplan even predicts American cities will resemble this model.

"West Africa is becoming the symbol of worldwide demographic, environmental and societal stress, in which criminal anarchy emerges as the real 'strategic' danger," he writes. "Disease, overpopulation, unprovoked crime, scarcity of resources, refugee migrations, the increasing erosion of nation-states and international borders and the empowerment of private armies, security firms and international drug cartels are now most tellingly demonstrated through a West African prism. West Africa provides an appropriate introduction to the issues, often extremely unpleasant to discuss, that will soon confront our civilization."

Kaplan says that environmental scarcity will be "the national-security issue of the early 21st century." Now I've been saying this stuff for the past twenty-five years, but here it is from a detached, objective, secular journalist.

Tell me if he doesn't sound like something I would write: "The political and strategic impact of surging populations, spreading disease, deforestation and soil erosion, water depletion, air pollution, and, possibly, rising sea levels in critical, overcrowded regions like the Nile Delta and Bangladesh—developments that will prompt mass migrations and, in turn, incite group conflicts—will be the core foreign-policy challenge from which most others will ultimately emanate, arousing the public and uniting assorted interests left over from the Cold War."

Kaplan also predicts, based on societal trends, that America will be "less of a nation than it is today." Again, does this not sound familiar? Is this not exactly what I have been predicting based on my study of prophetic Scriptures?

Global anarchy is indeed coming. It will be the prelude to a New World Order—a pseudo-peace and pseudo-stability offered up by a pseudo-savior. But the result won't be peace and stability but tyranny, chaos and war.

Let's see what the Bible has to say about that war—a conflict that will end forever man's suicidal bloodlust. Revelation Chapter 6 discusses seven seals that are broken to bring God's judgment on the world. The first of these is a rider on a white horse: **"And I looked, and behold, a white horse, and he who sat on it had a bow; and a crown was given to him; and he went out conquering, and to conquer."** This is the European Antichrist discussed earlier in this book. He appears at the beginning of a very special period that God has predicted in detail in many prophecies.

The time period is set by Daniel 9:24-27. Daniel says that the Jewish people were allotted by God 70 sabbatical years to accomplish the the things for which He created them. Of those 490 years, 483 have already been fulfilled in history. This rider on the white horse charges forth at the beginning of the last allotted seven-year period known as the Tribulation.

In Revelation 6:3-4, the passage jumps from the beginning of the seven-year period to the middle. The focus shifts to the last three-and-one-half years because it will be the most intense period of judgment. Verse 4 describes a rider on a red horse who takes peace from the Earth. Well, you cannot take from the Earth that which does not exist, right? So the scripture is telling us that there is peace—or, at least a pseudo-peace—on the Earth until this point. The rider on the red horse is given authority to take peace from the earth. Matthew 24:15 tells us what starts this war. The incident that sets off the last war is the European leader—the one who has instituted this worldwide pseudo-peace—taking a seat in a yet-to-be-built Temple in Jerusalem, declaring himself to be God.

Revelation 6:4 predicts the rider on the red horse will remove peace so that **"men should slay one another."** I was reading in the Greek text and I looked up the word "slay." It means *to butcher or slaughter.* It does not mean just to kill. It means a ruthless massacre.

So, we know how this war will start. We know who will start it. Zechariah 12:2-3 states that God is going to cause Jerusalem to be a burden to the whole world. It says that anyone who tries to lift that burden or solve its problems will be destroyed. I have devoted a good portion of this book demonstrating how and why Muslims will never be content until they have Jerusalem. Arafat has always said openly that the real issue of the peace talks is Jerusalem. It belongs to *Dar al Islam*, he insists. They claim it as the third holiest site of the Islamic faith.

How does this war begin? Stage one is depicted in Ezekiel 38:4. The prophet sees some highly mechanized and well-equipped armies moving toward Israel from the uttermost north. Remember, Ezekiel saw these visions with ancient eyes and described them in terms of the 7th century B.C. Ezekiel saw the prince of Rosh, Meshech and Tubal are from Magog. Bible scholars have long agreed that these are the ancient Scythians who later became the ethnic Russians. We know that part of these people settled on the European side of the Urals and the other went to the great plateau into Asia. They built the Wall of China that was originally known as *The Wall of Magog*. So, the Bible tells us these people will come in the last days. But they would not be a world conqueror. They would be a regional power with tremendous military power.

"And I will turn you about, and put hooks in your jaws, and I will bring you out, and all your army, horses

and horsemen, all of them splendidly attired, a great company with buckler and shield, all of them wielding swords," it states in Verse 4. The next verses tells us which countries will be joining Russia in this invasion: Persia, Ethiopia, Put, Gomer, Beth-togarmah.

Persia, is of course, modern-day Iran—but the ancient Persian empire was much more, including what is today Pakistan through Turkey and much of the true Arab world including Egypt. We have shown that Iran is one of the most dangerous forces in the world today—the heart of radical Islamic fundamentalism. A former general from the Mossad told me that stopping Iran now is more important than stopping Hitler was in the late 1930s. Remember this is a Jew saying this.

Ethiopia is a reference to part of black Africa—the modern Islamic nations of Ethiopia, Somalia and Sudan. So some of those nations will be a part of this coalition. The descendants of ancient "Put" are found in Libya, Morocco, Algeria, Tunisia and Mauritania. All of which are Islamic nations.

Gomer is an area in Eastern Europe—including several nations which have been under Russian influence. Togarmah was a son of Gomer. Part of his family settled in the Baltic states we now know as Estonia, Lithuania and Latvia. Others settled in Turkey. Turkey is surely being drawn into the Islamic world. Ataturk, the father of modern Turkey, some 70 years ago, by his own will took Turkey out of the Islamic world and tried to make it a western secular republic. By the force of his will, he outlawed the wearing of the fez. He put the clerics out of the government and so on. He set Turkey into motion to be a modern western-style country. They made formal declarations to join the

European Community. They asked for membership and were turned down. This happened five years ago. This immediately started the Turks to proclaim that they had forsaken their religion and traditions only to be rejected by the western world. They began reversing all Ataturk had done. They are now rushing headlong back into the Muslim world. The last election saw the Muslims win an unprecedented number of seats in their congress. Ezekiel foresaw all of this coming.

"The Hook" Of Deception

The hook in Russia's jaws could well be the treaty Moscow has already signed with Iran that commits the nation to support them in any regional war in the future. This attack is a surprise, and the proof is in Ezekiel 38:13. Here we see some people of the region demanding to know why this invasion is taking place: **"Have you come to capture spoil? Have you assembled your company to seize plunder, to carry away silver and gold, to take away cattle and goods, to capture great spoil?"**

Meanwhile, Back To The Future

Let's time-warp back to the present, for a moment, just to illustrate how close we are to a time like this. There is, as I have mentioned earlier, an ultra-nationalist leader in Russia today—Vladimir Zhirinovsky—who considers the independent states of Lithuania, Latvia, Estonia and other Russian neighbors to be part of "Greater Russia." He wants to restore the Russian empire to the boundaries of the former Soviet Union. He proudly calls himself a "dictator." And, as I have mentioned before, his grand design for a Russian renaissance calls for an imperial dash to the South.

In an interview after his big win in Russia's parliamentary elections, he painted an apocalyptic picture of regional conflicts in the Middle East and Central Asia. "These conflicts will make a hell of these regions, with war raging for 10 to 15 years," he said. "Cities and roads will be destroyed, epidemics will explode, millions will die and neither America nor the United Nations will be able to do anything about it. The world community will beg us to save what remains of those peoples in Central Asia, the Middle East and the Indian Ocean coast. We will be obliged to send our boys there, our army will then appear on the coast of the Indian Ocean."

I don't know if Zhirinovsky will be the man to lead Russia into this Final Battle. But I do think it's possible. If it's not him, it will be someone very much like him— someone capable of making a terrible blunder—a miscalculation that will cost the lives of tens of millions. The fact that we can even imagine an event like this today is significant. It tells me we are ever so close.

Ezekiel's View Of A.D. 2000

Verse 16 describes the Armageddon coalition this Russian dictator assembles—this **"mighty army"**—coming upon Israel **"like a cloud to cover the land."** Verse 19 indicates God will also cause a great earthquake in Israel to coincide with this invasion.

Picture this now: Ezekiel looking into the future with his ancient experiences sees this invasion force coming upon the Middle East like a cloud and sees a great shaking of the earth. Couldn't this well be a description of a nuclear strike? It could well be. Because listen to what follows:

"And the fish of the sea, the birds of the heavens, the beasts of the field, all the creeping things that creep on the Earth, and all the men who are on the face of the Earth will shake at My presence; the mountains also will be thrown down, the steep pathways will collapse and every wall will fall to the ground. . . . And with pestilence and with blood I shall enter into judgment with him; and I shall rain on him and on his troops, and on the many peoples who are with him, a torrential rain, with hailstones, fire and brimstone."

100 Pound Hailstones

Did you know that open-air hydrogen bomb tests have been accompanied not only by the intense fireballs and destructive radiation but also with hailstorms. The test ships that survived the thermonuclear explosion had large dents in their upper deck armor platings. The hailstones were apparently caused by the great atmospheric turbulence the blasts caused. A thermonuclear explosion is like a big compression hammer that instantly compresses the atmosphere and shoots it into the upper stratosphere. When you compress air with humidity, then throw it into the stratosphere at 60 or 70 degrees below zero, what happens? All of that compressed moisture instantly freezes, then falls back to Earth as big chunks of ice. It says, at one point in Revelation, that the hailstones falling down on men are 100 pounds apiece. I believe Ezekiel is predicting accurately the phenomena of an escalating nuclear exchange.

Nuclear blasts would explain the heavy rains, hailstones and fire of this great battle. But what is brimstone? Look it up in the dictionary. The definition is usually simple—sulfur. Now what would sulfur be doing out in this high-tech battlefield of the future? Well, in a previous chapter on the arsenal of this Final Battle, I discussed the likelihood of the deployment of chemical and biological weapons. Do you know what one of the principal ingredients of many chemical and nerve gases is? You guessed it—sulfur, or brimstone. This would also explain the pestilence that Ezekiel describes as a part of this attack. Pestilence means *plague.*

Super-plague, Courtesy Russian Chemicals, Inc.

Let me introduce some other information for you to think about. On March 27, 1994, the *Sunday Times of London*, perhaps the most prestigious newspaper in Great Britain, reported prominently that the Russian military is secretly developing biological weapons of mass destruction, including a *"super-plague"* for which the West has no antidote. The research and development is being carried out in defiance of President Boris Yeltsin, the paper reported. The plague is reportedly so potent that just 440 pounds sprayed from planes or using airburst bombs could kill 500,000 people. The paper cited evidence provided by three Russian defectors.

The continuation of the project makes a mockery of Russia's pretensions toward freedom and democracy, the paper said. "It also raises questions about the future intentions of the Russian military, who have used political capital and scarce resources to continue a program that remains a key part of their war plans."

But "fire" is most often mentioned as the destructive force in the Final Battle. Joel 1:19, 20, for instance, describes what is called the **"time of Jacob's trouble"** in Jeremiah: **"To you, O LORD, I call, for fire has devoured the open pastures and flames have burned up all the** trees of the field. **Even the wild animals pant for you; the streams of water have dried up and fire has devoured the open pastures.**" Let's cross-reference some of this with other scripture.

Daniel 11:40, is describing the same battle: **"At the time of the end the king of the South will engage him in battle, and the king of the North will storm out against him with chariots and cavalry and a great fleet of ships. He will invade many countries and sweep through them like a flood."** The King of the south is Egypt with the Muslim Confederacy. The King of the north is the descendant of Magog via the Scythians of the extreme north—the forefather of the ethnic Russians—described by Ezekiel, Chapter 38.

"He will also enter the Beautiful Land, and many countries will fall; but these will be rescued out of his hand: Edom, Moab and the foremost sons of Ammon," Daniel 11:41-43, continues: **"He will also invade the Beautiful Land. Many countries will fall, but Edom, Moab and the leaders of Ammon will be delivered from his hand. He will extend his power over many countries; Egypt will not escape. He will gain control of the treasures of gold and silver and all the riches of Egypt, with the Libyans and Nubians in submission."**

The **beautiful land** is Israel. **Edom, Moab and the sons of Ammon** include some of the tribal names of the Arab race plus the modern nation of Jordan. This passage hints that Cairo will be betrayed by their Russian allies who, along with North African Muslim nations of Libya, Moroco, Tunisa, Algeria and Mauritania (all descendants of Put) will simply overwhelm and occupy Egypt—at least for a short time.

In Ezekiel 39:1-6, the battle escalates to Stage Two and engulfs the world beyond the Middle East. Fire rains down on Magog—Russia—and on **"those who inhabit the coastlands** [literally, **continents**] **in safety."** This could well be a reference to nuclear attacks on the United States and the Western Hemisphere as well as Europe.

Perhaps you have become convinced by the news media and U.S. diplomats that Russia is no longer interested in attacking the United States and that missiles have been retargeted. Well, did you know the U.S. has no plans to verify the retargeting of the Russian missiles? The Clinton administration is only demanding that Russia agree to reaim its missiles and provide an explanation of how it would be done. And should Russia not stick to its word, the U.S. would make itself much more vulnerable to a surprise first strike.

It takes about 30 minutes for Russian missiles to reach the U.S. after launch. It could be as little as 22 minutes. Now it takes about 15 minutes for the U.S. to retarget missiles. That leaves only seven minutes to do the following:

- identify the attack;
- confirm the destination;
- locate the president;
- launch a counterattack;

Is that realistic? Or is the United States placing itself at a tremendous strategic disadvantage? Ronald Reagan had a pretty good credo when it came to dealing with the Russians: "Trust, but verify." Those are simple words to live by. Yet they seem to have been forgotten in the foolish euphoria of the West.

Back to the future. Daniel 11:44-45 describes the counterattack against the Magog alliance. The Russian leader is in the midst of wreaking havoc throughout the Middle East, but he's disturbed by rumors from the north and east. Apparently he becomes aware of the impending counter invasions from Asia and the European leader (pronounced Antichrist) and tries to finish off the Jews before they come, just as the German SS did in the final days of Nazi Germany. The final verse describes the Russians as coming to their end with no one to help them.

The Last War, Stage Two

Now, let's jump back to Revelation 6:5-6: This passage denotes the end of stage one of this war and the beginning of stage two with the breaking of the third seal. What these verses predict is that no one in the world can afford to buy oil or wine because they are so expensive and there are terrible food shortages. This will be the beginning of the large-scale famines I have described in other books, such as my latest, *Planet Earth—2000 A.D.*

Then the fourth seal: **"I looked, and there before me was a pale horse! Its rider was named Death, and Hades was following close behind him. They were given power over a fourth of the earth to kill by sword, famine and plague, and by the wild beasts of the earth."**

This seal unleashes mass death. The **sword** represents death by the weapons of war. **Famine** and **plague** are the war's aftermath of scarcity and probably biological weapons. **Wild beasts** are apparently driven from their natural habitat searching for food and against normal habit go after mankind. All of nature will be disrupted.

The fifth seal, revealed in Verses 9-11, predicts the wholesale slaughter of those who become believers in Jesus Christ during the seven year Tribulation period.

Nuclear Winter

The sixth seal is opened in Verses 12-15, **"I watched as he opened the sixth seal. There was a great earthquake** [shaking]. **The sun turned black like sackcloth made of goat hair, the whole moon turned blood red, and the stars in the sky fell to earth, as late figs drop from a fig tree when shaken by a strong wind. The sky rolled up like a scroll, rolling up, and every mountain and island was removed from its place. Then the kings of the earth, the princes, the generals, the rich, the mighty, and every slave and every free man hid in caves and among the rocks of the mountains."**

These verses describe some of the latter events of stage two of the Final Battle—a period so terrible for men that they pray for rocks to fall on them to hide them from their fate.

I believe this passage describes the initial stages of an all-out nuclear war. *"Seismos"* (σεισμοσ) in the Greek does not necessarily mean earthquake, as it is usually translated. It can also mean a terrible shaking of the earth by forces not known to the 1st century writer who witnessed it. As a result of this violent shaking on the earth, the **sun** becomes black like sack cloth and the **moon** becomes red like blood. This sounds remarkably like the "nuclear winter" scenarios that scientists predict will follow a thermo-nuclear war. The debris that is blasted into the atmosphere will blot out a great deal of light and heat from the sun and moon.

Note that John predicts that multiple **stars** fall out of the sky to earth. To a 1st century man, this would appear like falling stars. But he could have well been describing multiple independently targeted warheads blazing through the atmosphere as they streak toward their targets.

The clincher is **"the sky was rolled up like a scroll."** In a thermonuclear blast, the atmosphere is violently pushed back upon itself as a great vacuum is created. Then it rushes back into the vacuum with almost equal force. The double violent movement of the atmosphere is one of the great destructive parts of the bomb's explosion.

Just When Things Couldn't Get Worse . . .

Stage Three of this conflict is so horrible Jesus said if God did not stop it there would be no one left alive on Earth. The terrible escalation of the war is described in Revelation Chapter 8. Consider Verse 10, for instance: **"The third angel sounded his trumpet, and a great star, blazing like a torch, fell from the sky on a third of the rivers and on the springs of water. . ."** The word translated star (αστηρ) is the Greek word from which we get the word *asteroid*. It appeared to John to be a great blazing asteroid as it hit the earth's atmosphere and began to flame. Remember, this was a first century man actually witnessing the last great war, with its 21st century technology. He could only describe it in terms of phenomena with which he was familiar in the 1st century. This could literally be a nuclear warhead reentering the earth's atmosphere on the way to its target. Would an asteroid or a meteor poison the waters? No. But radiation from a thermonuclear explosion would.

Let's turn to Isaiah 13:6-13 for more detail of this terrible period: **"Wail, for the day of the LORD is near; it**

will come like destruction from the Almighty. Because of
this, all hands will go limp, every man's heart will melt.
Terror will seize them, pain and anguish will grip them;
they will writhe like a woman in labor. They will look
aghast at each other, their faces aflame. See, the day of
the LORD is comingæa cruel day, with wrath and fierce
angeræto make the land desolate and destroy the sinners
within it. The stars of heaven and their constellations
will not show their light. The rising sun will be darkened
and the moon will not give its light. I will punish the
world for its evil, the wicked for their sins. I will put an
end to the arrogance of the haughty and will humble the
pride of the ruthless. I will make man scarcer than pure
gold, more rare than the gold of Ophir. Therefore I will
make the heavens tremble; and the earth will shake
from its place at the wrath of the LORD Almighty, in the
day of his burning anger."

Notice that it says **mankind's faces will be aflame.** The
intense heat and blinding light of a great thermonuclear
blast can do this for a radius of up to 100 miles. A 25-
megaton air burst over Los Angeles could set people afire in
San Diego. The Russians have some 100-megaton warheads
in their present arsenal. Each one is equal to four times the
munitions used by all sides in World War II.

Also, the same phenomena described in Revelation
6:12-14 is predicted here—the **sun, moon and stars of
heaven** will be darkened and not give their light. Once
again, this could be a nuclear winter. I feel certain they will
play a major role in World War III.

Notice, too, how often the scriptures refer to the Earth
shaking in this final confrontation. This could, of course, be
the result of a series of actual earthquakes. We know

earthquakes are increasing in frequency and intensity and will continue to do so in the last days leading up to this Final Battle. But I believe at least some of this shaking and quaking is going to be caused by nuclear warfare—it seems plausible in the light of such widespread devastation and wholesale slaughter. The accompanying phenomena also lends weight to that idea.

Billions Killed In A Matter Of Months

As a result of all this catastrophe, Isaiah said that mortal man will become as scarce on earth as the pure gold of Ophir. Revelation Chapter 6, Verse 8 predicts *a fourth of earth's population* will be killed in the first stages of the final battle. Chapter 9, verse 18 predicts that *a third of the surviving population* will be killed in the second stages of this war by **fire, smoke and brimstone** which is unleashed by the great army that comes from east of the Euphrates River—Asia. This adds up to half of the world's population, or some three billion people.

Isaiah gives further confirmation of this destruction and great loss of life. It is certainly unlike anything that the world has witnessed before—even in the worst conventional world wars. Look at how the final war is described by Isaiah: **"Behold, the Lord lays the Earth waste, devastates it, distorts its surface, and scatters its inhabitants. . . The Earth will be completely laid waste and completely despoiled, for the Lord has spoken this word. The Earth mourns and withers, the world fades and withers, the exalted of the people of the Earth fade away. The Earth is also POLLUTED by its inhabitants, for they transgressed laws, violated statutes, broke the everlasting covenant. Therefore, a curse devours the**

Earth, and those who live in it are held guilty. Therefore, THE INHABITANTS OF THE EARTH ARE BURNED, AND FEW MEN ARE LEFT." (Isaiah 24:1-6 NASB)

200 Miles Of Radiated Blood

Let's jump back now to Revelation 14:19: This depicts the third and final stages of the war. It focuses on Jerusalem. There will be so much fighting that blood will flow for 200 miles. A ravine runs from Jerusalem to the Dead Sea area and the Jericho road runs through it. It is a steep ravine that runs down from Jerusalem to the great Jordan Valley. It happens to be almost exactly 200 miles from up at the northern region above the Sea of Galilee down to the Dead Sea, on down to the Wadi el Arabia (this is a dried riverbed south of the Dead Sea) ending at the Gulf of Eilat. This verse is saying that the blood will stand to the horses' bridle in this valley. I have traveled the entire length of this valley and it is long. It is almost impossible to imagine that valley covered with blood five feet high! Yet that is exactly what God predicts, and He always fulfills His Word. Some have asked, "Wouldn't the blood coagulate and not flow?" Blood exposed to intense radiation doesn't coagulate.

The End Of Earth's Present Ecology

John predicts the final stages of the Last Battle in Revelation Chapter 16. Part of this is a complete breakdown of the Earth's environment brought about, no doubt, by the thermonuclear exchanges and biological and chemical warfare:

"And I heard a loud voice from the temple, saying to the seven angels, 'Go and pour out the seven bowls of the

wrath of God into the Earth.' And the first angel went
and poured out his bowl into the Earth; and it became a
loathsome and MALIGNANT SORE upon the men who
had the mark of the beast and who worshiped his image.

"And the second angel poured out his bowl into the
sea, and it became blood like that of a dead man; and
EVERY LIVING THING IN THE SEA DIED.

"And the third angel poured out his bowl into the
rivers and THE SPRINGS OF WATER; and they
BECAME BLOOD. And I heard the angel of the waters
saying, 'Righteous art Thou, who art and wast, O Holy
One, because Thou didst judge these things; for they
poured out the blood of saints and prophets, and Thou
hast given them blood to drink. They deserve it.' And I
heard the altar saying, 'Yes, O Lord, the Almighty, true
and righteous are Thy judgments.'

"And the fourth angel poured out his bowl upon
THE SUN; and it was given to it to scorch men with fire.
And MEN WERE SCORCHED WITH FIERCE HEAT;
and they blasphemed the name of God who has the
power over these plagues; and they did not repent, so as
to give him glory.

"And the fifth angel poured out his bowl upon the
throne of the beast; and his kingdom became darkened;
and they gnawed their tongues because of the pain, and
they blasphemed the God of heaven because of their pains
and their sores; and they did not repent of their deeds.

"And the sixth angel poured out his bowl upon the
great river, the Euphrates; and its water was dried up,
that the way might be prepared for THE KINGS OF
THE EAST."

As I mentioned earlier in this book, it is now possible—without the direct intervention of God—to do most of what is predicted here. God may do some of these catastrophic events directly, but I believe that He, for the most part, simply ceases to restrain man from his evil nature. Serious damage of the already damaged ozone layer would cause the cancerous sores. The turning of all of both salt and fresh water to blood seems to be God's direct doing.

The fierce scorching heat could be the result of polluting the earth's atmosphere to such a degree that not only the ozone layer but also the earth's weather patterns are completely thrown into chaos.

Destruction Of Ancient Barrier To Asian Hordes

The drying up of the Euphrates River is not only possible but already set up. Turkey has already built dams at its head waters. Shutoffs and diverting of the River are being planned by Turkeyæfor political reasons!

"It is true," an *Atlantic Monthly* report in 1994 quoted Erduhan Bayindir, site manager at the Ataturk Dam, as saying, "We can stop the flow of water into Syria and Iraq for up to eight months without the same water overflowing our dams, in order to regulate their political behavior."

All Of World's Cities Destroyed

The Final Battle, thus, will be fought between what is left of the forces from the West and the vast hordes from the East. Now there is no way that the severely depleted forces of the European leader in Jerusalem could contend with the Eastern armies of 200 million men in a conventional war. I believe what comes next, then, according to Revelation 16:17-21, is a nuclear war that wipes out every major city in the world.

"And the seventh angel poured out his bowl upon the air; and a loud voice came out of the temple from the throne, saying, 'It is done.' And there were flashes of lightning and sounds and peals of thunder; and there was a great earthquake, such as there had not been since man came to be upon the Earth, so great an earthquake was it, and so mighty. And the great city [Jerusalem] was split into three parts, *and the cities of the nations [Gentiles] fell.* God remembered Babylon the Great [Rome] and gave her the cup filled with the wine of the fury of his wrath. And every island fled away, and the mountains were not found. And huge hailstones, about one-hundred pounds each, came down from heaven upon men; and men blasphemed God because of the plague of the hail, because its plague was extremely severe."

Zephaniah 1:15-18 confirms this scenario. It pictures civilians living in the world's cities struck down quickly and violently. But note there is no discussion of any attacking army. The destruction is related to a day of darkness and thick clouds (nuclear winter?). Again, it sounds just like the portrait you would expect if you transported an ancient prophet into the 20th or 21st century to witness a nuclear attack.

Plutonium Everywhere, And No Sane Guardians

Is there enough nuclear material in the world for this three-and-a-half-year conflict that will destroy every major city in the world? Once again, I turn to my friend Joseph de Courcy, for the answer: "Since the early 1950s approximately 380 tons of plutonium have been produced worldwide, 250 tons for military purposes and 130 tons for civil use. Of the military total, 70 tons is already thought to be in store, and extraction of plutonium from Russian and U.S. nuclear warheads under disarmament treaties are likely to add another 150 tons to the total in store. If existing plans for the construction of new nuclear processing plants go ahead, it has been calculated that there could be a combined civil and military world surplus of between 400 and 500 tons of plutonium in store by A.D. 2002."

Obviously, the entire world will be greatly affected by this protracted nuclear conflagration. No part will be spared suffering. But some parts will be utterly *destroyed*! Revelation 8, for instance, states that one-third of the trees will be burned up, one-third of rivers and springs dried up, etc. A fair question might be, "Which third?" There are some specific references made in scripture and we can make educated assumptions about others.

The land of Israel and the surrounding area will certainly be targeted for nuclear attack. Iran and all the Muslim nations around Israel have already been targeted with Israeli nukes. Russia clearly receives a knockout blow, probably in the form of a retaliatory nuclear strike. Russia's Eastern European allies would also likely suffer the same fate. All of Europe, the seat of power of the Antichrist, would surely be a nuclear battlefield, as would the United States, the world's second most powerful nuclear power (China is rapidly catching up). The Soviet Union had over 60,000 nuclear bombs, which are almost all now under Russia's control.

If you add up the square miles of the entire world's land mass, you get a figure representing about 56.8 million. If you add up the total land mass of the areas I just enumerated, you get a total square mileage of about 18.9

million—or roughly one-third of the world total. Quite a coincidence, wouldn't you say?

The Hatred Is Old; The Weapons Are New

All this destruction will be caused by the ancient hatred between Ishmael and Isaac—the smoldering flames of hatred that have existed for 4,000 years—the jealousy of Ishmael toward Isaac—the fact that Ishmael and his descendants have never been willing to accept the blessings that God gave them. God didn't give them the same promises He gave to Abraham's promised son, but He did give them great wealth and blessings. In spite of this, they have never been satisfied. They wanted Isaac's blessing. This conflict has gone on down through the ages, and it is what is going to touch off the war that will almost destroy the World.

Because of God's grace alone it will not quite destroy mankind. In Zechariah, chapter 14, we see that the Lord Himself will come back and fight those armies that have come against Jerusalem. He will personally deliver the Israelites who have believed in Jesus as their Messiah and will supernaturally protect them from destruction. He will stand on the Mount of Olives, exactly where He last stood on Earth in human form, and split it in two from the Dead Sea westward to the Mediterranean.

Zechariah gives an unusual, detailed account of how hundreds of thousands of soldiers in the Israel battle zone will die. Their flesh will be consumed from their bones, their eyes from their sockets, and their tongues from their mouths **while they stand on their feet** (Zechariah 14:12). This is exactly the sort of thing that happens from the intense radiation of a neutron type bomb. Perhaps this is what will be used. But God's power is certainly stronger than any nuclear bomb and could, if He chooses, do this and more. We do know that God will supernaturally strengthen and protect the believing Israelites so that they will survive the worst holocaust the world will ever see. Amen.

But, believe it or not, there's more to this story. The world is not over. Contrary to popular belief, the Final Battle is not about the end of the world. You've heard about the Final Battle—stay tuned for the way of escape and the present world's final era of a thousand years of Peace.

Chapter 13

THE
SPACE
RACE

"Brothers, we do not want you to be ignorant about those who fall asleep, or to grieve like the rest of men, who have no hope. We believe that Jesus died and rose again and so we believe that God will bring with Jesus those who have fallen asleep in him. According to the Lord's own word, we tell you that we who are still alive, who are left till the coming of the Lord, will certainly not precede those who have fallen asleep. For the Lord himself will come down from heaven, with a loud command, with the voice of the archangel and with the trumpet call of God, and the dead in Christ will rise first. After that, we who are still alive and are left will be caught up together with them in the clouds to meet the Lord in the air. And so we will be with the Lord forever. Therefore encourage each other with these words."

—1 Thessalonians 4:13-18

The Great Illusion

An acquaintance of mine works in the purified water business. He travels around the world and helps plan and build water-purification plants. Recently, I ran into him and asked him what he was up to—where his latest project was taking him.

"Palestine," he answered.

"Come again," I said. "Did you say Pakistan?"

"No," he said. "I'm helping to build a plant in Palestine."

"Forgive me," I said. "But there is no such thing as Palestine."

"Well," he said, "technically I guess you're right. But the United States government is encouraging American companies to begin businesses in the new Palestinian state. They're really pushing it hard. So, we've got an agreement to build a plant there."

"Well," I said, still perplexed by it all, "where will the plant be? In Gaza?"

"No," he said, "in Jericho. There's a little spring there, and Yasser Arafat wants some good water to drink. Peace is making all this possible."

It continues to amaze me just how many people don't get it—how the U.S. government doesn't get it, how the Western world doesn't get it. There will be no peace in the Middle East as long as the world entertains the Arabs' fanciful illusion of dividing and conquering Jerusalem and driving all the Jews into the sea. Peace will only be possible if, by some miracle, the Arabs realize that their ambitions for military and economic hegemony over Israel are delusional. But don't hold your breath until such a conclusion is reached without Divine intervention. It's just not in the script. Never before have we been able to see prophetic fulfillment so clearly. World events are playing out precisely as the Bible predicted they would. And the Bible is clear about how the current Middle East tensions will lead directly to World War III, climaxed by the return of Jesus the Messiah to Planet Earth.

Israel is facing world pressure like never before. Because the Arab world has been successful at framing the debate over the Middle East as a struggle between downtrodden Palestinians and powerful, heavily armed Jews, Israel is dangerously close to compromising its own security needs.

Israel's Fate Is Sealed

"Land for peace!" is the cry heard 'round the world. Even in Israel, more and more people seem willing to be blackmailed into turning over the lands of Judea, Samaria, Gaza, Jericho and the strategic Golan Heights. At "Jerusalem, City of Peace," a three-day seminar in Cairo in March 1995, the message was clear: "The world must understand that without a solution to the issue of Jerusalem there won't be peace, there won't be a normalization of relations," explained Faisal Husseini, in charge of Jerusalem's affairs for the Palestinian Authority. "If Palestinians get their rights, Jerusalem can be the warming sun in the Middle East, but if Palestinian rights are ignored, Jerusalem will become the black cloud that could swallow everything, including all hopes for peace."

262 THE FINAL BATTLE

Once again, it's evidence of that continuing irreconcilable dilemma: By "rights," the Palestinians mean they should control Jerusalem. The Jews can never compromise on the holy city. But, no matter. For while Israel will certainly face some perilous moments in the near future, the Jewish state's fate has already been decided. God doesn't make promises He can't keep. And God has promised the land of Israel to the Jews forever. Period. From the time of their miraculous rebirth until the Messiah comes to rule over them permanently, the state of Israel will be preserved—though it will undergo near annihilation.

Where Will You Be In All Of This?

But how about your fate? Has it been decided? It's in your hands. Jesus has given us all a way out of this mess just like He has provided a way of survival for His special nation of Israel.

The prophets made it clear that when the nation of Israel was reborn, as it was in 1948, that this historic event would mark the beginning of a countdown of specific events. It would signal that the Second Coming was very near. Jesus specifically said, **"Now learn this lesson from the fig tree: As soon as its twigs get tender and its leaves come out, you know that summer is near. Even so, when you see all these things** [all the signs that precede His coming], **you know that it is near, right at the door. I tell you the truth, this generation** [the one that sees the signs] **will certainly not pass away** [die] **until all these things have happened."** (Matthew 24:32-34 NIV)

Is This The Generation?

I put the explanatory notes within the above text in order to bring out clearly the context. Jesus promised that the generation that saw all the predicted signs coming together in concert would not die until they were all fulfilled in His visible return to earth.

Many biblical scholars have pointed to the fact that 40 years is generally regarded as a generation in the Bible. Some people have said that a generation has passed and nothing has happened. But note carefully, Jesus said the generation would not *"pass away* **until all was fulfilled."** In other words, many who saw the signs begin to come together *would not die* before their climactic fulfillment. Life expectancy today in the U.S. is about 76 years.

The very existence of Israel is a testament to the truth of the prophets and the fact that God keeps His word. And, remember, Jerusalem was reunified under Jewish control in June of 1967. This, taken together with the rebirth of the state of Israel, is of enormous significance. They represent a great miracle. Add to these the following important signs:

- Russia's agreement to fight on side the Muslims in future Mid-East war
- Russia's equipping of the Muslim world with the arsenal from hell
- Political union of Europe
- Decline of the United States
- Iran (Persia) leading Islamic revival to drive the West out of Middle East and to liberate Jerusalem while destroying the state of Israel
- Turkey turning back to the Islamic world
- Japan, China and Far East nations becoming hostile to Western interests and gathering vast arsenal
- Rapid increase in frequency and scope of famines, earthquakes, killer storms, volcanic eruptions, weather pattern changes, plague conditions, religious deception,

occultic revival, ethnic conflicts, international revolutions, etc.

All of these indicate that we are in the general time
(generation) of the Coming of the Messiah, Jesus of
Nazareth.

Hello. Is Anybody Listening?

As I mentioned before, my purpose in writing this book
was to jolt the believer and non-believer alike out of their
complacency—to say, "Hey, time is running out, folks!"
Never before in human history has mankind been faced
with a choice so clear: horrible torment and death or
everlasting happiness and eternal life. My goal was to paint
an accurate portrait of what life will be like on Earth in a
few years—a graphic, detailed depiction based on the best
intelligence information available as well as the prophectic
scriptures.

The good news is that Jesus offers a way out for
everyone! But it will be a lot less painful for those who
choose Jesus now—before the final countdown begins. If
you think conditions on Earth are bad now, let me tell you
something: You ain't seen nothin' yet!

In Luke 21:25-26, Jesus summarizes the kind of
tribulation the world will be facing very soon: **"And there
will be signs in the sun and moon and stars, and upon the
Earth dismay among nations, in perplexity at the roaring
of the sea and the waves, men fainting from fear and the
expectation of the things which are coming upon the
world." And, "For then there will be great distress,
unequaled from the beginning of the world until now—
and never to be equaled again. If those days had not been
cut short, no one would survive, but for the sake of the
elect those days will be shortened."** (Matthew 24:21-22)

It's easy to understand why men may faint from fear someday. I think I have described more than a few events in this book that would make me faint from fear—if I were around, that is. But I am not going to be here. And you shouldn't be planning to be around either. You see, there's an escape hatch for those of us who choose it. But it's only going to work once.

The Coming Great Mystery

One day soon, the Bible indicates that millions of people will just suddenly disappear from the face of the Earth. Just imagine what the freeways, and airports and subways and streets of the world will be like at that moment. Can you imagine what life will be like for those left behind? Pilots, drivers, conductors—people from every walk of life—just suddenly vanish. The world will be given an explanation that will be the beginning of the biggest deception of all history—so let me tell you what really is going to happen.

I've mentioned this event many times before. Especially in a taped series called, *The Rapture Factor.*

Removal Of Ambassador Equals War

This event is God's way of removing His ambassadors. When a nation recalls its ambassador, it usually means a war is about to follow. The Bible says that every believer is an ambassador for Christ, **"We are therefore Christ's ambassadors, as though God were making his appeal through us. We implore you on Christ's behalf: Be reconciled to God. God made him who had no sin to be sin for us, so that in him we might become the righteousness of God."** (2 Corinthians 5:20-21)

For almost 2,000 years God has sent His ambassadors to every part of the earth to implore the non-believer to receive

His gift of pardon purchased for us by the death of His Son, Jesus Christ. The Biblical meaning of reconciliation means to restore man to relationship with God by removing all the barriers man erected. The Lord Jesus removed all those barriers at the cross by dying under the judgment due our sins. Now their is only one barrier—it is our failure to receive by faith the pardon He purchased for us. Jesus made the one unpardonable sin clear when He taught what the Holy Spirit's primary mission would be, **"But I tell you the truth: It is for your good that I am going away. Unless I go away, the Counselor will not come to you; but if I go, I will send him to you. When he comes, he will convict the world of guilt in regard to SIN and righteousness and judgment: IN REGARD TO SIN, BECAUSE MEN DO NOT BELIEVE IN ME . . . "** (John 16:7-11) According to this Scripture, the only unpardonable sin is to die without believing in the Lord Jesus Christ, because the Holy Spirit only convicts the unbeliever regarding that sin.

The Great Snatch

All who simply receive that pardon and invite Jesus into their life with the view to His changing their life to God's plan, will be "snatched up" to meet Him and changed instantaneously into immortality.

When this great event happens, it will be God's way of declaring judgment on the world. His restraint of lawlessness and man's full capacity for evil will have been removed with the evacuation of His ambassadors. The Holy Spirit's special personal presence in the believers will be no more on earth.

God is going to remove the believers out of the world so that they will not have to endure the misery and trials that will beset the planet for the seven years that follow. So, what I'm saying is that there are millions—hopefully tens of millions or hundreds of millions—of people on Earth today who will not be around for the beginning of World War III, even if it should begin tomorrow. The Lord Jesus promised this, **"Since you have kept the word of My perseverance, I also will keep you from the hour of testing, that hour which is about to come upon the whole world, to test those who dwell upon the earth."** (Revelation 3:10 NASB)

"Those who dwell upon the earth" is a technical term used by the Apostle John to describe the non-believer in the book of Revelation. He uses it several times. They are identified as those whose names are not written in the Lamb's book of life in Revelation 13:8. So the purpose of the above world-wide judgment is to test the unbelievers. Believers of today are to be kept from *the time* of that testing. Great promise, isn't it?

Who Will Be Delivered?

Who then will delivered? It will be those who sincerely placed their trust and faith in the promises of God by acknowledging Jesus Christ as their personal savior. It doesn't matter what church you go to or to which denomination you belong. Your socioeconomic background will be irrelevant as will be your race, ethnicity or political beliefs.

You just have to admit you have come up short. Believers are the ones who are humble enough to understand that, without God, we can never be fulfilled or even understand our destiny—the meaning of life. What's the key? What is God's promise?

The simple answer is found in John 3:16: **"For God so loved the world that He gave His only begotten Son, that whoever believes in Him should not perish, but have eternal life."**

Paul told us how we can take advantage of that promise. In Romans 10:9-11, he wrote: "That if you confess with your mouth Jesus as Lord, and believe in your heart that God raised Him from the dead, you shall be saved; for with the heart man believes, resulting in righteousness, and with the mouth he confesses resulting in salvation. For the Scripture says, **'Whoever believes in Him will not be disappointed.'"**

Grace Before Judgment

Isn't it great to know that God is going to raise up a believing remnant of true Christians and give one last great offer of the free gift of forgiveness and acceptance in Jesus Christ before snatching us out of the world as it plunges toward judgment? Wouldn't it be great to be assured about your eternal fate?

If you have insecurities about your relationship with Jesus Christ, then this is the time to receive Jesus as your Savior and Lord. He has already purchased your forgiveness by bearing the judgment of your sins on the cross. If you are confused about details and don't feel like you understand it all, don't worry. The only thing you need to understand is that God offers a full pardon and new spiritual life for the asking. If you truly desire to receive Jesus into your life, then you are ready to thank Him for dying for your sins and invite Him to come into your life.

"Behold, I stand at the door and knock; if anyone hears My voice and opens the door, I will come in to him, and will dine with him, and he with Me," Jesus tells us in Revelation 3:20.

The door symbolizes your will. If you right now invite the Lord Jesus into your life and receive His gift of pardon, He will come into you to stay. He will begin to give you new desires that are according to His will. Through His presence in you, He will give you the power to do these new desires as you moment by moment depend upon Him. He also promises, " . . . **For I will never leave you nor forsake you.**" (Hebrews 13:5 NKJV)

Are You Playing Russian Roulette With Eternity?

When you have taken this step, Jesus wants to change your life and empower you to live for God. The more we learn of God's love and unconditional acceptance of us, the more we want to please Him and the more we are able to trust Him to work in us. That's all it takes. God makes it so simple—so easy to avoid the coming holocaust, so easy to take advantage of eternal life. So, if you haven't done so already, make that commitment right now—confess your sins to God and humbly and sincerely accept His promise of forgiveness and life everlasting. You don't want to miss that last race into space. This is really the main message of this book.

Can you imagine what it will be like immediately after the Rapture. That experience in itself ought to make some people faint with fear—especially if you have heard about this offer before but didn't get in on the action when you had the chance.

Muslims and Jesus

I spent a good part of this book describing the threat of Islam in the modern world. But, did you know that even the Muslims of the world fully expect a "second advent" of Jesus Christ in the world. They, too, believe He will usher in an age of peace and justice in which the righteous reign. Islam predicts that Jesus will return in the midst of earthly chaos, greed, depravity and plunder. He will "descend among you as a just judge," says the *hadith*.

"Not one of the People of the Book will fail to believe in him," predicts the *hadith*. "Spite, mutual hatred and jealously one of another will certainly depart, and when he summons people to accept wealth, not one will do so."

There are striking parallels between what the Bible prophesies about the Second Coming and what Muslims believe. There are also some even more striking *contrasts*. While Muslims see Jesus in a profoundly transcendent role, they do not see Him as God. They also deny that He died on the cross and was resurrected. Instead, they believe He never died and was taken up to heaven.

"Christ has a unique place in Islamic eschatology," says Muslim scholar Eqbal Ahmad of Washington's Institute for Policy Studies. Francis Peters, a New York University specialist on Islam, observes, "Jesus is seen as the prophet who didn't die."

The Koran calls Jesus a "sign," the "Word and Spirit of God," even the Messiah. *"And Jesus shall be a sign for the coming of the hour of judgment,"* the Muslim holy book says.

Once again, because there are some half-truths about Jesus in Islam, it makes it even harder to convince Muslims of the *whole* truth.

You And The Lord Jesus

Some people might be tempted to look at the material offered in this book and become depressed. If you are a Christian, you should not be pessimistic and drop out of the world in despair. We should rejoice in the knowledge that Jesus could come for the believer at any moment. This should and must spur us on to share the good news of salvation in Christ with as many as possible.

Even though He may come today or tomorrow, we should plan our lives as though we will be here on Earth for our full life expectancy. Don't drop out of the world. Don't stop working for righteousness on this plane. Make the most of the time we have.

As the world becomes more chaotic and troubled, we as believers need to be stable, because we know where things are headed. We can rest assured that Christ will protect us until His purpose is finished and then we will be taken up to be with Him in heaven. Let's take as many as possible with us, Okay?

THE
FINAL
PEACE

After the Final Battle, This is what the LORD promises
will follow:

"The LORD says . . . 'I have cut off nations; their
strongholds are demolished. I have left their streets
deserted, with no one passing through. Their cities are
destroyed; no one will be left—no one at all . . .
Therefore wait for me," declares the LORD, "for the day
I will stand up to testify. I have decided to assemble the
nations, to gather the kingdoms and to pour out my
wrath on them—all my fierce anger. The whole world
will be consumed by the fire of my jealous anger. The
LORD has taken away your [Israel's] punishment, he has
turned back your enemy. The LORD, the King of Israel,
is with you; never again will you fear any harm. At that
time I will deal with all who oppressed you; I will rescue
the lame and gather those who have been scattered. I
will give them praise and honor in every land where they
were put to shame. At that time I will gather you; at that
time I will bring you home. I will give you honor and
praise among all the peoples of the earth when I restore
your fortunes before your very eyes,' says the LORD."

(Zephaniah 3:6, 8, 15, 19 and 20 NIV)

Concerning the new world order that follows, the LORD says:

"**The LORD will be king over the whole earth. On that day there will be one LORD, and his name the only name. The whole land, from Geba to Rimmon, south of Jerusalem, will become like the Arabah. But Jerusalem will be raised up and remain in its place, from the Benjamin Gate to the site of the First Gate, to the Corner Gate, and from the Tower of Hananel to the royal winepresses. It will be inhabited; never again will it be destroyed. Jerusalem will be secure . . .** (Zechariah 14:9-11 NIV)

After the LORD Jesus judges the unbelievers who destroy the earth, He will then rule the world from a restored Jerusalem, with the believing remnant of the Israelites as His administrators and priests:

"**In the last days the mountain of the LORD's temple will be established as chief among the mountains; it will be raised above the hills, and peoples will stream to it. Many nations will come and say, 'Come, let us go up to the mountain of the LORD, to the house of the God of Jacob. He will teach us his ways, so that we may walk in his paths.' The law will go out from Zion, the word of the LORD from Jerusalem. He will judge between many peoples and will settle disputes for strong nations far and wide. They will beat their swords into plowshares and their spears into pruning hooks. Nation will not take up sword against nation, nor will they train for war anymore. Every man will sit under his own vine and under his own fig tree, and no one will make them afraid, for the LORD Almighty has spoken.**" (Micah 4:1-4 NIV)

Wars have been raging in the Middle East since the beginning of humanity. Of course, wars have been fought all over the planet, but the Middle East has always been an especially violent, contentious place.

Why? The answer, as hard as it may be to believe today in this era of supersonic transportation, digital cellular communications and satellite technology, is an ancient blood feud that began four thousand years ago in the tents of Abraham—the father of Ishmael and Isaac.

Here's what happened: God promised Abraham an heir. He promised him a son through whom He would bless all nations—one who would raise up a mighty people. But Abraham grew old— and impatient. Even though he had great faith, as time passed, he and his wife, Sarah, began to have doubts, wondering if, perhaps, they had misunderstood God's promise? So Abraham and Sarah hatched a back-up plan. Sarah told her husband to impregnate her Egyptian maidservant, Hagar, so that Abraham would have his heir. A son was soon born, and he was called Ishmael. This turned out to be the worst surrogate mother case in history.

So Ishmael was raised in the home of Abraham and Sarah. And Abraham grew to love his first son. But 14 years later, when Abraham was 100 years old and Sarah was 90, she gave birth to the legitimate heir, born in response to their faith in the miraculous power of God to keep His promise. They named him Isaac (Laughter). Conflict between the two sons of Abraham began almost from the start. In Genesis, chapter 21:9, it says the conflict began just after Isaac was weaned: "And Sarah saw the son of Hagar the Egyptian, which she had born unto Abraham, mocking."

Hagar and her son were banished. But the Lord had mercy upon them. He promised Hagar her son would beget twelve princes. Ishmael went to live in the wilderness region of Hejaz where he indeed had twelve patriarchal sons associated with the peoples known as Midianites, Edomites, Egyptians and Assyrians—all the desert peoples of the Middle East.

God's Mercy To Ishmael

As God always does, He provided many opportunities in this story for redemption of bad situations created mostly out of disobedience and lack of faith. Abraham agreed to impregnate Hagar because he doubted God would fulfill his promise to bear him an heir with Sarah. To be fair to Ishmael, God offered him a great kingdom of his own to the east of his brother. However, it was never enough. Thus, the descendants of Isaac and Ishmael have been at each other's throats for forty centuries now.

How do you solve an irreconcilable, 4,000-year-old blood feud? There's only one solution to this crisis—the heavenly policy that Jesus Christ Himself will institute when He returns to Earth to rule for 1,000 years.

That's just what the Lord Jesus is going to do. When He returns to Earth, he doesn't just bring to a halt the terrible bloodshed I described in this book. He also sets up His kingdom on Earth. He personally rules over the world from His throne in Jerusalem.

Perhaps after reading this descriptive account of the Final Battle, it's more difficult than ever to imagine a future age when the Earth will be restored, when disease will be unknown, when peace will reign. But that's just what follows the destruction—a literal 1,000-year reign of Jesus Christ on Earth.

Sometimes, perhaps, we believers focus so much attention on the events leading up to the return of Jesus to

Earth that we tend to overlook or misunderstand the
volumes of biblical references to what will be the most
exciting, glorious and fulfilling time in the history of man—
the period known as the Millennium. There are many
misconceptions about this period—one, for instance, is that
today's believers won't be a part of it. Not true.

Though believers will indeed be "raptured" out of the
world before the terrible events described in this book, *we
will return with Jesus and interact with the Millennium
world and population!* According to Revelation 21:9-27, the
raptured church will be living in a heavenly city right
above Jerusalem.

The New Jerusalem

Listen to this description by John: **"'And one of the
seven angels who had the seven bowls full of the seven
last plagues, came and spoke with me, saying, 'Come
here, I shall show you the bride, the wife of the Lamb.' ..
. And he carried me away in the Spirit to a great and
high mountain, and showed me the holy city, Jerusalem,
coming down out of the heaven from God, having the
glory of God."** (Revelation 21:9-11)

This "New Jerusalem"—a city so bright its glow lights
the world by both day and night—is where we, the
"translated" believers will be living in new eternal bodies.
Accordingly, we will have great freedom and great powers
beyond our imagination. We will be able to walk through
walls, for instance, disappear and reappear at will and to
travel at the speed of our own desires just as Jesus did in
His Resurrection body. We will live in a dimension
unimaginable to mortals.

Remember, Jesus walked the earth after He rose from the grave. His disciples could recognize him, touch him and feel his flesh and bones. Jesus, as you will recall, went out and did some fishing, prepared a meal for his followers and ate with them. Jesus was seen in this Resurrection body by somewhere between 500 to 1,000 people, according to the Gospel accounts.

How do I know we're going to be like the resurrected Jesus after the Rapture? According to Thessalonians 4:16-17 and I Corinthians 15:51, the dead in Christ shall rise first. Then, we're told, in the twinkling of an eye, we who are alive on Earth at the appointed moment shall be caught up to meet the LORD in the air—together with the resurrected Church age believers. At that point, we're changed to be like Jesus. We get our new glorified bodies. When Jesus comes He **"will transform our lowly bodies so that they will be like his glorious body."** (Philippians 3:21 NIV)

The Future Marvels

Like Jesus, our immortal bodies can be seen, be touched, partake of food and co-mingle with the people of the Earth. We will also be able to become invisible and move across the universe at the speed of thought. Our primary home will be the heavenly Jerusalem that apparently hovers in juxtaposition over the earthly Jerusalem during the millennial era.

Meanwhile, there will be people down below—on Earth—living in their mortal human bodies under the personal rule of the Lord Jesus, the King on David's throne. It will be a very different world than we know today. There will be real justice. Children will not die. Death will apparently only occur as punishment to unreformable unbelievers who are children of the all believers who repopulate this age. Isaiah gave us a hint about this, **"No longer will there be in it an infant who lives but a few days, or an old man who does not live out his days; for the youth will die at the age of one hundred and the one who does not reach the age of one hundred shall be thought accursed."** (Isaiah 65:20 NASB)

Life will be greatly extended—especially for those who live by faith. Satan will be bound in chains during this period. The world system will be under the Lord's direct control, so that it will promote righteousness instead of sin. The world will not be without temptation as the people of this time will still have their old sinful natures. But the means and spiritual environment for holy living will be there in a way never available before.

What The Millennium Is Really Like

The average Christian misunderstands this millennial period. He thinks that Christ comes back as the king and the world is a new creation—everything is perfect. This is not the case. Only after the thousand-year period, when new heavens and a new earth are created, as depicted in Revelation 21:1, will there be total perfection. The LORD will completely restore the earth to an unprecedented level of peace, but it will still be under the curse mankind will still be mortal.

During the millennial age, Jesus will regenerate the Earth. He gives it new life and beauty. Acts 3:19 refers to it as a time of **"refreshing."** Acts 3:21 calls it a time of **"restitution,"** or restoring the Earth.

Think of how long it took us to rebuild Germany and Japan after World War II. The Lord Jesus will have to restore the earth's ecology immediately, or no one could survive. This world is going to be virtually uninhabitable when He returns. Remember, it's going to be a toxic waste dump of nuclear radiation, and biological and chemical weapons residue. All the cities will be in ruins, the fresh water poisoned, the oceans totally polluted with all sealife dead. The trees and grass will be burned up, the atmosphere filled with debris. The weather patterns will be shifted, causing havoc with storms and rain in the wrong places.

Don't listen to those "allegorical alchemists" who twist the clear, normal meaning of the Scripture to say Jesus will come only after we prepare and restore the world and bring in the Kingdom of God for Him. Christ comes when things are at their worst and restores the world in the beginning years of the Millennium. The Bible couldn't be more clear about that.

The La La Land of Allegorical Interpretation

Those who deny the Millennium are called "A-millennialists,"—meaning "without or no Millennium." Then there are the "post-millennialists," those who theorize that we must help usher in Christ's return by first cleaning up the world and bringing in the kingdom ourselves. A-millennialists must simply ignore countless passages in the Bible to make their case. Post-millennialists must pretend that the Bible portrays Christ reentering a placid and tranquil world. Nowhere does Scripture describe a situation like that. It's clearly not going to get better before Jesus comes; it's going to get worse. Christ's reentry to this planet is to save it from self-destruction, not to ascend to a throne we have provided for Him.

Let me state this plainly: God doesn't need man's help to bring in His kingdom. Even with help of the Holy Spirit, it is impossible for man to do this awesome work. Man is not strong enough to cast out and bind Satan. Even the archangel Michael couldn't do it (Jude 9). God is sovereign. He keeps His promises. And, as promised, Jesus is going to come again in His own time and rule the world in His own way. And the time is coming soon—very soon.

God's "New World Order"

Jesus not only will restore the Earth during this time, He will also completely change the world order and system. The earth's moral and spiritual environment will be totally changed with only believers in Jesus, the Messiah, allowed to remain on it. It will be a time when war will be unknown. There will be no armies, no defense plans, no military camps, no arsenals of mass destruction. Globally, it will be a time of peace and prosperity.

Hospitals will be shut down. There will be no poverty, violence or crime. There will be no wastelands, no storms, no droughts, no crop failures, no floods. And at last, there will be no poor and homeless people.

Even the wild animals will be tame and harmless and will stop devouring each other.

The Lord promises, **"Never again will there be in it an infant who lives but a few days, or an old man who does not live out his years; he who dies at a hundred will be thought a mere youth; he who fails to reach a hundred will be considered accursed. They will build houses and dwell in them; they will plant vineyards and eat their fruit. No longer will they build houses and others live in them, or plant and others eat. For as the days of a tree,** so will be the days of my people; my chosen ones will long enjoy the works of their hands. They will not toil in vain or bear children doomed to misfortune; for they will be a people blessed by the LORD, they and their descendants with them. Before they call I will answer; while they are still speaking I will hear. The wolf and the lamb will feed together, and the lion will eat straw like the ox, but dust will be the serpent's food. They will neither harm nor destroy on all my holy mountain," says the LORD." (Isaiah 65:20-25)

Our Spiritual Battle Only On One Front

What happens to all the vices we are so familiar with today—the constant evidence of sin? Since Satan will be bound and the world environment no longer under his control, mankind will only have to contend with the temptations of his sin nature. And almost everyone will have the Holy Spirit to give him power to fight the old sin nature.

So with all of these assets going for man, Jesus just won't tolerate open rebellion and sinful life-styles. You've heard of the "zero-tolerance" attitude against drugs in certain communities? There will be a "zero-tolerance" attitude toward all sinful patterns developing in a man. It's going to be a period of real "tough love" for the world. In Revelation 19:15, we're told that the Lord will rule the world **"with a rod of iron."** That's the difference. Jesus will be here as a righteous and benevolent dictator. The world will be operating under a true theocracy—the only true benevolent dictatorship of all history.

Do you know what a "theocracy" is? We often think of it today as a government ruled by a church or religious

figure. But the root word, "Θεοσ," means "God." So the
Millennium will truly see the world ruled by God Himself.
Jesus instructed us to pray, **"Thy Kingdom come, Thy will
be done, on Earth as it is in heaven."** This is the period of
time that prayer is about. Think of that every time you pray
the Lord's prayer. While we won't know perfect
righteousness until after the millennial kingdom, this period
will literally see the Lord's will done on Earth as it is
in heaven.

Rebellion In Paradise—Again

During the Millennium, however, there will be children
born who will not receive the offer of salvation and will
reject Jesus as their Savior. At the end of the millennial age,
God will reveal this rebellion that has been suppressed in
their hearts. God unleashes Satan so that he can bring out
into the open the sinful unchanged hearts of these
unbelievers. The Devil will quickly find followers who will
be ready to launch an attack against the Lord Himself.

In other words, during the Millennium, some people
remain under control only because of the great advantages
I've noted above. But the wickedness of the human heart is
a sad thing. Even without the presence of Satan and his evil
world system, people will still go astray. They have no one
to blame but themselves. They can't say, "The devil made
me do it." All of humanity enters the Millennium righteous.
But they bear children who turn away from the LORD
Jesus—even though they can see Him and have direct
access to Him.

The Great Lesson Of Divine History

God shows us something by His order of history. Man began on this earth in perfect environment. He will end his history on the earth in near perfect environment. In both cases man rebels. It shows us that *environment and economic security are not the problems.* God's only answer is "We must be born again spiritually." God must give us a new spiritual nature that will always desire fellowship with Him and desire His plan for our lives.

As long as we are in these mortal bodies, we still have a sin nature that will lure us out of God's will, but the nature God causes to be born in us will always make the true believer so unhappy that he will come back to the way of faith again. If we don't respond to our spiritual nature or God's loving Fatherly discipline, we might get an early trip to our heavenly home.

If you have gotten this far and still have not received the pardon that Jesus died in your place to provide, do it now. You may be saying, "I don't understand the Bible—I'm not sure that God is real." Jesus says, **"I tell you the truth, no one can see [understand] the kingdom of God unless he is born again . . . Flesh gives birth to flesh, but the Spirit gives birth to spirit. You should not be surprised at my saying, `You all must be born again.' The wind blows wherever it pleases. You hear its sound, but you cannot tell where it comes from or where it is going. So it is with everyone born of the Spirit."** (John 3:3-8)

All of us are born physically alive but spiritually dead. Knowing God and understanding the Bible is not a matter of intelligence, but of having the right kind of life. Only those who have a spiritual nature can understand and know God personally.

You see illustrations of this phenomena everyday. Whenever you turn on the television set you are using something that a native from the jungles of Africa would call a miracle. Suppose you would bring in a native and explain to him that there were people speaking, dancing and singing in the air all about him. He would think you were nuts until you turn on the TV and adjust the channel so that it picked up the signals from the air and reproduced them. Then the native would see the phenomena, though he couldn't understand how it was done.

In the same way, God is very near and around you. But unless you have the same kind of life He has, you can not perceive Him. The moment that you receive the pardon for your sins and ask Jesus to come into your life and give you a new heart, you experience a miracle that you cannot explain. But you can see the results of it. It is like Jesus said, you can hear the wind, you can see its effect on the trees and grass, etc., but you cannot see the wind itself. So you will progressively see and understand the things of God, though you cannot see the Holy Spirit who is doing these things. You will experience a new set of desires that make you want to follow God. This is what the new birth is all about.

If you pray and ask God to do what I've just explained, then you will not be here for the Final Battle. You will be in heaven with Jesus. We will witness this terrible period of history from the presence of God.

With all my heart, I pray that will be your experience.

Until then—Maranatha, Tally Ho and good fishing! (Luke 5:9-10)

To receive a FREE Catalog
of Audio & Video Tapes and
books by Hal Lindsey,
or if you would like information
about Hal's Tours to Israel or
Prophecy Conferences,
Call Toll Free

1-800-TITUS 35

or write to:

Hal Lindsey
P. O. Box 4000
Palos Verdes, CA 90274

Hal Lindsey's
International Intelligence Briefing

This Monthly Inside Report Uncovers and Explores Worldwide Events

If you'd like to discover how worldwide events are pointing to the last days . . .

. . . then you should be reading *Hal Lindsey's International Intelligence Briefing* — the amazing newsletter that gives you an insider's view and perspective on world events.

The Significance of World Events

Every day our worldwide intelligence network scours the world for little-known, but significant news events. The information is then studied and analyzed by Hal Lindsey and his staff to uncover its Biblical significance.

Then every month we put together a concise, insightful report that reveals how these events fit together and what they could mean for your future.

Many of them are in the news every day. For example, you'll get up-to-date reports on . . .

• What's happening in the Middle East? Is peace around the corner? Or war?

• The true state of our military. Are we prepared for the next conflict?

• What's next for the economy.

• Military hot spots and world conflicts.

News Events That Impact Your Future

But it's not just everyday news. We delve deeper and interpret lesser-known news events for you.

• Killer viruses are back. Are they part of the great plagues prophesied for the Last Days?

Matching the News With Biblical Scenarios

Hal Lindsey relates these events to Biblical prophecy, and shows how many of them fit the scenarios laid out in Ezekial 38-39 and Matthew 24.

You'll learn which events are setting the stage for the final battles as described in the book of Revelation.

With Hal Lindsey's *International Intelligence Briefing* you'll know what's happening right now and what to expect in the future. It's your indispensable source for the news of the world from a Biblical perspective.

A one-year (12-issue) subscription to *International Intelligence Briefing* is just $40. And you're fully protected by our . . .

Money-Back Guarantee

Read your first three issues of *International Intelligence Briefing*. If you aren't completely satisfied then let us know within 90 days and we'll send you a full refund of every penny you paid.

To subscribe just pick up the phone and call TOLL-FREE:

1-800-848-8735

Or write your name and address on a piece of paper and mail it with your check of $40 to HLM, P.O. Box 4000, Palos Verdes, CA 90274.

With Hal Lindsey's *International Intelligence Briefing* you'll know what to expect in the months and years ahead. Subscribe today. And don't forget the money-back guarantee. Thank you.